"Author Paul Boge delicately wea[...] grim reality of human trafficking [...] and social culture of ignorance a[...] [...] this book is a must-read for everyone who cares about the safety and well-being of our nation's children and the systemic malevolent sickness that targets them."

—Steve Bell, Singer-Songwriter & Author

"The powerful stories in this book shine a light on the very dark, insidious reality of human trafficking here in Canada. It could happen to anyone and presents a risk to all. This is not just a threat that happens somewhere else to children we will never know or see; this has spread to neighbourhoods in every corner of Canada. This is a clarion call to action and should inspire us all to be aware and to do all that we can to stop it."

—Hon. Peter MacKay, Former Cabinet Minister, Partner at Baker & McKenzie LLP

"Thank you, Joy Smith, for giving Canada a reality check on the horrific crime of human trafficking. Your steadfast perseverance to give a voice to the voiceless and put a big spotlight on this crime has opened up the minds and hearts of Canadians to identify how they contribute to the problem and most importantly how they can become part of the solution. You have oftentimes stood alone in this hard fight for justice, and we will be forever grateful that because of you Canada is a safer place for women and girls!"

—Diane Redsky, Executive Director of MaMawi Wi Chi Itata Centre Inc., Project Director of the National Task Force on Human Trafficking of Women and Girls in Canada (2011 to 2015)

"*The True Story of Canadian Human Trafficking* seen through the eyes of survivors will be an educational tool for Canadians. We cannot get enough education and awareness on this poignant issue."

—Scott Kolody, Assistant Commissioner, RCMP Manitoba

Dear Amy, be blessed and encouraged in your ministry in loving people. I pray this book encourages you in what God is doing. Many blessings to you,

THE

TRUE STORY
OF CANADIAN HUMAN
TRAFFICKING

BY PAUL H. BOGE
FOREWORD BY PAUL BRANDT

2018

The True Story of Canadian Human Trafficking
Copyright ©2018 Paul H. Boge
All rights reserved
Printed in Canada
ISBN 978-1-927355-95-4 Soft Cover
ISBN 978-1-927355-96-1 E-book

Published by: Castle Quay Books
Tel: (416) 573-3249
E-mail: info@castlequaybooks.com | www.castlequaybooks.com

Edited by Marina Hofman Willard

Cover design and book interior by Burst Impressions
Printed at Essence Publishing, Belleville

Library and Archives Canada Cataloguing in Publication

Boge, Paul H., 1973-, author
      The true story of Canadian human trafficking / Paul H. Boge.

ISBN 978-1-927355-95-4 (softcover)

      1. Human trafficking--Canada. 2. Human trafficking victims--
Canada. 3. Human trafficking victims--Canada--Biography.
4. Human trafficking--Law and legislation--Canada. I. Title.

HQ281.B63 2018   364.15'510971   C2018-900585-8

CASTLE QUAY BOOKS

foreword

There are people you meet who change the course of your life. While that is rare, it is rarer still to meet people who, while changing your life, also change the course of world history.

My friend Joy Smith is one of those people to me.

She has a fire, a passion, and a vision to pursue what is right, true, good, and noble.

My eyes were first opened to the topic of human trafficking through the Dateline NBC documentary *Children for Sale*, first aired in 2004. Dateline went undercover and detailed a brothel raid to free child sex-trafficking victims in Cambodia. The raid was organized by the International Justice Mission (IJM) in co-operation with the Cambodian Ministry of Interior. The television special is still available online, and while the raid has been surrounded with controversy and criticism as to its efficacy, especially in relation to the well-being of the victims, it was arguably one of the most important international "tipping point" moments in raising public consciousness to this horrific crime.

In late 2004, my wife, Liz, and I were offered an opportunity to travel anywhere in the world to participate in Samaritan's Purse's "Operation Christmas Child" delivery program, a yearly event that reaches over 90 war-torn and impoverished nations around the world. Through OCC, children around the world receive a practical, free, unconditional gift. The gifts are packed, delivered, and sent with love to children of all ages who would otherwise never have an opportunity to receive such a gesture of hope. Having been impacted greatly by the Dateline special and wanting to learn more about human trafficking and how we could be a part of solving the problem, we immediately requested southeast Asia. The next OCC trip available to us was delivering to Cambodia.

Cambodia changed our lives. Its people, food, and natural beauty are all incredibly compelling. Early historical accounts show Cambodia as a potential crown jewel of Asia. There were few other kingdoms on earth more poised with potential and promise. It's a beautiful country with a more recent tumultuous and genocidal past, and we struggled to comprehend as we learned of the atrocities of Pol Pot and his Khmer Rouge regime. We walked the killing fields and sensed the voices of millions of victims crying for justice from beyond the shallow burial pits. We witnessed the bones, teeth, and bits of clothing still evident on the ground, brought up each time the rains fall and fail to wash away the sins of the past. We could feel the ripple effects of generations of trauma, abuse, and disregard for the sanctity of human life. The beauty of the jungle and Angkor Wat's impressive architecture contrasted sharply with a history of slavery, dishonesty, coercion, murder, and abuse.

We met a spirit in Cambodia, and its hatred for human life knows no bounds.

While visiting, we were introduced to a fledgling NGO working to free child sex slaves. We listened as their organizer explained that because they were vastly under-resourced, all they could afford at the time was to pay traffickers the going rate for these children so that they could take them from the brothel for the day. They would bring the children to a safe location, feed them, let them play with toys, and let them be kids; but at night, they had to take them back to their owners.

I never lose grasp of the fact that Cambodia was once a prospering nation. No one could ever have imagined the horror that would befall it. It's estimated that around 3,000,000 died during the rule of the Khmer Rouge, and the stage was set for an incredibly vulnerable population to be exploited. As Edmund Burke so eloquently stated, "The only thing necessary for the triumph of evil is for good men to do nothing."

Since Cambodia, we've been advocates in the fight against human trafficking and sexual exploitation. We've travelled to many countries, and while we've seen hope and joy expressed through the perseverance of the human spirit, we've also seen abject poverty and lawlessness. I remember returning to my home in Nashville from one such trip. I was scheduled for a lunch with a business associate, and I immediately began to share with him stories of the need we had witnessed. He stopped me midsentence.

"I don't want to know."

He then went on to share his dreams for parties he was planning, events he was attending, and investments he was considering. I was dumbfounded, but I suppose at least he knew the kind of person he wanted to be. He understood somewhere deep inside that with knowledge comes responsibility, and he naively believed that by ignoring evil and injustice, they wouldn't be his problem.

My experience has shown me that this is not how it works. Ultimately, to fight against human trafficking and sexual exploitation is to take a stand for the limitless value of human life. It is to uphold human dignity. To ignore this issue is to erode the very foundation of democracy and civilization. Society crumbles under the weight when evil is ignored. It's been proven throughout history time and time again.

Liz and I were introduced to Joy Smith and her foundation's work through new circles we were running in of those who were equally convinced of the significance of the fight against human trafficking. Through events we've attended together and conversations we've had, I have always been impressed with Joy's ability to fight tirelessly on behalf of victims and to bear the burdens of human trafficking survivors. She is a true Canadian hero, but, more than that, she is a champion of humanity. She has changed our nation and through the introduction and support of Bills C-268, C-310, and C-36 has provided us with an opportunity. We can sit idly by as a nation while lives are destroyed, or we can remain on the right side of history, which has always been about justice, equality, and freedom. Since the days of William Wilberforce this has been the choice facing humanity when faced with slavery. "You may choose to look the other way but you can never say again that you did not know" was his battle cry, and he and Joy have been history-makers who have encouraged me to raise awareness and fight against what is still one of the world's largest industries. As of the date of publishing, there are more than 40 million slaves in the world today, and research and evidence have proven that sex trafficking is a growing issue in Canada. Aided by the fast pace of technology, perpetrators and those who would sexually exploit our population's most vulnerable have the advantage. While sex trafficking affects all parts of Canadian society, Indigenous women and children are disproportionally represented as sex-trafficking victims. Although only 4 percent of Canada's total population, the First Nation's population represents 51 percent of those trafficked for the purpose of sexual exploitation.

Not many books can save lives. This one can. *The True Story of Canadian Human Trafficking* is an important account of a trafficking victim, a trafficker, a john, and a woman who decided to take a stand on behalf of our population's most vulnerable.

Even though the purchase of sex is a crime in Canada, our ability to affect change related to sex trafficking and sexual exploitation admittedly seems small. Operation by organized crime syndicates and a seemingly endless demand can make this feel like an insurmountable battle. While studies are showing that education, research, and awareness are key, as Joy states in this book, "we need to admit that the battle starts in our minds and in our hearts." While stopping the atrocity of human trafficking seems complicated, never have I heard a more appropriate and elegant solution than that offered by one of emancipation's first pioneers: "Let everyone regulate his conduct ... by the golden rule of doing to others as in similar circumstances we would have them do to us, and the path of duty will be clear before him" (William Wilberforce).

—Paul Brandt
Founder of The Buckspring Foundation
Founder of Not in My City
Member of Canadian Country Music Hall of Fame

preface

Human trafficking is having a devastating impact on Canada. When people hear of human trafficking, they often associate it with foreign girls who are brought into our country. This is happening, and it must be stopped. Yet many are shocked to learn that human trafficking is happening to Canadian girls on Canadian soil.

Our girls—from all backgrounds and all financial statuses across our country—are being lured into human trafficking for the purpose of sex slavery.

And they are being used by Canadian men.

Human trafficking is a network of good versus evil that includes girls who are lured into trafficking, the traffickers who control them, the "johns" or men who use the girls for sex, and the many citizens, organizations, police, teachers, religious leaders and politicians who are fighting to stop it. People like Joy Smith.

I have known Joy for many years. We were seated together at a fundraising banquet in Winnipeg for street children in Kenya when we discussed the possibility of a book on human trafficking in Canada. I knew next to nothing about it. I had assumed that the men who used girls came from low incomes and lived at or near the streets. But she corrected me by saying that johns come from every walk of life in Canada and are mostly commonly 30 to 60 years old with a good job.

I felt the blood drain from my face. She was describing men who are in the same age bracket as me.

How in the world does a man who should be helping destitute girls get himself into a state of mind where he misuses his power to cause such devastation in the life of a young girl?

Moreover, I wondered how a Canadian girl could be deceived into the world of human trafficking.

The best way for me to find out was to sit down with Canadian survivors of human trafficking to hear their stories from the very beginning, through every unimaginable detail of their ordeal, to discover how human trafficking works and what would have helped prevent them from entering into that world in the first place.

There is much to be done in our nation in combatting human trafficking. And in spite of this darkness, there is more reason to have hope. It is my hope that this book will in some way be an encouragement to save one girl's life, to prevent even one girl from being lured into human trafficking, to have one Canadian man stop using girls once he sees that the girls do not want to be there, to have one human trafficker change his ways, or to have one person enter law enforcement, politics or an organization in an effort to combat human trafficking. If any of these happen, I will consider this book to have been a success.

Please note: in this book, I have combined true stories of testimonies of human trafficking survivors into one main character. I have also combined stories of traffickers and stories of johns. I have compressed timelines for the sake of space. I have changed most of the names to protect people. In certain circumstances, I have changed locations.

————

My sincerest thank you to each of the Canadian survivors of human trafficking who spoke with me in the preparation for this book. I am humbled and grateful for your willingness to share with me the unimaginable damage that was done to you. I admire each of you. I admire your courage to confront the dangers of human trafficking in Canada and your desire to protect young women in our country from being deceived into this evil. Thank you for sharing your stories.

Thank you to those survivors who, for many reasons, were not able to talk with me directly. The pain they had to endure was still too raw to be able to meet with me face to face, yet they wanted to contribute.

And so they provided their testimonies and answers to my questions, on condition of anonymity, through Joy Smith, whom they knew personally.

Thank you to the reformed trafficker and the men who once used girls who spoke with me. Your insights helped me understand how a man can go down that path. And that there is hope for restoration and redemption from such a lifestyle.

This book would not have been possible without the constant support and encouragement from my friend Joy Smith. She has spent countless hours with me to help me learn about human trafficking. We would meet in her home, where I would take notes, often in disbelief at the scope of this unimaginable tragedy in our country.

I am grateful to Joy's son Edward for his help. And also to Joel Oosterman, whom you will get to know in the pages of this book. I am grateful for every police officer, politician, non-government organization and the many volunteers who offered their insights.

My thank you also to so many of you who have been praying both for this book and for human trafficking to end. Thank you to each person who read the various drafts of the manuscript. Your comments and questions have made this a better book.

And as always, my sincerest thank you to Larry and Marina Willard for their willingness to publish this book. I appreciate your dedication and passion for combatting human trafficking in Canada.

Thank you for your interest and your time in reading this story. But be forewarned about learning about human trafficking in Canada. I close with the words of William Wilberforce, who spoke of slavery in Britain years ago when he said, "You may choose to look the other way but you can never again say you did not know."

—Paul H. Boge
Winnipeg, Manitoba
February 8, 2018

introduction

Human trafficking happens every day in Canada. But many people do not recognize it or want to understand it or admit how frequently it occurs in our country. I myself could hardly believe the prevalence of human trafficking until my son Edward Riglin, a police officer, opened my eyes to what was really happening.

Young women and girls who service men with sex are often called "prostitutes." Yet many are *being* prostituted and are victims of heinous crimes. Many had no idea that one day they would be forced to service men sexually and sold on the open market. Many live in fear of beatings or worse if they do not comply with the traffickers' demands. Predators target and lure the vulnerable young, showering them with gifts and novel experiences, claiming to love them, promising to marry them. And the overriding allure is money: traffickers make $260,00 to $280,000 per victim per year.

Human trafficking is a dark, evil crime targeted at our youth. It is the modern-day slave trade.

As a teacher, I started to give seminars on how to protect children when they are on the internet. What I didn't expect were the testimonies of many young girls who showed me their tattoos and told me they belonged to one of the traffickers whose identities were well-known. I was appalled at what was happening.

In response to these horrors, and with God's grace, I went to Parliament to pass laws to combat this crime against our youth. At first, many MPs worked against my efforts to pass the laws to combat human trafficking. Why? Because they did not know about it. Yet, in time, these same people became champions in the fight against human trafficking.

Now, trafficking rings are being taken down every single day. I am grateful to our police forces at every level across this country. I commend them and the frontline workers, the NGOs, and most of all the survivors who have so courageously told their stories. They are real heroes.

Education is our greatest weapon against this crime. I am grateful to Castle Quay Books and to the author, Paul Boge, for taking up the cause to educate the public and publishing this book. It is the real story that needs to be told here in our country.

My hope is that *The True Story of Canadian Human Trafficking* will save young lives and reveal to Canadians human trafficking for what it is.

—Joy Smith

chapter one

For some people, their favourite place is a specific location in the world. A spot where they can relax. Feel at home. Unwind. For others, it's an imaginary place in their mind where they can explore, invent and create. Each person seems to have a place where they can let their guard down. Where they can be themselves. Where they come alive. Where pressures disappear, worries fade away and they can experience the freedom and safety that comes with forgetting the past and living in the present moment.

For 16-year-old Abby Summers, that place was a soccer field.

Abby opened the door and walked out of her high school in Markham, Ontario, with the other girls from her gym class. The bright sunshine blinded her a moment, causing her to squint against its glare. When her eyes adjusted, she saw the green pitch freshly marked with white lines. Pristine condition. She would have spent the rest of the day there if she could.

The physical education teacher split the group of girls into two teams and instructed them to partner up for a passing drill. With an odd number of players on her side, Abby was left to practice by herself. She watched as her teammates passed to each other and tried to shrug off the sting of being left out. It was just the luck of the draw, she tried to convince herself.

Again.

Abby kicked a red-and-white ball out from the ball bag. She rolled it onto the front of her foot and flicked it up. Alternating between feet, she juggled and got 40 in a row. Not bad. Her record was 100. She glanced over at her teammates, thinking it strange that not one pair of them offered to modify the drill to allow her to join in. She attempted again to shake off that feeling, but like a heavy snowfall in a Canadian winter storm, what little she managed to brush away soon piled back onto her again.

The sun felt like a million degrees as she waited for the pre-game preparations to end. The teacher finally blew her whistle. Abby exhaled in relief, taking her position in centre-right midfield. This felt better. On the field. Together as one team. Ready to play.

She tightened the ponytail of her shoulder-length blonde hair. Felt her pulse quicken. Felt herself focusing. Already anticipating where the ball would go first. The thrill of the game about to start.

The teacher blew the whistle.

The game began.

The striker passed the ball back to the centre midfielder, who passed it over to Abby. Abby dribbled it up, returned the pass to the centre midfielder, and moved forward into open space. Her eyes darted around as she looked for any possible opening, thinking two, three and four moves ahead, as if the soccer pitch were a massive chessboard.

She noticed the defender cheating forward to intercept a possible pass to the striker and saw her opportunity. With her wingers out on the side, Abby bolted right down the middle. Her centre midfield teammate read it perfectly. She chipped the ball high in an effort to lob it over the defender so it would drop down out of reach in front of the goalie.

Abby looked over her right shoulder for the ball, but a bright flash of sunlight blinded her again. She turned the other way, glancing over her left shoulder, and saw it arriving in a perfect arc. Out of the corner of her eye she caught a glimpse of the goalie rushing out to cut down the angle. Abby checked her run, getting ready to strike the ball. She timed her approach perfectly.

Without warning, a defender suddenly came in, attempting to head the ball away. But the defender missed completely. In an instant, Abby went from thinking she had a clear shot on net to feeling the horrific impact of the defender's forehead cracking against her nose. Her body shot out an immediate painful burst of adrenalin. She felt herself crash to the ground. It was as if someone had momentarily turned the lights off.

When they came on again she found herself stunned, lying on her back. The shock of the injury pulsed through her. *How bad is it? How bad is it? Am I going to be okay?* These first few seconds were critical. Her brain assessed if she was in danger of falling unconscious. Her head began to pound. She became deaf to any sound around her. It was as if she had been enveloped in her own private cocoon of unimaginable pain. It was the worst she had ever felt.

Up until then.

Instinctively, she covered her face, being careful not to touch her nose. She felt blood dripping down off her chin, staining her white jersey in bright red blotches.

"Abby? Abby, are you all right?" Her teacher spoke in a calm tone, like she had seen this before, giving Abby the reassurance she needed that she would be all right.

She tried to regulate her breathing, but her staggered breaths seemed to take an eternity to get under control. Someone brought her tissues. She held them under her nose, forcing her head up to keep from choking.

"Abby?" the teacher said again as she sat up.

"I—" She interrupted herself to listen to her body. She'd fallen once while trying to learn skateboarding. Another time she felt dizzy after a ride her mom took her on at Canada's Wonderland. But nothing like this. She'd never given any thought to how fortunate she was to have been free of injuries this long. But now that it was here, it was hard to remember what it was like *not* to be hurting.

"I never saw it coming," Abby said.

"It's all right, Abby. Just take your time."

"One second I'm fine, and the next she's like right in my face."

"Abby, you okay?" the defender asked. Abby nodded. "I'm so sorry."

"It's okay," Abby replied in a muffled voice, her nose stuffed full. She breathed in and out through her mouth in slow, measured breaths. When her head began to clear she saw the extent of the red staining on her shirt. All that blood caused her to feel woozy and nauseous. The teacher helped her to her feet. Abby heard the faint sound of applause and a cheer from her teammates behind her.

Sitting down on the bench, Abby watched as the game restarted. It felt surreal. As if she were looking through a pane of glass at a world she could no longer access. Strange to be so close and yet so impossibly far away.

She stuffed increasing amounts of tissue under her nose until the teacher blew the final whistle. She stood up, the ground felt firm beneath her, and she nodded to her teacher when asked how she felt. The class walked back to the school building. Abby was last.

She walked alone.

Using a wetted paper towel, Abby cleaned up her face in the girls' washroom. She looked at a reflection of herself in the mirror.

"It doesn't look that bad," her friend Kedisha said.

"Yeah, not until it turns colours," Abby replied.

They both laughed. Abby tilted her head slightly from side to side. Looked at the soft light blues of her eyes, then the whites around them to see if there was any damage. She tried to take a short breath in through her nose, felt the sting of what would surely become a bruise, exhaled, then threw the paper towel in the garbage.

"You should try hockey next," Kedisha said. "It might be easier on your body." She gave Abby a playful jab in the shoulder. "See ya. Gotta head off to chem lab."

"Have fun."

Abby looked back in the mirror as Kedisha walked out the door.

Abby spun her combination and opened her locker. She reached in for her brown paper bag lunch. The moment her fingers made contact she was reminded of the argument she and her mother had that morning as Abby took her lunch bag from the kitchen counter. It was a silly argument—as arguments sometimes seem after you've had time to reflect on them and you realize there was nothing to get upset about.

The cafeteria proved to be every bit as loud and full as always. And, as always, Abby felt a sting of nervousness inside her, wondering who she'd be able to sit with. Towards the back she saw a group of classmates sitting together. She tried to convince herself that they were friends. Wanted to believe they were friends. But when you don't have the solid confidence that people have your back, when you feel you need a bit of a performance to get them to take interest, you begin to wonder if you have what it takes to be accepted by them.

She forced herself to walk towards them, hoping this would not get awkward, and passed a younger girl with fire-red hair walking the other way. She sat down and said hello.

"How's your nose?" the girl who accidentally smashed into her asked.

"I'm still alive."

That drew a chuckle from the group. Success.

"I'm really sorry," the girl repeated.

Abby shrugged it off. "It's not your fault. Besides, there could be a lot worse things in life, right?"

The discussion shifted to an upcoming concert. Abby indicated she liked the punk band, though if the group could have seen into her heart they would have realized she hated that group. She smiled, nodded and said the kinds of things people say when they essentially repeat back what they've heard and mimic the behaviours, unique words and mannerism of others in an attempt at being accepted by them.

"Hey, you guys want to drive over to the mall?" the girl beside Abby asked. Designer jeans, perfect makeup, flawless skin, easy confidence.

Money.

The group agreed. Then the rich girl realized her mistake. "Sorry, Abby, we only have enough room in the car for—"

"Hey, that's cool. I have to eat lunch anyways," Abby said, trying to sound nonchalant but knowing full well she would have rather gone without food for a week if it meant hanging out with them. "Have fun."

The rest of the group left. Abby touched the bridge of her nose. Yeah, that was going to leave a mark. She opened her brown paper bag, unwrapped her sandwich and felt what it was like to be in loud, crowded room all alone.

As she bit into her turkey sandwich, she thought it strange that her having to sit there by herself came down to a lottery of how many girls were at the table a moment ago and how many seats were in that rich girl's car.

Abby stepped off the school property onto the sidewalk and immediately felt the relief that came with knowing she could be herself. Why was it so difficult to just walk into school, say what you thought, be accepted by your friends, have an interesting day—without getting your face smashed in—and then come home? Why was this walk always the best part of the day?

She walked the four blocks to her home. Every step took her farther away from the memories of the day, save for the throbbing in her nose. She walked up the driveway of her red-bricked house. She entered the garage code on the keypad and glanced up at the basketball hoop. It had been underused since her dad started the habit of working later and later each evening. For a moment she remembered the fun times they used to have playing ball. When she was young she could barely get the ball up to the basket. Then she grew taller, but he was around less, and that hoop just stood there as a testimony to what was, instead of what should be.

Opening the door she heard her mother call out from the kitchen. "Hi, Abby!"

"Hi, Mom," Abby replied, forgetting the reason for the argument they had that morning. What had it been about again?

She turned the corner. Saw her mother, Talia. Spunky smile. A true older version of Abby.

"You were right. I was wrong," Talia said.

"No problem."

"I'm off to help at the shelter tonight. Have a great time—" She stopped. Stepped into better light. Saw Abby's nose. Her mouth dropped open. "What happened to you?"

Is it that obvious?

"Soccer."

"Is it broken?" her mom asked, putting her hand on Abby's shoulder to get a better look.

"It's not broken, Mom."

"It might be."

"I'm fine, Mom."

"Let's go to emergency."

"We're not going to emergency."

Her mom exhaled. "You're sure?"

Abby looked into the kitchen. Didn't smell anything cooking. "What's for supper?"

"Supper? Your dad, that's what's for supper. He's taking you out tonight. Remember?"

"Right."

"Have fun."

Her mother walked into the garage. Abby heard the car starting, then the rumble of the garage door closing.

Cool. She and her dad. Spending time with him could make up for the bad day. She went upstairs, got changed into nicer clothes. Sat in front of the mirror, doing the best she could with makeup to hide the start of the blue forming on her nose. Interesting, she thought, how it matched her eyes.

She sat down on the living room couch and checked her various social media accounts. She had spent an hour there when her dad's number came up.

"Hey, Dad," she answered.

"Abby, how are you doing?"

"Doing good. How about you?"

"Excellent. Good day at school today?"

She heard it in his voice. Sensed it right away. *An excuse is coming. Please, Dad. Just cancel whatever came up, and let's go out for dinner.*

"It was fine," she lied.

"That's great."

His voice was too upbeat. He was setting her up for the fall. She supposed that by now she should have gotten used to it, but she hadn't. Every time he bailed was a letdown. This would be no different.

"Say, Abster, I'm really sorry, but it's not going to work tonight. Can we switch it around to another night?"

No. No, we can't. You made a promise. You said you would be here. Just stop telling me you're going to be here when you can't.

"Sure thing. No problem."

"Thanks. I am still in a meeting out here in Barrie. I won't be home for a few hours."

Fine. Okay. Fine. But can you just do me a favour? Before you hang up, can you just say you love me?

"Okay, safe travels."

"Have a great evening, okay?"

"You too, Dad."

I love you. I love you. I love you. Can you say it?

"Take care, Abster. Talk soon."

Talk soon?

The line went dead.

She shrugged her shoulders, but the crushing weight didn't leave. She felt disappointed that she wasn't strong enough to brush off her dad cancelling on her. *This shouldn't bother me so much.*

Should it?

She grabbed some ice cream out of the freezer. Dairy free. Vanilla. She glanced at the clock. Perfect. A soccer game was about to start. For every door that closes—

Her phone pinged. Putting down her ice cream, she pulled out her phone from the back pocket of her jeans. A new contact request. She looked at his picture.

Good-looking guy. Wow. Who is this?

She clicked on his image. Jake. Brown eyes. Brown hair. An easy, unforced smile.

Forgetting about the game she grabbed her ice cream and walked up to her bedroom. She closed the door, even though the house was empty, and sat down on her bed. She put her ice cream on the nightstand beside her clock-calendar, keeping her eyes on the new interest in her life.

She flipped through various social media platforms, trying to learn what she could about him. Then she returned to staring at his picture. They had a few acquaintances in common. No one close. She didn't recognize him from school. *Maybe he's a nice guy who reaches out to a lot of people.* But the longer she looked, the more interested she became. To respond or not respond? She decided to wait a while. Best not to look too desperate. She flipped through his pictures and read the comments.

A while later, she heard the garage door open. Probably her dad. She noticed how her hurt feelings about being stood up by him had been melted away by her interest in Jake. She glanced at the time. It surprised her how long she had been thinking about her new potential friend. A stranger who earlier today had no place in her life.

She put her phone down. Opening her door, she walked down the stairs to say hi to her dad. He smiled as best he could, but she read the exhaustion in his eyes. He apologized again. Said he would make it up to her. Whatever she wanted. She said that would be fine. She knew the routine. He went to the kitchen for a drink—whisky, his favourite—and headed for the couch.

Abby went back upstairs. Looked at Jake's picture again.

And wondered what kind of person he was.

chapter two

He was the first thought on her mind when her alarm clock woke her at 6 a.m.

Normally she would have touched the snooze button. Normally she would have gone back to sleep. But she didn't normally receive friend requests.

Not from guys like Jake.

She looked at his picture. Felt an unmistakable connection with him. Like he could breathe a sense of calm into her life. She cycled through his photos, touching the screen longer than she usually did.

What do you know about him? Why did he contact you?

Part of her wondered if he was one of those guys who reach out to dozens and dozens of people to broaden their network of contacts and loosely defined friends. The other part of her wondered if, hoped, it was more than that. Hoped it was real. Hoped he saw something about her that interested him.

It wasn't until she got into the bathroom and looked in the mirror that she remembered her injured nose. A light blue line ran across the bridge where it was bruised. She touched it. It didn't hurt. Not that much.

She had other things on her mind.

The morning at school went faster than usual. When her class before lunch ended, she pulled out her phone and gazed at him again. She focused on him with such intent that she didn't even notice Kedisha walking up to her.

"So how's Toronto's latest UFC fighter doing?" Kedisha asked, catching a quick glance of Jake before Abby hid her phone from view.

Abby looked up. Laughed. "Good. Doesn't feel that bad. What's new?"

"Who's the guy?"

Abby felt her pulse quicken. Her face flushed. She sensed a rush of blood through her nose. What to say? She raised her shoulders as if it were no big deal. As if he hadn't been the only thought on her mind since last night.

"Just some guy."

"I don't think so. Who is he?"

Abby clicked off her phone, then felt in a strange way that it was disrespectful to do so.

"Want to go for lunch?"

"I'll meet you there. Need to talk to my band teacher."

"Sounds good," Abby said, hoping Kedisha would let it go.

At least until she had sorted Jake out in her own mind.

Abby walked into the crowded cafeteria and for the first time had no concerns about sitting by herself. Leaving her lunch unopened on the table, she put a knee on the bench and kept standing as she studied Jake's face. Yes or no? Accept or decline? She looked into his eyes. Soft pools of golden brown. Maybe. Maybe this could become something. You never know unless you try.

Abby accepted.

She flicked through his profile to other pictures of him. Skateboarding against a backdrop of the setting sun. A selfie of him in a Mustang. Red. Convertible. One of him at Niagara Falls. With the large Horseshoe Falls behind, of course. That one was her favourite. He seemed so happy. So content. She felt relaxed just looking at him.

A message popped up from him. Her heart jumped.

"Hey, Abby. How are you doing?"

"So, you going to take boxing lessons next?" Kedisha asked with a laugh. Abby clicked off her phone. Part of her was glad to see her; part of her was annoyed that her friend had inadvertently cut short a great moment.

"Boxing? Me? No."

"You sure? You can take a pretty good beating and keep on ticking."

"Energizer bunny. That's me."

"Some of us are finishing our lunch break out on the field. Want to join us?"

Abby hesitated. It caught Kedisha off guard. Something wasn't right.

"You go ahead," Abby said.

"Everything okay?"

"Fine," Abby replied, her attention already back to her phone, even if she was still looking at Kedisha.

"Okay. If you change your mind, you know where we are."

The moment Kedisha left, Abby turned back to Jake's message.

"Doing great. How are you?"

She waited. Was his message a typical one he sent to all the people he reached out to, or was this specific to her? Was this the beginning of greater things to come, or would he fizzle out like the dew on an early morning that the sun burns off, leaving no trace of what was once there?

Abby took out her sandwich. Was about to take a bite.

"I'm well. Thanks for responding. How's your day going?"

Abby smiled. If there still was a crowd of students making noise in the cafeteria, they had all disappeared as far as Abby was concerned.

The bell rang. What? So soon?

"Going great. Thanks. Gotta run off to class. Chat later?"

She watched. Hoping for a response. Come on. Come on.

"For sure."

Yes. Abby took her uneaten lunch and put it in her locker. Grabbed her books and headed off to class.

The walk home today felt different. Better. Much better. She stayed focused on her conversation with Jake. She reached her house, passed under the basketball hoop, not noticing it this time, said a quick hello to her mom and went upstairs.

"Hi, Abby," her mom called out, watching her round the corner up the stairs. "Who are you texting?" she asked, trying to make conversation the way mothers do when they want to stay involved in their children's lives and have a slight, or possibly exaggerated, fear that perhaps they are drifting apart.

"A friend," Abby said. She entered her room and closed the door, shutting out her mother.

Abby got onto her bed, pushed her back up against the pillows and headboard and stretched out her legs in front of her. She messaged him back.

"So I'm curious, how did you find out about me?"

"A gorgeous girl like you?"

Gorgeous. When was the last time someone had said that about her? "Thanks."

"I saw you following one of the same people I follow."

He gave the name. She recalled.

"Cool. Thanks for reaching out."

"How could I not? You seem fun. What kinds of things do you like?"

A knock at the door. Her mom poked her head in. "Want to grab some ice cream?"

"No, I'm okay."

"You sure?" Abby nodded. "Nose okay?"

"Yeah, thanks."

"If you change your mind, let me know." Her mother closed the door.

"I like playing soccer."

"Me too. You have a favourite team?"

"Bayern Munich. Real Madrid."

"I love Real Madrid."

"What kinds of things do you like?"

"I'm a big soccer fan too. I love the feeling of being in a packed-out stadium. What else do you like?"

"Movies. Music."

"What kind?"

"All kinds. Depends. I like trying different kinds out. You?"

"Yeah, I like all kinds too. Fun to try different things out. Lots of great stuff out there. You like hockey?"

"Yes! Go Leafs! I think this might finally be our year. Think we'll finally do it?"

"Absolutely. We have to keep believing. You been in Toronto your whole life?"

"Yup. Born and raised. You?"

"Same. My parents too. Yours?"

"Yeah."

"Your parents work close to your home?"

"I wish. My dad is away a lot with work."

"That's a bummer. He doesn't know what he's missing."

"He's great. Just not around much."

"You had a good week so far?"

"School's been okay. Homework. Other than that, not much."

She wondered if she should have said that. Did that make her sound like she didn't get out much?

"Nothing fun? No one to go see a movie or watch a game with?"

"Nope."

Back and forth they went. She usually went to sleep around 10:30. He finally said good night at 1:30. She lay down in bed. Her alarm woke her four and half hours later, leaving her with the groggy feeling of a short night's rest.

She didn't discuss the texts with her mom over breakfast. Not with Kedisha over lunch. She rushed home that evening and threw herself on her bed with her phone, feeling the comfort that comes with being able to share your thoughts with someone who cares.

"I've been thinking about becoming a nurse," she typed.

"You would be great at that." His response came so fast. She smiled.

"I don't know. It's a lot of schooling. I'm not the best student."

"It's high school. Boring. Once you're doing something you love you will be great at it."

"You think so?"

"I know it. Your nose all better?"

"Still a little bit of a bruise. But I hardly notice anymore."

"It's been fun getting to know you."

"It's been fun getting to know you too."

"You're a really honest person. I've never met anyone like you."

"I've never met anyone like you either."

She watched the screen for his next response. Waited. Waited. Waited. Wondered if he had forgotten about her. Then it came.

"So, would you like to get together sometime?"

chapter three

Rain pounded the jet bridge as travellers from Winnipeg to Ottawa Macdonald-Cartier disembarked from the plane. Drops pelted the roof and glass, creating a loud reverberating beat. Joy Smith, wearing a black coat over a black pinstripe pantsuit and pulling her carry-on suitcase, stepped off the walkway into the airport. Ever since her early morning flight took off, her mind had been processing all the many tasks she had to accomplish today.

And that list was about to get much, much longer.

Her phone rang. She brushed a strand of white hair away from her ear and checked the number. It was unfamiliar to her.

"Hello," she said, in a tone conveying both gentleness and strength. The line was quiet. "Hello, how can I help you?"

"Is this Joy Smith?" a teenage girl's frantic voice asked.

"Yes, it is. May I ask your name?"

"Are you the member of Parliament who's helping victims of human trafficking?"

"Yes, I am. Please tell me how I can help you."

"I ... I ..." The stressed voice on the other end tried to continue. Erratic. Accompanied by heavy breathing. Like someone who was about to pass out.

"It's going to be all right. Tell me where you are, and I will get you help."

"I think ..."

"Yes."

"I think I'm a victim. I need ... I need ..."

"Are you safe right now?"

"I ... I ..."

The girl was becoming hysterical.

"It's going to be all right. May I have your name?"

The line went quiet again. As if the girl on the other end was wondering if saying this over the phone was safe.

"Samantha."

"Samantha, where are you?"

"I'm at Ottawa Hospital in emergency. The one by the experimental farm," she whispered, feeling perhaps she had now gone too far in giving out both her name and location. "A man who said he was my friend forced me ... He's in emergency ... This is the first phone call I've made in months ... Please help me. Please help me."

"Samantha, do you see a security officer?"

The line went quiet. "No, I—wait—yes."

"I want you to go that person and tell them that a member of Parliament is coming to see you. Can you do that? I'm coming to you right now."

"Please hurry. I am so scared. If he knows I phoned someone he'll ... he'll ..." Deep, heavy breathing. Then a chilling whisper. "If he knows I phoned someone he'll kill me. Do you understand me?"

"I'm on my way."

Joy heard the line go dead.

Joy parked her car, then hurried in the pouring rain through the emergency entrance. She approached the security desk, scanning the area for a fragile, terrified teenager.

"Joy Smith?" a voice said.

Joy turned to her left. A shell of a girl approached her. Dishevelled red hair. Pale white skin. Blue miniskirt. Skimpy grey shirt. Sunken cheeks. Lifeless green eyes. She looked like a ghost. There was so little left of her that her frail appearance made it seem she could disappear into thin air.

"Samantha?"

She nodded.

"Everything is going to be all right."

The moment Samantha heard those words, something in her relaxed. Like she was in the presence of safety. Like she was a young child and her mother had come into her room to calm her fears of a lightning storm.

Joy turned to the short, well-built security officer, introduced herself, and asked if there was a private room they could use. The officer led them to a small room with a table. Seeing a vending machine nearby, Joy pulled out her wallet and inserted her credit card.

"What kind of drink would you like, Samantha?"

She seemed shell-shocked by the question. Her brain tried to imagine what it was like to be given a choice. She tried to recall something as simple as making a decision for herself.

Joy understood the look of indecision in her eyes. "Whatever you like, Samantha. What's your favourite?"

She stalled. Blinked. Her mind tried to turn into gear. It was like getting a car started that had been left frozen over winter. Her difficulty breathing spoke of the unbearable trauma she had experienced. She sounded like a wounded child when she asked, "Is there a sports drink?"

"There is. Any particular flavour?"

She bit her lip, as if she feared repercussions if she asked too much. "Red?"

Joy hit the button. She gave Samantha the drink. They sat down. Joy closed the door.

"Thank you for calling me, Samantha. That took a lot of courage. Can you tell me what happened?"

Samantha's hands began to tremble. Like a voice inside her mind was warning her of impending doom. That perhaps she wasn't as safe as she thought. She leaned her elbows on the table, placed her hands on either side of her head, and gripped tight, as if it was the only thing she knew how to do to keep it from exploding.

"If he knows I'm here, I'm going to die."

"You're safe now. I promise you that. I have many, many friends, and I assure you I will get you to a safe place. Everything is going to be all right."

Tears began to stream down Samantha's face. How did it ever come to this? She covered her eyes, as if doing so could prevent her from looking back into her past. She stayed that way so long it was as if she had turned into a statue frozen in unimaginable grief and pain. Then, finally, she let out a breath.

"I met him online. Then we met in person. Became friends. It all seemed so great." She gripped her head even tighter. All those awful memories. It was bad enough to have experienced them all one by one. But now, sitting here, it was like having to relive each of those moments combined in one instant.

And it proved to be an unbearable task.

"Then everything changed. I was forced to have sex with so many men." It all became too much. She shook her head. Pushed herself to continue. "It was awful. I worked for him for months. Eating when he told me to eat. Sleeping when he told me to sleep. I was beaten so often. There were times I was sure I would die. My friend Crystal wanted to leave. So…"

She rubbed her temples. She looked straight ahead, focusing not on Joy but on some imaginary point behind her. She was so exhausted, her bloodshot eyes seemed slightly crossed. She closed them. "He strangled Crystal to death with an extension cord."

Samantha became silent to honour Crystal's death. It felt wrong to continue speaking until she had at least tried to remember her dear friend in a sombre moment.

"He told me he would do the same to me if I ever tried to leave." She stared at the red drink on the table. Desperately thirsty, yet somehow unable to make the connection to reach out and take it. "He got into a fight a few hours ago. He got knifed. Badly. I rushed him to emergency."

She looked at Joy. A curious expression came over her. She blinked. Focused on Joy. "Strange, isn't it? Trying to save the life of someone who will kill you?"

She reached out and grabbed the bottle. Twisting off the cap, she chugged half of it. "Now he's in surgery, and the doctors tell me it doesn't look good."

Voices in Samantha's head spoke to her.

He's not dying. He's going to get off that operating table, grab a scalpel, find you here in this little room and finish you off once and for all.

"He told me if I ever went to the police he would kill me. But he didn't have to threaten me. A friend of mine in the game tried that once. But the

33

police said they had nothing to charge him with, and she had to live with the fear of him finding her. I never heard from her again."

This woman can't help you.

She finished the bottle. "Word on the street was that you help girls like me. Is that true? Does a person like you help someone like me?"

You're making a mistake.

"Samantha?"

The caring tone, contrasting so much with the negative voices in her head, was too much for Samantha, and she couldn't meet Joy's eyes.

"Samantha?" Joy asked again.

Something in Joy's tone encouraged her to take a chance. She looked up. Their eyes met.

"I believe you, Samantha. I believe everything you told me."

Samantha broke down. She squished her eyelids together, forcing out a stream of tears.

Joy put her hand on her shoulder. "And I am going to help you. All right?

"Thank you."

"I have friends with the Ottawa Police who are going to help you. Then we're going to find you a safe place to live. And Samantha, I'm going to be with you every step of the way."

Samantha wiped the tears from her eyes. "You think I can get out of this?"

"I know it."

The police arrived, and Joy stayed with Samantha while they reviewed her case. Afterwards, Joy connected Samantha to a safe house outside of Toronto run by a humanitarian group specializing in helping survivors of human trafficking.

Joy drove onto Parliament Hill, passed through security and entered her parking area. She walked to the building and showed her special MP ring to the security guard. Every MP receives a special pin, and some choose to have them made into rings. A unique number has been stamped into every member's ring ever since the ring was first introduced as part of a security measure in 1979. Inside Joy's ring was number 1301.

Joy entered Parliament through a door reserved only for MPs and staff. Opening the door to her office suite, she smiled at her assistant.

"Good morning, Karen."

Karen had short blonde hair and wore dark pants and a white shirt. She smiled in a way that was both pleasant and tough. Human trafficking awards and major news articles decorated the wall behind her.

"Hi, Mrs. Smith. How is Samantha?"

Hearing the conversation at the door, Joel Oosterman stepped out of his office, finished wiping his glasses with a cloth and put them back on. His dark grey suit matched the clouds through the window behind him.

"Good morning, Joel."

"Mrs. Smith." He nodded to her.

"Samantha's a survivor." Joy said, hanging her coat on the rack.

"Excellent," Karen said, her voice quiet. A relief to hear about someone surviving after others had not.

"That is great news," Joel said.

"It is great, isn't it?" Joy said, walking to her private office. "All right, let's continue working on our bill."

Joy entered her office, Joel and Karen followed, and she sat down at her desk filled with papers. Brushing a stack to the left she glanced at a quote on her desk by William Wilberforce that often gave her inspiration. Wilberforce served as a member of Parliament in England and dedicated his efforts to abolishing slavery. He regularly introduced bills to ban the slave trade and faced extreme opposition by those earning vast sums of money from it. Wilberforce never gave up. Some 18 years after he started, the Abolition of the Slave Trade Act passed in 1807, ending slavery in the British colonies. The House stood and cheered at its success.

Wilberforce's quote read, "You may choose to look the other way but you can never say again that you did not know."

This truth gave Joy hope. On difficult days in particular. It would remind her that change takes time. That even doing the right thing can be difficult. Especially when money and power are at stake.

Her computer was to her right. Across from her stood a chesterfield and two chairs. Behind those, a TV. Her office also featured a tea and coffee service, and she offered those beverages to every guest who entered as a symbol to honour them for visiting her.

Joel sat down on a chair and Karen opposite him. They had been working long days drafting a bill that, if passed, would result in a minimum sentence of five years for human traffickers. It would mean that judges would be required to give at least a five-year sentence for a human trafficking offence. A law already existed that provided for a maximum sentence, but there was no minimum. This resulted in instances where judges gave convicted human traffickers light sentences of one year or even less. If Joy's bill became law, it would encourage victims like Samantha to come forward and identify their traffickers, knowing that their traffickers would be prosecuted and jailed for a sufficient length of time for them to hopefully get their lives back in order.

The bill would include a summary sheet as well as a substantial amount of supporting information. The hope was that if Joy, Joel, Karen and the many other members of the team could assemble a well-researched and organized bill, then a majority of members of Parliament across party lines would support the bill.

They discussed further details of what they would research today. Joel took notes. When they had laid out a plan for the day, Joel leaned back in his chair.

"Something bothering you?" Joy asked.

Joel paused, always careful to deliver a well thought through response. "Joy ... the chances of this bill going through are ... well, let's just say it's highly improbable. We either need a minister to take this on—and that's not likely to happen—or we need to get our name drawn in a private member's bill lottery. And even then, we would have to be drawn early."

Normally bills were brought forward by a cabinet minister. Joy served as a member of Parliament but was not in cabinet. Her first option, and the one most likely to succeed, was to get a minister interested in carrying the bill forward. Human trafficking would normally fall under justice, so the justice minister could champion it. The trouble was that the government had already laid out which bills they wanted to bring forward. And there would not be time to add another one into the mix. A government initiative would need to get dropped in order to make room; otherwise her initiative would get outright refused.

But she had a backup plan.

If a minister could not be found to bring forward a human trafficking bill, then a member of Parliament could introduce a private member's bill.

A private member's bill was a massive long shot. The House of Commons spends most of its time on business related to government. There's only a small amount of time allocated to discussing private members' bills. Members of Parliament who are not cabinet ministers can submit a private member's bill. And many would like to. The question arises of how to decide which bills get attention in the House of Commons and which don't.

Enter the lottery.

Every session, the names of those members of Parliament qualifying for private members' bills (some 240) are drawn at random. Of those, normally only the first five will have a decent chance at presenting a bill. And even if a member gets their name drawn high enough, they face the arduous task of getting that bill approved through three separate readings. At the end of each of the second and third readings, a vote is taken. If the bill doesn't pass at either one of those readings, the bill fails. Bills that deal with relatively minor items pass more easily. Of the 127 private members' bills that received royal assent (became law) between 1945 and 1993, a staggering 96 of them dealt with inconsequential items like changes to the names of constituencies.

On top of that, Joy was in a minority government that might only stay in power for two to three years and could end at any time.

That meant if you were a regular member of Parliament like Joy, you had to first count on your name being drawn high in the lottery. Then, if your bill dealt with something of significance, like protecting victims of human trafficking, you had the next massive mountain to climb of convincing the other parties—and, sometimes, your own party—to vote for your bill. And you had to hope that the government stayed in power long enough to get your bill through.

It was like climbing Mount Everest and then reaching the top only to discover a second Mount Everest waiting for you.

Most private members' bills are put on the order paper in the hopes of getting immediate attention but typically fade into nothing.

"We have to get the justice minister on board," Joy said. "He says yes, we're off to the races."

"He's our best shot," Karen said.

"He's not going to do it," Joel interjected.

"Sure he will. He just has to be encouraged with facts," Joy replied.

"He may want to do to but might not be able to do it. It doesn't fit into the government's agenda," Joel said.

Joy leaned back in her chair and thought. "I don't see how he could say no."

"The best chance is for him to be given a good reason," Karen said. "We have the research. We have evidence that traffickers are being convicted and given light sentences. But even if—"

Joy stood. "I'm going to have a private meeting with the minister of justice," she said. "Time to find out our chances with this bill."

chapter four

It was time to make a decision.

Ever since she had received the message *Do you want to meet?* Abby had been a nervous wreck. Her mind and heart flipped back and forth about what to do, what this meant and how, when or (gasp) if to respond.

Her English teacher talked about Victorian writers. That interested her. She looked forward to reading a new book. But during most of the class her mind was on Jake. What would he be like? Would she measure up? Would he still have interest in her after they met? Would she have staying power? The little bit she did catch of class included an assignment on choosing two books, each from a different author during the reign of Queen Victoria in England. So many to choose from. So many she had already read. The last class of the day proved to be the longest.

Finally, the bell rang.

She left class and immediately looked at her phone. Had he re-sent the request? Had he given up on her for taking so long to respond? Why was this so hard to decide?

What's the big deal? Get together and go for a fun time. If it doesn't work, it doesn't work. No problem.

But what if I go and I do like him but he turns me down? What if I don't make the right first impression? What if I'm myself and he doesn't like me? Do I pretend to be someone else at first and be the person I think he wants me to be? Or do I just go as myself? If I go just as I am, will that be enough?

Will he love me for who I am?

Maybe I should talk this through. Maybe I should give this a second thought. Who to talk with? Mom? Mom would be all right, I guess, but this is teenage stuff. She wouldn't get it. Dad? Forget it. He's not around, and besides, it's still teenage stuff. Then again, he is a guy. He would have advice, wouldn't he? Forget it. He won't be home until late, and I would need him to respond now. Kedisha? Yeah. Kedisha would be cool. She would promise to not say anything. She would be able to help me out with what to do.

Glancing down the hallway through a maze of students, Abby saw Kedisha at her locker. She was about to call out to her friend when she noticed Kedisha's boyfriend approaching her. The two of them talked for a brief moment, Kedisha laughed at something he said; then the two of them walked down the hall in the opposite direction from Abby.

No matter. I can make up my own mind.

Abby pulled out her phone. But just as soon as she had done so a battle began inside her mind.

You can do this.

But what if he doesn't end up liking me?

What's not to like? Stop being so pessimistic. You're a great girl. And he's a great guy.

A guy I hardly know.

A guy you've gotten to know in cyberworld, and now it's time for real life.

I don't know.

Message him back and say yes.

We don't have anyone in common. I might not be who he thinks I am.

Three letters. Y-e-s.

No. No. O-k-a-y.

Okay? That's way too casual.

She typed in "It would be great to meet!"

Did that sound too excited? She erased the exclamation point and replaced it with a period. Was that too serious now?

Arrgh. Just send it.

Abby reread her last message. People passed in front of and behind her, like an endless stream of traffic on the 401. Now or never. She pressed send before she could change her mind.

She put the phone in her pocket. Walked down the hallway towards the nearest exit. Pushing the panic hardware on the door, she released the catch and let herself out into the afternoon. Her phone beeped. She recognized the tone. She looked at the message. Jake.

"Great. 7:00 tonight?"

That was fast. What she busy tonight? Did it matter?

"Sounds great!"

He texted the name of the restaurant. She sent a thumbs-up. Looking up, she thought the sky had never looked so blue before. But if she had looked farther in the distance, she would have seen rain clouds approaching.

Abby had changed her clothes four times and was now further away from making a decision than when she started. She sat on her bed. Glanced at the clock. *Just make up your mind.* But so much was riding on this first impression. *What if I don't meet his expectations? What if I gave a certain impression online and now he meets me in person and he doesn't like me? What if …*

She settled on a dark pair of jeans and a long-sleeve grey shirt. She searched through the mess on her closet floor and dug out a light jacket despite the heat. She put it on. Kedisha had commented the other day that the blue brought out her eyes. She checked and rechecked her makeup. Hair down. Poker straight. *Here goes nothing.*

The subway ride to the Yorkdale Mall station seemed shorter than normal. She was both excited and terrified to meet him. She hoped the excited part would win out.

She knew the restaurant. It was at the mall. She had never been to it before. Too expensive for her bank account.

What am I doing?

I'll be fine. It's just a get-together.

Wait a minute. Who else knows I'm here?

It's a restaurant. It's public. But whatever you do, don't go back with him. Don't accept a ride. No matter how nice you find him. You don't know him that well. If he offers, just politely decline. Now go and have some fun.

She arrived at the restaurant. Soft lighting. Dark furniture. She looked in and saw a tall hostess in an all-black dress that hugged her body. Black pumps. Toned arms. And tanned legs that stretched from here to Vancouver. *Great. I can understand why they have models at these restaurants, but would it be possible to have ones that don't totally show me up? First date, too. Like I'm not dying already with potential comparisons. Relax. Relax. It will be all right. Wait. He hasn't seen me yet, and I could just bolt. If I go now, I can catch a movie. What's playing tonight?*

"Are you meeting someone tonight?" the 10 at the greeting station asked.

Yeah. And don't steal him from me, okay?

"I am," Abby said. "We have a reservation—"

"Abby?"

Easygoing. The voice was as soft and low as she had imagined. Something in our perception of sound attaches personality to a voice. And when Abby heard his, she relaxed. She turned around. *Here goes nothing.*

A picture come to life. Tall. Well, taller than her. Golden-brown eyes that looked even better to Abby in person. An unmistakable genuine vibe.

"Jake?"

"You look great. Thanks for coming."

Any thought of backing out was swept from her mind.

I'm glad I followed through on showing up. Who knows? We'll see where this leads.

"You too."

Did that come out right? Did my "you too" mean I think he looks great too, or did it mean that I was thankful he came here as well? Or did it refer to both? Wait! Add this: "Thanks for asking."

"Of course. Want to get a seat?"

"Sure thing."

"Restaurant or lounge?"

Restaurant. I don't want to be rated against all those girls in the lounge.

"Whatever you prefer."

"How about the lounge?" he said to both her and the hostess. The hostess nodded with a smile that revealed to Abby that she was exhausted, yet she put on a good front despite her condition. "The soccer game is on," he added to Abby.

"Great." That word came out in a high pitch instead of the casual tone she had intended. Her stomach did a somersault.

The bar was done in a light blue marble that oddly matched her eyes to perfection. Straight-backed chairs surrounded mahogany tables. Wide-screen televisions hung around the room. Low volume. The kind of place where you could spend a lot of time talking without having to shout.

They sat down at a table. Abby half-expected, half-hoped he would hold her chair for her, then dismissed the thought when he didn't. *Guys don't do that anymore. Get with it.*

A waitress approached the table, just as stunning as the first but with creamy skin and spun-gold hair. *Do they have a model-making machine back there?* The waitress smiled and asked for their drink orders. She hid her exhaustion better than the hostess. Jake smiled back. Abby felt a flash of jealousy.

"I'll have a vodka martini," he said.

Awkward. He's clearly drinking age. His age wasn't totally clear on his profile. I'm going to feel like an idiot when I say Coke. Or even worse, I try to order an alcoholic drink, she asks my age, and I feel like the kid playing soccer by herself. What to do. What to do.

"Do you make a good cappuccino by any chance?" Abby asked.

"The best."

Crisis averted.

The waitress left to fill their orders.

"It's great to see you in person," Jake said.

"You too."

Seriously? Come on, girl. Can't you say something besides "you too"?

"And it's really nice of you to have taken all that time to message with me."

Don't you dare say it.

"I've really enjoyed getting to know you."

Okay. That wasn't great, but at least it was a complete sentence. We're into a conversation now. First few awkward moments behind us. Lift-off was good, and we're about to reach cruising altitude.

"Thanks. You're a great person, Abby. It's easy to connect with you."

Flutter. Flutter. The waitress brought their drinks. Abby said thanks. Jake didn't acknowledge her, never taking his eyes off Abby. Was he into her?

"So what kind of food do you like?" he asked.

"Oh, everything."

"You like lobster?"

She loved lobster. Had it with her family at her last birthday celebration. They took a picture. She posted it online, though she had since forgotten.

Abby smiled. "I do."

"Lobster and steak combo. Calamari to start. What do you say?"

"I'm all in."

"Perfect."

They talked about her schooling. Her soccer. The books she had read. When the food arrived, they alternated between laughing, eating and cheering at the soccer game. She found herself at ease with him. *What was I so afraid of anyways?* And despite all the other girls walking around, she felt the comfort that came with being with someone who valued her, who cared about what she was saying. He wasn't just listening because he had to. He had chosen to be there.

Just before the second half kicked off, after all the food was gone and just before he received his second drink, he looked at her in the soft light of the lounge. Their eyes met. The nervousness of having to talk to fill silent space left them. She could just be herself. No pretending to like bands she really hated or plastering a smile on her face. Just herself. And when he saw her, she knew the verdict was coming. He could have other girls. No problem. She was convinced of that. But did he want her?

"You're beautiful, Abby."

She'd never heard that. Not from someone outside her family. Her dad had said it. A while ago. A long while ago, in fact. But this felt different. This was an objective point of view. It came from someone who didn't have to say it. Parents sort of do. Jake didn't.

Did he?

He moved on to talk about World Cup qualifying, but his words kept running through her mind.

They were still engrossed in each other long after the postgame show finished. How do three hours go by so fast? Then came the lull in the conversation when both people realize it's time to call it a night.

"Thanks for a great evening, Jake."

"Sure thing. Can I give you a lift home?"

Oh boy.

Logical Abby and In-Love Abby began arguing with each other.

Remember your plan.

I do remember my plan, but it's different now. He's a good guy.

Subway. Then bus. End of discussion.

He's a great guy. I'll offend him if I don't.

Try to keep some objectivity about this guy. You had a nice evening. Call it a night.

"I'm okay, thanks."

"You sure? You know we Canadians are always being too polite."

"Eh?" she said.

"Eh?"

They both laughed.

"I almost forgot!" He reached into his jacket and pulled out a box wrapped in black wrapping paper. "For you."

Abby sensed the guilt people feel when someone gets them a gift and they don't have anything for them in return.

Just be honest with him.

"Jake, you shouldn't have. I … I feel bad. I didn't get you anything."

"Sure you did. You came here tonight. What more could I ask for?"

"This feels awkward. I don't know what to do. Do I open it now?"

"Only if you want."

She unwrapped it. Opened the box. *Oh my.*

A gold necklace with a small purple stone reflected the light back at her. Thin enough to be elegant. Large enough to carry value.

"Jake."

"Just a small thank you. Have a good night, okay?"

"You too."

Speechless, she followed him out to the parking lot. Said goodbye. Smiled back at him over her shoulder as she walked towards the subway entrance. He waved back. Soon he was out of sight. Despite the cool air,

Abby felt the warmth that comes with being in the presence of someone new who also turns out to be someone great. The ride home could have taken forever. She had all the time in the world as she thought back about her evening.

When she arrived, her mother asked her where she had been.

"Out with friends," she said.

That was odd. She had a friend in Kedisha. But *friends* plural was slightly out of the normal. Abby didn't want to involve her mom. Not yet. She wanted to trust her own judgment. Make up her own mind before reaching out to her mom for confirmation.

Retreating to her room, she placed the necklace on her bedside table and put her phone showing a picture of Jake beside it. *So this is what it feels like? This is what it feels like to be a girl in love.* She stared at her phone until the soft draw of sleep came over her.

Abby drifted off to her dreams.

chapter five

Joy watched the minister of justice stand in the House of Commons and head towards the lobby. She followed him, hoping to catch him before he became engrossed in another conversation. She walked through the door and entered the government lobby.

The House of Commons is split into two sides. The government sits on one side and the opposition on the other side. Behind each side is a lobby. The government goes to their side. Opposition to theirs. The lobbies are secluded places for members of Parliament only. The spaces are furnished with tables, sofas, chairs, computers and phones—everything members need while they are sitting in the House and don't have time to get back to their office. Party whips (those assigned to keep the members in line, hence the title "whip") assign staff as needed in the lobbies. Access to a given lobby is highly controlled by security.

Creating a perfect location for a captive audience.

Joy entered the long, narrow lobby. Other members of Parliament from the minority Conservative government talked on their phones, with each other, with staffers. Joy searched through the crowd. Caught a glimpse of the minister of justice.

"Hi, Joy. Good to see you again," a fellow MP from Manitoba said, hoping to catch a word.

Joy greeted him back. "Good to see you, too. Are you coming by my office later today?"

"Absolutely."

"Good," Joy said with a smile. "I'm looking forward to meeting with you. Thank you for fitting me into your schedule."

There was an art to being polite and staying focused on a mission without unnecessarily offending people.

Joy reached the minister, only to find him engrossed in a conversation with another member. She moved just to within eyesight of him, hoping to catch his attention. He saw her. Joy smiled and raised her eyebrows in a way that indicated she wanted to speak with him. The next reaction he gave would prove critical. So much in personality is involuntary. A person can only hide so much. If he acknowledged her right away, it would be a good sign. If he went back to his conversation, it meant he had other pressing issues that would not allow him to divert his attention.

He nodded.

Joy waited, using the time to rehearse in her mind. The point of this conversation was not to get lost in all the details. Stay focused, and figure out where the minister stood on the issue. Would he take on this kind of bill? If not, could he be encouraged to take it on?

He finished his conversation. Others wanted to talk with him. Joy moved in.

"Hello, Arthur."

Some made the mistake of calling him Arty. But Joy knew better.

"Hi, Joy."

"I wonder if you have a few minutes to talk."

"Of course." He pointed to a couch. They walked over and sat down.

"Thank you. I know how busy you are."

"Not at all."

"As you know, I'm involved in the fight against human trafficking."

"Well done."

"I wonder if at some point it might be worthwhile to look into a bill."

"A bill? Why? You already have your Motion M-153."

Some three years earlier Joy had drafted M-153 on human trafficking. It was part of a long and dedicated process in the fight against human trafficking. An event back home in Winnipeg had opened her eyes to the evil hiding in plain sight. An event that included her son Edward had propelled her into this fight.

When she came to Parliament her first official act to defend victims of trafficking started with calling on the Standing Committee on the Status of Women to initiate a study of human trafficking in Canada. Nearly a year later the committee passed the motion, and the study began. The result of that study was a report entitled *Turning Outrage into Action to Address Trafficking for the Purpose of Sexual Exploitation in Canada*. It was tabled in Parliament that same month.

The report's key priorities focused on the prevention of trafficking, protection of victims and prosecution of offenders. It called on all Canadians to stand up for victims and implement the proposed recommendations. Joy made a motion in 2006 calling on Parliament to condemn the sex trafficking of women and children across international borders and implement a comprehensive strategy to fight the trafficking of persons worldwide. In March 2007, the House of Commons unanimously passed Joy's Motion M-153. It was victory. But it wasn't enough.

"Exactly," Joy said. "The House gave one hundred percent support. That means they understand there is a problem."

"Across international borders. I agree. And that's an implementation issue for our border security."

"But what if this isn't just about victims coming into our country?" Joy asked. "What if it is about victims from *within* our country?"

"Again, it's a matter of border security to ensure that all those coming in are coming in for lawful purposes."

"I'm referring to girls born and raised right here in Canada."

The minister stopped his train of thought. Had he heard that right?

"Girls not being brought into Canada but girls who are already Canadians?"

"It is true that human trafficking is happening from outside to inside. Foreign girls are being lured in under false pretenses and are then used for awful purposes by men who have deceived them," Joy said. "But trafficking is also happening to the girl next door. Your average girl. Every income bracket. Every skin colour. Every neighbourhood. Canadian girls are victims of human trafficking."

"Impossible."

"No."

"I simply don't believe it."

"I've seen it."

"Joy—." Another MP walked by and nodded to Arthur. Arthur returned the greeting. "Joy, human trafficking …" he seemed momentarily overcome with information. Like his mind was trying to process something it had not believed was possible. "Human trafficking is not on the government's agenda."

"Maybe it should be. The motion was carried unanimously."

"Joy, your motion was impressive work. It really was. But no one would ever have voted against that motion. It's so generic and calls on people to do what obviously should be done."

"Exactly."

"Joy, there are many important issues we have to deal with. Human trafficking is one of them. But the government doesn't have time to address everything at the same time. You understand that."

"I do. And I understand the many items you have to balance and move forward. Don't think I don't appreciate the magnitude of your position."

"The government doesn't have time to—" Something caught his attention. Another MP waiting her turn to speak. He nodded at her in acknowledgement. "You said it exactly right. Condemning human trafficking across international borders."

"And now I'm asking to go a step further. To condemn it *within* our borders. To protect Canadian girls."

That caught him off guard a second time. Like his mind had already chosen to disregard Joy's earlier comment. He physically leaned back. Not a great distance. Had someone not been part of the conversation they might not even have noticed it happened. But Joy noticed. Even if he did do it involuntarily.

"Human trafficking is not happening to Canadian girls," he said. It came out as more of an attempt to assure himself of what he knew. Or at least what he thought he knew. He fought against his cognitive dissonance. Then wondered. "It isn't happening, is it? Not to our girls."

"What if it is?"

"Joy, human trafficking as it relates to Canada is people being brought in from outside."

"In part. But what if there's more to it than that? We're talking about a new crime here, Arthur. Something we have closed our eyes to. I'm not sure why. But we just don't see it. Or maybe we don't want to see it."

Members started re-entering the House of Commons. The minister stood. Joy, too. He looked apologetically at the other member in waiting. Then to Joy, quietly enough that it would not be heard by others, "Joy, the information you're giving me is ... is staggering to say the least. I'm going to look into it. But I need to be clear with you. We are not going to put a bill forward on this." He turned his hands palm up as an indication of a man already swamped with responsibilities who had become accustomed to rejecting new and good ideas that would capsize the boat if he took yet another task on. "But keep up the good work," he said.

"Thank you for your time," Joy said as the minister departed.

She took in a breath. How many conversations had there been in this lobby over the years? How many members had both good news and bad news delivered to them there? How many historically significant conversations had taken place there?

She wondered if this might have been one of them.

When the session ended, Joy returned to her office. Karen looked up from her desk. Joy motioned to her office. Karen followed her in.

"And?" Karen asked, sitting down.

"I think we have a very big battle on our hands, Karen."

"He's not going to support it?"

"It doesn't look that way. He's just ... I don't know. We passed the motion. Why is he not seeing this?"

"We can show him the bill. We can go through the evidence."

"He's not interested," Joy said.

"Well, he's the best chance we have at getting this thing through, so we have to get him interested." Joy's mind was already working through other scenarios. "If the minister of justice can't be convinced, we're in serious trouble," Karen finished.

"He doesn't believe there is a problem," Joy said.

"Then how do we convince him he's wrong?"

"He's not going to put the bill forward. There has to be another way."

"Well, not without him. If he is not willing to support the bill, all that's left …"

She didn't want to say it. The other route was just dumb luck. It was basing your plan on a lottery ticket. It was a joke of a way forward.

"You can say it out loud, Karen. A private member's bill."

"Lotto 649."

Joy became quiet. The room became quiet. Almost eerily so. It felt strange all of a sudden. Like all the weight of the history of Parliament Hill was coming alive in their room.

Joy spoke quietly, her tone both soft and strange. "Can I let you in on a little secret, Karen?" she whispered.

Karen leaned forward. She titled her head slightly to the left the way she always did when she was giving someone her undivided attention.

Joy became still. All the experiences, all the many challenges, in her life and in her political career seemed to come to bear in what she was about to say.

"I know I'm going to get called in the top three in that lottery."

Okay, that's a little spooky. Karen didn't know how to react. Didn't know what to say. She felt a shiver. Like there were more people in the room than just the two of them. But what impacted Karen more than what Joy said was the conviction that Joy might in fact be right.

"That's impossible."

"Is it?"

Karen swallowed. "You can't know something like that."

"I can't?"

People can be optimistic. Even overly optimistic. But to actually *know* something in advance?

No one could hear their conversation. No one could pick up on what they were saying. Still, Karen chose to whisper as well. "How could you possibly be so sure of this?"

Joy paused. Like every leader, she had experienced her scars. And those scars had taught her how to be measured. How to listen. How to discern.

"My father inherited the family farm. It was a big, successful operation," she said. "But he squandered it. He had no idea what he was doing. We sank down to poverty. It was so embarrassing."

She shook her head as if doing so could somehow get the emotions of those painful memories out of her mind. "I remember being teased at school because we were so poor. One day at recess my brother was being beaten. I didn't have the guts to intervene, so I ran to the schoolhouse, and a teacher came to stop the fight. By the time the teacher got there, my brother had been beaten so badly that he was full of blood and bruises."

Joy squinted her eyes a moment as if she were right back there, trying to block out the image of what she was seeing. "I told myself that day that I would never turn away from someone who was suffering. Years later we managed to scrape enough together, and I went to university. Got a master's degree. Began teaching. Then my son Edward changed everything for me. He was the catalyst."

The thought entered her mind to share more about Edward. But she decided against it. Now was not the time. "I started teaching about the dangers of human trafficking. Started helping girls wherever I could. Got involved in politics. And here I am in Ottawa. Now let me ask you this question, Karen. A poor little farm girl from Manitoba becomes a member of Parliament. Does that sound like an accident to you?"

It was rhetorical. Karen knew it. Joy knew it. So they waited, both of them absorbing what she was saying.

"This thing is far bigger than me, Karen. I can't do this on my own." Joy glanced past her. It had been an exhausting day. Still, in the tiredness of her life, her mind focused every last bit of energy on this single issue until things became crystal clear. "I can't convince the minister of justice. I just tried. That leaves one other option. The only way forward is a private member's bill. If I don't get called early in the lottery, the bill has no chance. No one else knows what I know. No one else feels what I feel. No one else will take the bill forward. And if there's no bill, then thousands upon thousands of Canadian girls will continue to suffer in shame."

She stopped. Squinted again. Thought even deeper. "But if there is a bill, if I do get drawn, then thousands will be saved." She leaned forward. Put her elbows on her desk. Folded her hands beneath her chin. "And that's how I know I'm going to get my name called."

It was preposterous. Wasn't it? Wasn't it just simply too much optimism? Or was it more? Had she tapped into something? Had she received some conviction somehow, someway, of what would actually take place in the future?

Joy nodded her head ever so slightly. "You watch and see."

chapter six

No doubt Kedisha knew something was different.

Abby could tell her friend was noticing changes in her. Even when they were just hanging out, she felt Kedisha observing her, studying her. Abby had experimented with different makeup, different hairstyles and different clothes. The changes weren't obvious from one day to the next, but over a week, over a couple of weeks for sure, they compounded into significant changes. Abby seemed altogether different.

Like a patient who gets a sudden new lease on life after a blood transfusion, Abby felt like she had been injected with a drug that made her into a whole new person.

She noticed it herself the most when she approached the lunch table occupied by her peers. Before she had felt apprehensive, even scared, about sitting down. *Will they get up? Will they make fun of me? Or worse, will they even know I'm here?* But now it was different. Now she was self-assured—she had a confidence that enabled her to approach them and not live and die with someone else's reaction.

"So who is he?" Kedisha asked as Abby spun the combination at her locker. She pulled on the lock and opened the door.

"Who is who?"

"You know who. How did you guys meet?"

Abby avoided eye contact. "We're just friends."

"So there *is* someone," she said, raising her eyebrows. "Name."

"None of your business," Abby whispered, hoping Kedisha would do the same and not draw attention to their conversation.

"Come on. Out with the details. How did you guys meet?"

"I have to get to class."

"You're smart enough. You can afford to skip a few minutes to give me the—"

"We met online," she said, thinking that giving Kedisha a few details would get her to stop her inquisition. "A friend of a friend."

"Is it that guy I caught you staring at on your phone? Cute. What does he do?"

"He's graduated."

"And doing what now?"

"Lots of questions, Kedisha," Abby said, grabbing her biology textbook and closing the door.

"What do you really know about this guy?"

That didn't go over well. Abby did little to hide her reaction. "Thanks."

"That's not what I meant."

"Can always count on you, Kedisha."

"Abby."

"Always seems to be so fitting that you have a super guy with you all the time, but poor, pathetic Abby, she couldn't possibly get a guy. So when she does, he must be a creep."

"Abby, I'm just curious."

"No, you're not. You're surprised."

The walk home usually gave Abby a chance to let her mind wander— to explore places without any restrictions. But today, the memory of the conversation she had earlier with Kedisha plagued her thoughts. She tried to get rid of it the way people do when they want a particularly awkward or painful event out of their mind. But the more she tried, the more it came back. Like a boomerang returning. Every time she attempted to throw that thought away, it seemed to come back twice as strong, until it felt impossible to shake loose.

Why was I so defensive around Kedisha?

It's her fault. The tone in her voice was so judging.

She's a friend. She's just asking.

Yeah, asking how I could possibly find a great guy.

She punched in her code in the garage door—the basketball hoop may as well have been invisible—and entered the kitchen. The moment she did, her phone buzzed. A message. A jolt of excitement ran through her. She checked. Jake.

"Canada's Wonderland tonight?"

"Hi, sweetheart," her mom said from the kitchen. The words were normal. The tone was not. To any outsider it would have seemed like any other greeting on any other day. But when people know each other well, and for a long time, even the slightest nuance in how they say things conveys much, much more than the simple words themselves.

Something was wrong.

"Hey, Mom," Abby replied, wondering if her own tone conveyed that she had discovered something odd in her mother's tone.

"How was school?"

Sucked. It was awful. My friend doubts that I can have a boyfriend— Come to think of it, Mom, do you doubt the same thing? Do you think I deserve a good guy? Would you believe me if I told you this great guy took me out to a super nice restaurant, called me beautiful and gave me a—

"It was good."

"Your nose a hundred percent?"

"It's fine," Abby said, heading up to her room to respond to Jake.

Her mother poked her head around the corner. "Why don't you come sit down. Let's catch up. I haven't seen you a while."

Haven't seen Dad either. He always comes home late and is so bagged. Business. I know. Pay for the mortgage. I get it. He has lots on the go.

"I was just going to go out tonight," Abby said, stopping on the stairs.

"Great. With Kedisha?"

"Maybe. Some other friends."

I just lied. Why did I lie? Big deal. She wouldn't understand ... Or maybe she would?

"Supper is in a bit. You want to get washed up?"

No. Not really. I just want to get out of here and hang out with Jake.

"Sure."

Abby's mother smiled and returned to the kitchen. Abby looked at her phone as she went to the back hall sink.

"Hey, Jake! Canada's Wonderland sounds great!"

"Super. I'm looking forward to seeing you again."

"Me too! It'll take me a while to get there by bus."

"Bus? Not my girl. Let's go by car."

"That's a long way to go."

"Your worth it."

"Awwww. Thanks. And by the way it's spelled you're as in you are."

"You see. Pretty and smart."

"Want to pick me up at my house?"

"Would love to."

"Super."

She put the phone in her pocket and was about to head to the kitchen when it buzzed again.

"Actually, want to meet at the Richmond Hill Centre platform? That might make it faster for both of us."

She admired his ingenuity. If she took the train towards him and he drove towards her, that would speed up the time for them to meet. It reminded her of math. If a bus heading towards Jake leaves in half an hour and travels at an average speed of 50 km/hr, and Jake drives a car towards Abby travelling at an average speed of 70 km/hr, what time would they—It didn't matter. Even if it didn't make chivalry sense, it did make romantic sense. People doing what they could to see each other as soon as possible.

"For sure. See you there."

She entered the kitchen and saw her mother blowing on dough in the oven.

"Sorry," she said. "I tried to rush the process. Wanted us to have fresh garlic bread for supper. Ruined it."

"No worries."

She sat down with her mom. Spaghetti and meatballs. Her favourite. How to eat and not get sauce all over herself? It didn't usually bother her. Not until recently.

She ate faster than usual. They talked. Exchanged words, really. Talking takes sharing of each other's opinions. Opening up. Allowing people to see in, or at least as far as you're willing to let them.

Her mother felt it. Felt the distance. Felt the words that sounded like she was listening to a recording and not to her daughter. That happens.

She looked at Abby. Wondering what was going on inside that mind of hers as she wolfed down her food.

Abby tried hard not to look obvious while glancing at her phone sporadically. No phones at the dinner table. That was the rule. But parents have to pick their battles. Better to keep her and her phone at the table than lose them both, right?

Abby was almost finished eating, and her mother felt she was about to slip away. There never is a good time to broach some subjects.

"That's a nice necklace you have in your room."

But there's a good way to do it. And try as she might, Abby's mother hit the wrong tone.

"What were you doing in my room?"

Torpedo. Torpedo. Torpedo.

Where are the countermeasures?

"I was just walking by," she lied. It was a half-truth, and both of them knew it. She was concerned. Abby was never one to buy herself a necklace. Not like that. That kind of necklace is a gift. Not from a shopping spree. That would defeat the whole purpose. You have it because someone wanted to give it to you. Because someone considered you valuable enough to have it. That necklace was a whack of dough.

And it concerned her.

"You went through my stuff?"

"It was lying beside your bed. The door was open. It's a nice necklace."

The words were fine. Her tone implied otherwise.

"A friend gave it to me." Abby got up from the table, said a half-hearted thank you, which came out more like *Stop interfering in my life*, and left, trying the best she could to leave on good terms.

She got off at the station. The conversations—with Kedisha, the one with her mom, the non-existent one with her dad—all vanished. She looked around and found Jake. His face buried in his cellphone. It bothered her.

Is me showing up not worth waiting for compared with that screen?

But she shut that voice out.

It's normal. Everyone looks at their phone. What's he supposed to do, stare at the entrance for you? Smile. It's Jake.

"Hey, stranger," she said.

"Hey, gorgeous!" They hugged. That felt better. He noticed her gold necklace. "Hey, you're wearing my necklace."

She touched the cool metal with her fingertips. "I love wearing it. It's beautiful, Jake. Thank you again. I don't know what to say."

"Anything for my girl." He pulled back from her. "Ready?"

She nodded. They held hands and crossed over to a parking lot. She was ever conscious of his fingers around hers, hoping her hand didn't feel clammy. Up ahead she saw an older Honda SUV. Black with rust around the wheels. They approached. She slowed down, expecting him to go to the driver's side. But he kept walking. She was caught off guard and had to quicken her pace. Strange.

Then she saw another car. Oh yeah. Forget the Porsches. The BMWs. The Mercedes. Bayern Munich was enough Germany for her. Besides, nothing, absolutely nothing, beats a red Ford Mustang.

Convertible to boot.

"This is yours?"

He got in. She opened her door. He started the engine. She loved the sound. That Mustang low rumbling was the most characteristic engine sound she had ever heard. She had wondered if the red Mustang in the photo was his or someone else's. Now she knew. What a rush. What a car.

She sat down in her black leather seat. Took in the new-car smell. She closed the door. No clunky sound. Just a perfect click like a sound chamber closing—a sound that separated her from the rest of the world.

"Easy Lover" by Phil Collins came on the pristine sound system. The speakers were placed perfectly for the music to envelope her. *"She's the kind of girl you dream of—dream of keeping hold of."*

Jake hit the gas. The car took off. Abby glanced up at the gorgeous streaks of red painting the sky. She wondered how it got that way. *"You're the one who wants to hold her—hold her and control her."*

He parked the Mustang, and they walked to the gates at Canada's Wonderland. He paid for their tickets at the entrance. Cash. Two one hundred dollar bills. It caught her attention. The amount and the bill. She remembered her history class. Prime Minister Robert Borden's image was on it. He served in office during World War I, one of the most difficult times in Canada's history. She had learned that Canada had conscription, and it gripped her soul to know that people were forced into battle. Many of them faced horrific violence.

And death.

He reached for her hand. He didn't have to go far. Hers was already outstretched waiting for his. He smiled and raised his eyebrows. She looked out at the amazing park and followed his lead inside.

They reached the Medieval Faire section and stood in line. Leviathan would be first, of course. A massive roller coaster reaching speeds of close to 150 km/hr. She told him she had never been on it before. A first time for everything.

"How was your day?" he asked.

Did it matter now? How did Shakespeare from her English class put it? All's well that ends well. She was with him now. "Great," she said. "You?"

He nodded. "Thanks for hanging out tonight."

"Are you kidding me?"

"Means a lot. You could have been doing a lot of other things. Thanks for coming here with me."

"I'd go with you anywhere."

Their turn came up, and he motioned her in first to the front of the coaster. Four across. She sat down on the end. Jake beside her. Two beside him. One wearing a retro Winnipeg Jets jersey, the other a Leafs jersey.

The coaster lurched forward and began its slow climb. Higher and higher. An unsuspecting person would have no reason to know what was about to happen. But anyone with experience knew full well what was coming.

It reached the top of the climb and began to level out. Then, without warning, it began to tip over the precipice. She looked over. Fear and excitement consumed her. Her car leaned over. Steeper and steeper. *That's not possible. It can't go vertical, can it? We'll fall off. We'll be killed.* It didn't matter to her that rides like this had been engineered. Tested. Safety checks performed. All that science goes out the door when you're seized with emotion.

Leviathan raced down to the bottom. Abby screamed like she was heading to the pit of hell. A high-pitched shrill of sheer terror. Jake laughed. Time of his life. Abby felt her head spinning. Like she was in the ocean and a huge wave had crashed over her, making her spin around, causing her not to know which way was up. A rush of adrenalin raced through her. The coaster rolled into a curve, and Abby felt her stomach return from her throat, back to where it belonged. The scream changed to a cheer. When the ride ended she found herself relieved the whole thing was over. And considered herself strong for surviving.

"Want to go again?" Jake asked. His chill sense of humour putting her at ease.

"That's a lot of people," she said, hoping to indicate she would go again if the lineup wasn't so long.

"You want to try Night Mares?"

She knew the ride. It starts off like a Ferris wheel fallen over on its side. But then it spins faster and faster as it rises up.

Abby tried to decide and felt a tug of war within her.

Do I make him think that I'm a chicken and go for something else, or do I go on Night Mares and show him I'm not scared?

What's to be scared of? It's a ride.

"Let's do it!" she said.

He put his arm around her shoulders as they headed off to the ride.

When they stepped in she grabbed his hand. That felt better. The ride started, and they began to lift up. She alternated between looking at the clouds and at the ground. It spun so fast she just let go and let the ride take control. Why fight it? It would be over soon.

Wouldn't it?

"You okay?" he asked as the ride slowed down.

"Yeah. I think so," she said, trying to figure out if she was scared or feeling ill.

They both laughed.

"Time for something to drink?"

"Definitely."

Abby followed his lead. As Jake ordered drinks, Abby sat down on a bench and glanced around at people. Couples mostly. She saw a family heading back to the parking lot with a little boy in a stroller. Late for a child to be out.

Jake came back with two beers. He sat down and gave her one.

Uh, Jake, you know I'm underage, right?

He read her expression perfectly. "You look at least 19. If they're going to ask anyone for ID, it will be me."

She laughed and drank a gulp of her beer. It splashed against the back of her throat, and she felt the bitter and refreshing sensation as she swallowed. She'd gotten tipsy at Kedisha's house when her parents weren't home. Beer tasted good then. But not as good as this.

Abby felt herself as relaxed as she had ever been. She heard Avril Lavigne's "Hot" playing through the speakers. *"Now you're in, and you can't get out … You're so good to me baby."* Somebody once said that when love happens you know it. She didn't know what they meant by it then. She did now.

They talked. Connected. She relished the feeling of being herself, of sharing, of speaking her heart and mind. And she felt the same from him as she got lost in his eyes. She loved being there for him. For his points of view. For his thoughts.

She finished her beer. Oh, that was good. She wanted a second. But it would be rude to ask. Wouldn't it?

"I really like you, Abby."

"I really like you, too, Jake." Was that her talking or the alcohol? It was one lousy drink. That wouldn't be enough. But it might have been enough to loosen the fears a bit. Now might be the time to do Leviathan again.

"I think we have a future together," he said, his voice quiet.

"That'd be great, Jake."

They stayed locked in each other's eyes. She wondered if there was a slight bit of hurt in his. And wondered if she would have what it would take to make right whatever might be bothering him.

"I have something for you," he said, reaching into his jacket pocket. He pulled out a small purple-wrapped box with a white ribbon. Abby's heart raced. She knew what came in tiny square packages. Okay, granted, it wasn't an engagement ring. Heaven knows it was too early for that. But it was a ring. She tried to fight back tears.

Don't cry. Don't cry.

Wait a minute. Why not? Why not cry? You have a guy who is taking an interest in you. Why not let this moment sink in?

"Jake."

"It's not what you think. I just hope you like it."

She unwrapped the box. Lifted the lid. Oh my.

A gold band with a row of diamonds and another row of pink sapphires. *Abby and Jake* engraved inside. She slid it over the ring finger on her left hand.

"It fits?" he asked.

She looked up at him. Her eyes moistened. She touched the ring with her thumb. "Perfectly."

He gave her a hug. She felt embarrassed for crying and wiped her tears with her sleeve. She stared at the ring. Absolute beauty.

They walked out under starry skies, crowds of people passing by them.

"Thanks for a great evening," Jake said. He stopped. She did too. Their eyes connected. Abby felt a sudden rush of nervousness come over her. Then, just as quickly as it came, it left again. He leaned forward and kissed her. She put her hands on his waist, her new ring pressing against her finger.

"I got a crazy idea," he said.

"Yeah. What? Like taking me on Leviathan again?"

"Exactly!"

"No!" she said, louder than she normally would have.

Jake smiled. He was about to ask her something, but he stopped short.

"Jake?" she asked, reaching out and touching his hand.

She felt him hold her slender fingers. A strong, comforting grip.

"This is crazy," he said.

She nodded. "Uh huh. You mentioned."

"Okay."

"Well?"

He thought a moment. "You want to take a road trip with me to Montreal?"

"What?" Absolute craziness. Montreal? But then, as wild as the idea initially sounded, it changed to a rush of excitement. La belle province with Jake. Riding in his red Mustang from Toronto Leafs country to the domain of Habs fans in Moe-ray-ahl. Wasn't that how her French teacher taught them to say it? She smiled.

"So, what do you say?" Jake asked. "It'll be a great time."

chapter seven

Neither of them had to say it out loud.

Joy and Joel often worked on the bill preparation late into the evenings. Weekends. Later evenings. Then even longer weekends. They did everything they could to provide research for the bill. The next step was to craft a summary of it. How to put this whole thing together in two sentences so that anyone would be able to read it and understand? They were working together with the Legislative Services Branch of the Office of the Law Clerk and Parliamentary Counsel to draft the bill. There was a ton of hard work going into all of this. But it was all going to be for naught if Joy's name didn't get called in the private members' lottery.

Joy knew it. Joel knew it.

No need for discussion.

Though Joy was more convinced than anyone about the result.

Late one evening in her office, Joy finished a call with her husband. Joel did the same with his wife from his office. Both had supporting spouses. No easy feat in Ottawa, where the divorce rate among MPs is twice the national average.

Joy sat at her desk. Joel entered.

"We have to put forward a bill that targets child traffickers with a minimum sentence," Joy said. "Otherwise, victims won't have the security to come forward and testify against their traffickers."

"But you think minimum sentences might scare off some MPs from voting for it?"

Joy took off her glasses. Rubbed her eyes. "I don't know what it will take to get them to vote. And yes, I know there is resistance to minimum sentences." She exhaled and squinted, as if doing so could help her see the light at the end of a dark tunnel. "If we put minimum sentences in, we'll get pushback and we might risk losing the bill. If we don't put it in, the bill will lack teeth, and the girls won't come forward."

"Then we have to find a way to get those MPs to vote for it in spite of their differences."

Joy angled her chair to the side. Looked out at the eternal flame.

"What does every politician want?"

"To do a good job and serve the country," Joel said. "And to stay out of trouble," he added with a laugh. It was needed. The tension in the room lifted momentarily.

"There are a few MPs who are only driven by re-election," Joy said. "But even those who aren't still think about re-election. So how do we craft this bill to ... encourage them?"

She felt the answer in the back of her mind. Allowed it to formulate as the thought worked its way forward.

"You're thinking of inserting a clause they can't vote against no matter what."

The room stayed quiet. She felt the thought arrive.

"We target the bill to protect children," Joy said, remembering a conversation she and Joel had with Ben Perrin, a Canadian lawyer who had spent a lot of time bringing the issue of human trafficking in Canada to light.

"That's excellent," Joel said. "We can use it in two ways. First we can appeal to an MP's sense of logic to protect minors. But it can also be used to put a potentially dissenting MP behind the eight ball. Which MP wants to be seen as someone who votes against child safety?"

"Precisely."

"That might work," Joel said. "But then the bill won't specifically protect those being trafficked who are 18 and over. Strictly speaking, it would be for 17 and under."

Joy closed her eyes, touched the bridge of her nose and prayed silently for wisdom. "If we leave out the part about the bill addressing minors—if we say it targets everyone who is being sexually exploited—then, on the one hand, we cast the net of trafficking as wide as possible to protect all victims. But then we won't have a carrot, or stick, for the MPs to be encouraged to vote for the bill. On the other hand, if we add in the clause about it being addressed to protecting minors, we may lose some of the power to protect adult girls, though we definitely increase the chances of the bill being passed."

Joy sighed. Why was doing the right thing so difficult?

They stayed quiet for a while. Thinking. Evaluating. For two people who were in arguably the most talkative profession, they both found the kind of solace that only silence can bring.

"We're already facing pushback on a bill that amends the Criminal Code, and we haven't even introduced it. We also know some people are opposed to the idea of minimum sentences." She stopped. Time to make the decision. "I think we are better off being more sure of passing a bill that targets minors than we are being less sure of passing a bill that targets all victims. It is what it is. The path forward is to have the bill amend the Criminal Code to include a minimum sentence of five years for anyone trafficking someone under the age of 18. Thoughts?"

The logic was sound. It made sense to Joel. "I agree, Joy."

No, it wasn't the best answer. But better off to get a result than to aim too high and risk total failure. Joy smiled. Joel wondered where her reservoir of optimism came from.

"Isn't politics great?"

Joy was stepping off a plane in Ottawa when she received an email. The subject line read "Private Member's Bill Ranking." She clicked on it. Took a breath. She skipped the preamble and scrolled down to the list. She wasn't first. She wasn't second.

Then she looked at the next one. Her heart pounded. She smiled.

She recognized the name.

Joy walked down the hallway to her office. Her steps echoed on the marble floor. The thrill of being selected third only served to reinforce her mission of getting the bill through. It was an important step, but it was just the beginning. Base camp of the first Everest. Now came the challenge of getting the bill through. She had to convince people.

Including her own party.

She saw Joel approaching from down the hallway. His mouth dropped open slightly when he saw her. He raised his hands in amazement.

"Third. Third!" he said.

"You seem surprised, Joel," she said with a laugh that reverberated louder than her steps.

"I just ... I ... It's incredible."

"Not really," she said.

They opened the door to her office. A recent addition to her team, a political science grad in her early twenties, rose to her feet. The nervousness on her face betrayed her concern. "Congratulations, Joy," she said, unable to hide what she really wanted to say.

"What's the matter?" Joy said, picking up on cues she had learned while being a mother to six children.

"Justice Department. They're waiting in your office."

Joy smiled. Turned to Joel. "You see? The battle begins. Shall we?" she said with a laugh, motioning to her office.

She opened the door to her personal office. Two men in their mid-thirties, wearing dark suits, identical short haircuts and black polished shoes, stood from their chairs. They did so in unison, as if they had done this many times before. Somehow the Justice Department always managed to have a similar kind of person working in their system. Like they had a factory somewhere that cranked these guys out.

"Mrs. Smith," they both said at the same time, forgetting their advance plan of who was going to do the talking.

"Call me Joy. You've met Joel, my chief of staff?" They could not recall Joel at first but did a good job of indicating they had. So many faces. So many names on the Hill. How could anyone keep it all straight? They all shook hands. The men in suits introduced themselves as Brennan and Ferris.

They sat down. Joy took her seat behind her desk, just to make sure there was no doubt in the two men in dark suits' minds about who was in charge here.

"Congratulations on your placement in the private member's bill lottery," Ferris said.

"Thank you," Joy said with a smile. *And you're so excited that your first order of business was to come all the way down here in person to congratulate me.*

They continued with pleasantries with each side knowing it was only a short matter of time before the fake air of niceties would have to be dispelled with some measure of truth. Joy offered them coffee, tea, water. They declined.

"Any thoughts about what your bill might be about?" Brennan finally asked.

Tough one. Such a direct question. How to respond without lying?

"Well, there are so many important items facing Canada today."

"And which ones in particular are you interested in?" Ferris asked as more of a statement than a question. Joy was convinced he had been in conversations with the justice minister. Why else would he be there?

Joy wanted to respond to him by name, so she waited the split second for her mind to recall it. Yeah, hundreds and hundreds and hundreds of introductions. It was a unique name. Her mind saw that famous wheel in an amusement park.

"Ferris, I'm going to have to give this some serious thought."

"I want to be clear, just so that there is no misunderstanding here," Brennan said. If they looked similar on the outside, they were different on the inside. Ferris was the good cop. Brennan clearly the bad one. "As a member of Parliament for the Conservative Party you have been instructed not to introduce any justice-related bills. I'm here—" He caught himself. "*We're* here to remind you of that."

"I'm glad you did. It's important that we have rules and that we work together."

"Your recent conversation with the minister of justice about human trafficking might indicate otherwise."

"I think the minister gave good insight into the issue."

"The plan is to keep this government on track. To complete the items we have set forward. We're under a lot of pressure," Ferris said.

Like the girls who are being trafficked? That kind of pressure?

"We just want to make sure we are all on the same page," Brennan added, readjusting himself in his chair. She expected Ferris to do the same, but he didn't.

That factory sure had tight quality control.

"Thank you, Brennan. I'll keep it in mind."

"We're not asking you to keep it in mind. We're asking you, reminding you, to comply."

First off, nobody tells me what to do. Least of all not in my own office. And second of all, don't go up against me. I'm not going away. And I'm not backing down. Not to you. Not to the justice minister. And not to—

She caught herself. *Be disciplined. Be rational. This is a long race. No point in getting them upset. At least not now. Now to change the subject.*

"I'd be curious to know, what kinds of private members' bills are important to the Conservative Party?"

I have to switch your train off the track you're on. That factory where they came from had the two men so focused on their agenda that Joy realized there was no point in arguing. Not now. Her suggestion changed the temperature of the conversation. The men seemed to think they had won. Brennan and Ferris looked to each other to see who was going to respond. For the first time they seemed ill-prepared.

"That would be a matter for you to resolve with the House leader."

Good move. Fall back on protocol. Joy expected them to do nothing less.

"Thank you. After all, we don't want to put a bill forward that won't get passed, right?" she said with a smile and a laugh. The men nodded. In unison.

She saw them to the door.

"Thanks for stopping by," she said with a smile. They said goodbye. When the door closed, her smiled faded. Joy and Joel returned to her office.

"We have to keep this thing totally quiet," Joy said.

"Understood. It stays with us and with those drafting the bill until it gets tabled in the House of Commons. And then it's all going to break loose. There's going to be a lot of angry people. Including the guys who just walked out the door."

Joy turned and looked out her window at the Centennial Flame. She often took inspiration from it as a reminder of the sacrifices that had been made throughout the years to preserve Canada's democracy. And it reminded her of the need to press forward to combat human trafficking.

Even as the flame burned under the golden sun, Joy felt herself fueled by a strong conviction that people should not be bought and sold. *Third name drawn on the list,* Joy thought. *If that isn't confirmation, what else would be?*

"Get ready, Joel," Joy said. "This is going to be a very bumpy ride."

chapter eight

Considering how many ways she could be caught, Abby found it surprisingly easy to set up her plan. *Tell Mom I want to sleep over at Kedisha's place Friday night. That won't be so much of a stretch. But then I have to make up a lie about Saturday night, which will be tougher. Maybe Kedisha has a friend who has a friend ... No, that's a bit too far removed, and Mom would get concerned. Keep it simple.*

Let's say Kedisha's grandparents have a cabin up in Muskoka. On Saturday after the sleepover they invite me for a day trip up there with them, but then they think of staying for the night, and I don't want to spoil their fun by making them come all the way back. Besides, what's the big deal? I'm with Kedisha. Unless of course Mom asks to speak with Kedisha's mother to see if it really is all right. Such is life. You can't cover every angle.

Besides, she figured, there was enough in there for a believable story.

She packed a change of clothes, toiletries, makeup and a second pair of shoes into her backpack. She would meet him on Friday. Come back Sunday night.

Abby left school before lunch. Kedisha caught a glimpse of her heading out the door. Found it strange that Abby's backpack was so stuffed. Thinking back on it, Abby seemed excited yet distant that morning. Wore a nice ring to go with her new necklace.

The bright sunshine warmed her as she walked through the doors. She took in a breath of fresh air. The beautiful weather would have been enough to put a smile on her face. But what really made her happy was seeing that red Mustang out front with the top down and a hot guy in the driver's seat waiting for her.

"Hey, beautiful!" Jake said. Abby threw her bag in the back seat and opened the door. It felt like a bank heist. They had the money. They were into the getaway vehicle. Now it came down whether they could take off without being caught.

"Hey, Jake!"

They kissed. Jake wanted to hang on longer, but Abby pulled away.

"Go, go, go!" she said, sensing that the armed guards from the bank were about to come out shooting. Jake gunned the engine. She felt the rush of air around the car, enveloping them in their own private world. She counted to five. That would be enough time. If she was going to be caught, it would have happened by now. She looked back. Saw the school disappear in the distance.

"Yes!"

She felt the seat against her back. The smell of leather was intoxicating. Jake turned on music. The Tragically Hip's "Blow at High Dough" pounded through the speakers. She twisted the ring he gave her as they sang the words.

… Yeah, I can get behind anything.

She reached out and touched his hand. They locked fingers. Without looking, she reached into her jeans pocket with her right hand and turned off her cellphone. She glanced over at Jake. He wore brown sunglasses, a button-down shirt rolled up the elbows and clean designer blue jeans. She wanted a pair just like them.

Wooo, baby, I feel fine, I'm pretty sure it's genuine.

"We can take the 401 all the way there," Jake said. "Or we can cut down at Port Hope to Highway 2 for part of the way. It'll add a little time, but it's a nicer ride."

"That'd be great. I've never been out that way."

"Something new then."

Sometimes the faster it gets the less you need to know.

They pulled off the 401 at Port Hope and ordered takeout. Jake, a hamburger and fries. Abby, a sandwich, salad and bottled water. Jake paid in cash again. They ate a picnic table near the waterfront. After lunch, they took the alternate route. Abby saw the sign that read "The King's Highway 2 Ontario." It reminded her of a Tom Petty song. The drive proved to be slower with a speed limit in some places of 80 km/hr and reduced further in towns. But for Abby the view of Lake Ontario was worth it. So wide and blue and beautiful.

As they switched back towards the 401 at Belleville, Abby gazed back at the water. She watched it fade into the distance like the school earlier.

They arrived in Montreal at seven that evening. Abby loved the vibe she sensed in the city, full of old stone buildings that spoke of culture and history. They drove down Rue Notre-Dame Ouest, passing the Notre-Dame Basilica. She remarked to Jake how beautiful the church looked. It stretched so high to the sky, as if in direct communication with the Almighty. She noticed how the architectural designers of the city found an ingenious way of preserving the old buildings alongside brand new skyscrapers. She previously thought cities should be all one or the other. But seeing them together worked in a way that made Montreal seem timeless. Like the old had just as much to offer the present as the new.

Perhaps even more so.

Jake stopped outside a beautiful five-star hotel. Abby stayed in her seat, hoping to risk embarrassment if this was just a brief stop and not the hotel they would be staying at. The valet attendant came to the car. He opened the door for Abby.

"Thanks," Jake said, handing him the key and a tip. Abby stepped out. Grabbing her bag out of the back seat, she accepted Jake's outstretched hand and followed him into the hotel. She noticed the marble floor first. Tan-and-black checkered pattern. The lobby stretched up three storeys, giving her the feeling of freedom that comes with an open sky. A large spiralling staircase wound its way up to the second level. Couches and chairs in an old French colonial style matched the elegant carpet.

"Wait for me here, okay? I'll get us checked in," Jake said.

Abby nodded and sat down on a green couch with gold trim. The polished brass casing surrounding the bottom of a nearby column cast her reflection back at her. Straightening her back she sat up, edged her way to the front of the sofa and smiled to herself, thinking for a moment that this was what French nobility must have felt like. She admired her reflection. Despite the road trip, she liked the way she looked. Then she thought perhaps the brass helped to hide her imperfections, like an effect on a computer program to enhance her image.

"All set?" Jake asked, holding a key card in his hand.

They took the elevator to the sixth floor. When the doors opened, Abby noticed that the hallway decor matched the style of the lobby. She loved it, finding it tasteful to see a hotel take as much care designing and maintaining the consistency in the higher floors as they did the lobby.

They walked down the hallway. Jake looked at the numbers and stopped at their door.

Abby felt her pulse in her throat quicken. A jolt of nervousness shot through her stomach.

Jake opened the door.

Oh, wow.

French doors off to the side led to a separate suite. The king bed in front of her revealed a colonial style. She dropped her bag on the ground and approached a large window with a glass balcony door beside it offering a view into the clear Montreal night.

"This is amazing, Jake," she whispered. Pulling the curtains back farther, she looked out at the glimmering lights and felt the city convey both a vibrant and a peaceful atmosphere. Like it could pick you up if you were down and bring you to a state of fun and enjoyment. Opening the balcony door, she stepped onto the concrete floor. She leaned against the railing and breathed in the night air. She took in the aroma of a steak restaurant nearby. A knock at the door. *Strange. We don't have any luggage coming up.*

She looked to Jake.

"A little surprise," he said.

She couldn't read his expression.

Jake walked to the door. Abby watched from the balcony. Police? Hotel attendant bringing something Jake forgot at the counter? Her parents?

Couldn't be. The knock didn't sound like a parent's knock. It would have been more deliberate. Authoritative. This was timid. Almost weak. Like the person on the other end was unsure of themselves.

Jake opened the door. She couldn't see the other person. The conversation was quiet and brief. Jake came in. Turned around.

Abby smiled.

"Now you have to be careful," Jake said. "The last time I opened a bottle I nearly broke a window. So watch out."

She laughed as Jake aimed the champagne bottle top at the open balcony door. Abby playfully pushed him to the side. "You can't shoot that thing outside! It might hit someone."

"A cork. Big deal."

Pop. The cork flew outside. He poured them each a full glass. They clinked glasses and sat down on the brown wicker balcony chairs. She felt the soothing burn of champagne go down her throat. It seemed like the drink knew exactly how to reach into every part of her to bring her a tingling sensation.

"I love you, Abby." Jake looked into her eyes. She was so taken by his comment, she found herself unable to respond. Jake poured them each a second glass. Abby felt disappointed in herself for not responding to him. The obvious reply was *I love you, too.* She wanted to ask something else but fought for the courage to say it.

She felt a sense of wooziness in her mind. That was one quick drink. But who cared? They weren't in a bar. They weren't going to have their ID checked. Weren't going to have any parents or friends walk in on them.

She took a large drink of her second glassful. Whatever the first glass had figured out to do for her, the second one did it even better. She hoped she hadn't let the silence drag on too long.

"Why?" Abby asked, her eyes shy, looking for that stamp of approval. She looked into his brown eyes with all the nervousness and honesty that filled her and allowed him into her heart to validate her if he wanted to. "Why do you love me?"

She felt the affection of his gaze. "Because you're the most beautiful woman I have ever seen in my entire life."

He leaned forward and kissed her. She leaned in, wanting more. He pulled back and poured her another glass.

Abby didn't feel any different between the second and third glass until she stood up. It felt like the blood had drained from her face. She steadied herself on her chair, and Jake put an arm around her waist and helped her inside. She hugged him. He brought her over to the bed. She felt herself relax in his arms as they slept together.

When they were finished, she felt the comfort that came with not having a worry in the world. She rested her head against her pillow. She could not remember ever feeling this comfortable. Her stomach growled. He laughed. She laughed.

"Time for something to eat?" he said.

Yes and no.

Yes, I'm starving, and I would love to go out and eat with you. No, I don't want to leave this feeling.

They showered. Changed clothes. "I only brought one other set," she said. "Sorry." She felt awkward. She had better clothes back home, but he said she only needed to bring enough to fit in her backpack.

"That's the whole point of rue Sainte-Catherine," he said in his best French accent. "Let's go shopping!"

If Montreal had atmosphere during the day, then it became positively electrifying at night. She imagined it was what Europe would feel like if she ever got there. Walking down the street Abby had the distinct impression that in spite of, or perhaps because of, living in a metropolis, the people still took time for themselves. For each other.

Montreal made time for life.

They discovered a jeans store with pictures of famous actors and rock stars on the walls. "Pick whatever you like," Jake said. And for the first time Abby went shopping without looking at the price tag. Her head still spinning from the champagne, she found herself almost giddy.

She grabbed a pair of jeans with rips across the front and brought them to the dressing room to try on. They fit like they were custom made for her. She picked out a long-sleeved shirt and a leather jacket made of lighter material. No point in going heavy this early in the fall. She looked in the mirror. If that brass reflection earlier in the hotel made her feel good, the reflection here made her feel positively runway quality.

"Gorgeous," Jake said.

And she believed him.

She changed out of the clothes and handed them to Jake. He counted out the bills. More brown ones. Like the ones he used to pay for their tickets to Canada's Wonderland. She gasped when she saw the total on the till. The cashier asked if she wanted to wear it all now. She looked to Jake. He nodded. The cashier cut the tags, she got changed, and she came out looking and feeling like a model.

"You see. No need to pack clothes when you come to Montreal!"

They walked out into the night air. It had just enough of a chill for him to put his arm around her. She breathed in the smell of new leather. It reminded her of his car.

She looked into the window of an elegant restaurant in a Victorian-style mansion. Jake noticed and tugged on her elbow towards the door. She felt bad a moment for looking, thinking he was going to have to shell out even more money because of her expensive tastes. But the speed with which he took her up the stairs and into the restaurant reassured her.

A hostess led them towards the front. Abby didn't notice this time if the hostess was a ten. She herself was a ten. Jake loved her. So what competition was there? They sat down at a table with a view overlooking the street, which filled up with an ever-increasing flow of foot traffic.

"You having fun?" Jake asked.

She closed her eyes a moment. "Time of my life."

"That's great. I can't believe I found you. I mean, I was so nervous when I first contacted you."

"You were nervous! How about me? I had a hard time breathing."

"I'm glad you and I can be here together."

"Me too, Jake."

"No trouble getting away. You see, you got guts."

"It wasn't hard. Gave my mom a story about hanging out with friends."

Jake paused a moment.

"Your dad?"

Oh, great, had to bring him into this.

"He wouldn't care. Neither of them would, really."

"Your parents holding you back?"

"They're okay, I guess."

Jake ordered appetizers. When the four Montreal smoked meat mini sandwiches arrived, Abby had a hard time resisting taking more than her half. Jake laughed and offered one of his, which she accepted. They talked about what to do after dinner. Catch a movie? Jake hinted at heading back to the hotel for some more fun. Maybe they would take a tour of the city tomorrow and do more shopping. Sunday would take care of itself.

The meal arrived. Lobster for her. Chicken for him. And a red Quebec wine to accompany both. The waiter placed the bottle on the table.

When they had eaten and were into their second glass, Jake paused and looked at her. "It would be great to build a life together with you, Abby."

"I would love that," she said.

"What kind of life would you like?" he asked.

She leaned her head back. Imagining. "A house, cars, kids."

"What kind of car?"

"Red Mustang."

They laughed. "I think we already have that."

We. She loved the sound of that.

They took a drink of their wine. "We could have it, Abby. We could have it all."

"You think so?"

"I know it."

She retreated to the comfort of her wine glass. Having a guy pay this much attention to her made her feel shy. But it was something she was looking forward to getting used to.

"You're sure?"

"Abby, we can have everything." He poured the rest of the bottle into her glass. If the waiter cared about her age, he did nothing to interfere. "But it's going to cost us a lot of money, Abby. Having a nice house and cars and things. We can do it. We can live anywhere we want. We just need money."

"Okay," she said.

"I bring in some money. But if we really want to have a good life, we need to bring in a lot more. We have to figure out a way to make a lot of money. Then we can have it all. You and me, Abby."

She nodded. "Whatever it takes, Jake."

He paid the bill in cash, and they walked outside. She took in a deep breath, as if doing so could somehow help her absorb the incredible character of the city. Ah, Montreal. Or, rather, Moe-ray-ahl. It sounded so much better with a French accent. The unique ambience of Montreal made it feel like a whole new world for Abby.

They grabbed dessert at a street-side café, then headed back to the hotel. He ordered up wine. They got drunk and put on a movie but didn't get very far.

They had other ways of entertaining themselves.

chapter nine

The phone calls, emails and personal visits Joy received became so frequent they were now embarrassing. Everyone, the Justice Department in particular, wanted to know the contents of Joy's bill. Any change to the Criminal Code, Joy? Because we all know we can't have that. She avoided, delayed and talked around the issue the way only skilled politicians can. They were all going to find out. And soon enough. And when news of her bill got out, there were going to be a lot of ticked-off people.

Parliamentary counsel certified her bill, giving Joy the green light to provide the required 48 hours advance notice of her intention to introduce the bill. She did so immediately. The following appeared in the daily House of Commons *Notice Paper*:

Mrs. Smith (Kildonan-St. Paul) —
   Bill entitled "An Act to amend the Criminal Code (minimum sentence for offences involving trafficking of persons under the age of eighteen years)."

Joy and Joel strategized about how to get the maximum effect out of the introduction that would take place three days later. They coordinated their efforts with newspaper columnists, non-governmental organizations (NGOs) and lawyers who had been working with Joy on the bill.

The morning Joy introduced the bill at first reading she issued a press release: "MP Joy Smith tables a bill to introduce mandatory minimum sentences for the trafficking of children."

She was pleased with the wording. Who could argue with protecting children? The first hurdle of getting her name called in the lottery had been accomplished. Next, she had found a fairly truthful way of sidestepping the Justice Department, at least for now (their fury was sure to come). This brought her to the first reading.

Easy enough. You stand up there. The bill gets introduced, and nobody really says much else. But then it goes to second reading, and a vote is taken. If it passes, the bill gets referred to committee for review. After committee, it goes to third reading, where there is debate, and the final vote. If it passes the House, the bill then needs to go through three readings in the Senate. Once the bill passes both houses, it becomes law by receiving royal assent—a formality by the governor general. But even then, the bill call be challenged at the Supreme Court level.

Walking out of her office, she headed to the House of Commons. This was the next step in a long battle. She put the length of the journey out of her mind and focused instead on the task at hand. No point worrying about winning the seventh game of the series when you're only in the first period of the first game.

Joy entered the House and took her seat. All chairs were covered in green, modelled after the House of Commons in England. The other members and the Speaker of the House entered and took their places. Session started, and as she waited for her bill to come up, Joy thought about her son Edward. About how his life had inspired her in all of this. That one conversation that changed it all. She thought about Samantha. On the path to rehabilitation. She thought of all the girls she had rescued from this dark evil. About the thousands and thousands who still needed help. And she thought about the fight that was going to explode when she finished her speech.

The Speaker of the House rose. "Introduction of private members' bills, the member for Kildonan-St. Paul."

Joy stood.

"Thank you, Mr. Speaker. Bill C-268 seeks to amend the Criminal Code to include a minimum punishment of imprisonment for a term of

THE TRUE STORY OF CANADIAN HUMAN TRAFFICKING

five years for offences involving trafficking of persons under the age of 18."

The Speaker asked for a seconder. Steven Fletcher, MP for Charleswood-St. James-Assiniboia in Winnipeg, seconded her bill. Joy had gone to Steven in private because she knew he would have the courage to stand by her when many others wouldn't.

"Mr. Speaker," Joy continued, "This is an extremely important bill because in Canada there are no mandatory minimum sentences for human trafficking convictions, not even for children. The October report of the Canada-U.S. consultation, in preparation for the world congress against sexual exploitation of children and adolescents, recommended that Canada amend its Criminal Code to provide a mandatory minimum penalty for child trafficking. In Peel County right now numerous trafficking charges are on the table, hopefully with convictions, and this kind of bill would ensure that traffickers have very stiff sentences. This is very mandatory.

"As members know, last year a Niagara man was convicted of human trafficking. He earned $350,000 off a 15-year-old girl over the period of two years. He only received three years and received a credit for 404 days of time already served. These mandatory minimum sentences for trafficking of children are of paramount importance here in Canada."

Joy sat down. It was out in the open now. She could have rescinded her bill earlier today if she wanted to. Could have cheerfully withdrawn it. But now the subject of Joy's bill was clear in everyone's minds. There was no going back.

When session ended, Joy walked back to her office. She opened the door. Karen had a worried expression on her face.

"They're waiting," she whispered.

"Wonderful," Joy said with a smile. She motioned for Joel to join her.

She opened the door to her office and smiled like nothing was wrong. She greeted them as if they were old friends.

"Ferris. Brennan. Good to see both of you today." She was about to add, *Did you see me introduce my bill this morning?* but stopped herself.

"You promised us, Joy." Ferris started. It was clear he wanted to be in charge of this meeting. And it was equally clear that both he and Brennan, and the people they represented, were not pleased with her dissention.

"Strictly speaking, no, I did not," Joy said. Her tone was altogether tougher. She showed no signs of fear. No indication that she needed their validation on this, or any, work she was involved in. She and Joel sat down. "In our last meeting, you gave your point of view that no bills concerning the Criminal Code should be introduced, and I listened intently to you. You then drew the erroneous conclusion that I was in agreement with you. I was not. So in case today's bill introduction left any room for doubt in your mind, let me be perfectly clear. I am not taking this bill down, and you are not going to convince me otherwise."

Poor Ferris was about to explode. MPs did what they were told to do. That's how the game worked. Everyone knew this. What was Joy's problem?

"Nobody's happy about this, Joy."

"Really? Because I'm thinking there are a lot of trafficked girls out there who are thrilled that this bill has officially been put forward. What do you think, Ferris? Think they can count on us to help them? Or is that a bridge too far for you?"

"That is not acceptable."

"My behaviour or human trafficking? To which are you referring?"

"You are part of a larger system, Joy."

"So are you. You and I. All of us. We are part of a system that is turning our backs on these girls. And it stops now."

"You are going to stop this bill, Joy. I am here as a humble favour to you. This is going to get ugly if you don't take it down."

"Oh, give it a rest. Why don't you—"

Joel stepped in. Damage control. "I think what Mrs. Smith means is that we are as settled in our position as both of you are settled in your position. We have a difference of understanding, and it's important for us to try to learn from one another as to why we hold these positions. We're all good people. And I'm sure we can work this out."

"Don't bet on it, Joel," Brennan said. "You guys are way out of line."

"You see, there you go again," Joy said. "You're totally missing the point. It's the traffickers who are out of line. Is it possible for the two of you to make that connection in your minds?"

"There are systems. There are protocols. There are ways in which we operate to make the system work."

"And it's a system that traffickers benefit from. No action."

"You're saying that the government—your own party's government, Joy—is not doing a great job."

"In many things, they are. In this, no."

"We're going to fight you, Joy."

"I'd like to see you try."

"Open your eyes," Brennan said.

"I offer you the same advice. Why don't you direct all your disappointment at sex slavery in our country instead of aiming your guns at me?"

"You're impossible."

"You are both excused," Joy said.

"This is not over, Joy," Ferris said, standing to his feet. Brennan followed.

"You're quite right. This bill has to pass second and third reading, and then it has to pass the Senate."

"That's not what I meant. Stop twisting my words around."

Joy looked them both in the eye. They meant well. No doubt they had other fish to fry. Not bigger, though. Just other fish. What could be bigger than rescuing trafficked girls? But she acknowledged to herself that while they were experts in legal matters and political policy, they were rookies in the world of human trafficking. She felt no sympathy for their stance. They had to come around. At stake was the future of many Canadian girls. And these guys and their masters had to get that through their heads.

Hopefully sooner rather than later.

The duo left. The door closed. Joy and Joel sat back down.

"Congratulations," Joel said. "The bill is out in the open."

"We have a lot of support so far," Joy said with a laugh.

Joel thought back to the first reading of the bill. "Step number one is done. Yes, we have a long way to go. But we got this far. You did well, Joy. You didn't back down."

"And I won't back down," she said. She brushed off the compliment. It was no big deal to present the bill. No big deal to go toe to toe with Brennan and Ferris. She wouldn't quit on her girls. No chance.

But Joel wanted her to see the success. It was a major milestone. And he felt she needed to celebrate. Scoring a goal doesn't mean you won the game. But you still cheer. You celebrate the achievement. Then you get ready for the next faceoff.

"Think about it this way," Joel said. "How many people in any party would have the guts to stand up to a directive?" He was quiet a moment. "Joy, this came from the PMO."

PMO stood for Prime Minister's Office. Under that office was the Department of Justice. Inside that, and under the minister of justice, were Brennan and Ferris. Sure, it took courage to stand up to them. But she didn't want to have to stand up to them. Why couldn't they all just agree on this and move forward? It was bad enough facing the world of human trafficking. Now she had all the political infighting to deal with on top of it.

What would be next?

"Thanks, Joel," Joy said. But she didn't dwell on it long. "Now, let's get back to work. We have to send out a message to every MP about why this bill is important and why they have to vote for it." Joel nodded. "And then we have to think through how we are going to fight within our party. No doubt we're going to be … encouraged further to take this bill down."

She leaned back on her chair. Her eyes focusing. "But I'm not going to take it down," she said. "No matter who comes against me."

chapter ten

Abby placed her hand on the wall and felt the chill of the ice against her palm. Strange. Ice was normally never this clear. But this was. Clear as glass. She turned to the right and felt another transparent wall made of ice. Not the thin kind, mind you—like that filmy layer on a cool fall morning that covers a puddle, and you tap on it with your boots and the whole thing shatters to reveal the water beneath. This was impenetrable. Frozen stiff.

She had the illusion of being able to see the world around her but was completely incapable of communicating with it. She pressed her hand against all four sides of what should have been open space, but she was blocked by the ice wall. Locked in above and beneath. As if in a hollow, transparent cell of ice. On the other side people walked around. Some of them appeared to be upside down. How did they do that exactly? They walked farther and farther away. She shouted at them. Knocked on the walls as hard as she could, but no one paid any attention.

Abby opened her eyes. Her head throbbed like when she collided with that soccer player and got a bleeding nose. She waited in bed until Jake woke as well. He had drunk more than her. She'd never seen someone pound it back like that before.

She heard a knock at the door. Then it came again. She heard the door open.

Her heart exploded. *Mom found me. Dad, too. Finally, he takes an interest. They're going to scream when they see I'm sleeping with a guy and in a foreign city. Foreign? This isn't foreign. It's Canada, for crying out loud. Moe-ray-ahl, remember?* The hangover made everything woozy. *Who's in our room?*

The Filipina housekeeper opened her mouth in shock. She raised her hands in apology and backed up. "It's all right," Abby said. Jake woke and saw her leave. He and Abby both laughed. For Jake, it was funny. For Abby, it was relief that it wasn't her parents. *Relax, will you? There is zilch to worry about. Take a breath.*

Abby fell back onto her pillow. She heard Jake get out of bed. "I've got a surprise for you tonight," he said.

"Really?" she said with a smile, momentarily forgetting the banging in her head. "What?"

"Bacon and eggs for breakfast."

"That's the surprise?"

"Coffee, too."

"Whatever you say," Abby said.

"It will help with the bags under your eyes."

That comment stung. She didn't like her bubble being burst. She shook her reaction off but realized he had a point. A heavy night requires rejuvenation. What helps a hangover? Coffee? Water? Rest? Exercise? She reached over to her night table, grabbed a bottle of spring water and downed it. Jake placed an order with room service and told Abby it would be there in half an hour. He went into the bathroom. She heard the shower water run.

Abby checked her phone. Message from Mom: *"How was the sleep-over?"*

Best not to respond. No point in getting into a conversation until she claimed to remember to turn on her phone while on the way to Kedisha's grandparents' cabin in Muskoka, right? Get to the point of no return.

She put on the white courtesy hotel bathrobe and looked outside at the Montreal morning. Her mind began to sway back and forth. Like when she had too much to drink last night and felt as if she might fall over.

You can leave it all behind, Abby. Just forget your old life in Markham altogether.

Yeah, right.

Yeah, exactly right. You've got Jake. You've got a future. He loves you. You going to turn that down? You going to risk that?

What? Run away?

No. Not run away. Run to. Run with. You have nothing back home. Not really.

My mom would flip. She would go absolutely berserk. My dad, too.

Your dad. Yeah. No offence, but he wouldn't notice for the first month. Maybe not the second month either.

Fine. But my mom would. I can't let her down.

Fair enough. But you could try it out.

For a day? I'm going home Sunday.

She thought that with as much confidence as she could, but she did a poor job of convincing herself. What a relief it would be to cut the rope anchoring her to the dock and just cruise off. She glanced at the clock. Breakfast would be there in 20 minutes. She joined Jake in the shower.

The afternoon consisted of Abby trying to get rid of her hangover by overdosing on water. They walked hand in hand to Mount Royal—the small mountain west of downtown that Montreal got its name from. As they climbed up, Abby saw the Mount Royal cross at the top. The steel cross was erected in 1924. It commemorated an original wooden cross of 1643 built by Paul de Chomedey to thank God for sparing the colony from threatening floodwaters.

"Want to sit down for a break?" she asked, pointing to the foot of the cross. Jake hesitated. Turned away. "We should head back down. My surprise is waiting, remember?"

"Jake? What is it? Come on!"

"I think you're going to like it."

"Jake!" she insisted.

He walked away, and she followed after him.

"Okay, okay," he said, stopping once the cross was out of view. "You ready?"

She raised an eyebrow at him. "This better be good."

"I got us tickets tonight for the Montreal-Toronto game."

"What?!"

"They're pretty high up. They were nearly sold out."

"I love the Leafs!"

"You'll be outnumbered. You might be the only person there who wants something different from all the others."

"What about you? I can count on you to be on my side, right?"

"I'll be right there with you."

She tightened her arm around him. A breeze blew into the holes of her jeans, which normally would have chilled her. But with him at her side, she didn't notice.

Abby felt the excitement and energy of the Metro car crammed with Habs fans. They pushed and squeezed against her, with every stop picking up more Les Habitants faithful. She loved the feeling. How infectious. Born and raised a loyal Hogtown Leafs' fan, still she found herself being pulled into the sea of red surrounding her. "Wait until you get into the arena," Jake said. "Nothing like it. Not even Toronto."

Impossible.

They stopped for poutine and hotdogs at a restaurant near the Bell Centre. Abby glanced up from their table and saw two girls in short skirts and short leather jackets coming in. Their flawlessly made-up faces and blonde hair made it seem like they had just finished a model shoot. Jake noticed her gaze and turned around.

"Wonder where they got their money."

"Jake." Abby tried hard not to laugh with a mouth full of food.

"I'm just saying." Jake bit into his hotdog. His mouth was full. But she could make out the words. "They make enough money."

"What?"

"What do you mean, what?" Jake said, laughing. He had the most relaxing smile. "Those girls make good dough."

"How do you know?" Abby asked.

"Montreal is the porn capital of Canada. Girls like that will do anything. And they get paid big bucks for it."

"Like how much?"

"But that's not where the real money is."

"How do you know?" Abby asked again, curious how her man had the inside track on this.

"I hear things."

"They make good money doing porn?"

"Porn? Porn is cheap. The real dough is in—" He shook his head. "Forget it. Come on. Let's watch the Leafs. Or the Habs. Whichever."

"Leafs! You promised!"

Jake stood. Abby followed him out, glancing at the girls in short skirts. She should have been focused on the game. On the ultimate Canadian hockey rivalry. Instead, her mind stayed on those girls, wondering how much money they made.

They found their seats just as the anthem began. The booming male voice pounded out the first half in French and the second half in English. Abby quietly sang to herself all in English.

"O Canada. Our home and native land. True patriot—"

She glanced around as she sang, engulfed in a sea of red Canadiens jerseys, hearing the echo of the singing.

"The True North strong and free ..."

She turned to Jake. Whatever he said about the seats being high up must have been relative. Fine. They weren't glass. But Abby loved these seats in the corner about 20 rows up. High enough to see the play develop. Sometimes when you sit so far down, you're too close to the action to see what's developing in the rest of the game.

"God keep our land glorious and free ..."

When the anthem ended, they sat down. Fans began cheering as the players took their places for the opening faceoff. The ref raised his hand and received confirmation from the goalies. He dropped the puck.

The game proved to be every bit as amazing as she had imagined and more. The fans chanted *"Go Habs Go"* as if they were one person, bellowing out with a passion and fervour she had never known. She had toyed with idea of cheering for the Leafs, but being in an all-Montreal section, she decided against it. Even though she figured no harm would come to her, she had this quiet reserve about her to just go with the flow, to not cause a fuss and to not risk potential confrontation with a drunk fan.

They took the Metro back. Fans cheered and chanted. A Habs' win. When they came out of their station Jake picked up a bottle of booze at a store and then a pack of cigarettes at a street vendor up the road. That seemed odd to Abby. *He smokes?*

"Reminds me of when I was younger," he said, opening the pack. He lit a cigarette. Offered her one. Why not? She took the cigarette into her mouth. He lit it for her. She felt the unmistakable buzz as she inhaled the burning sensation into her lungs. Wow. That went right to her head. What a rush. She coughed slightly. Caught herself laughing at her inability to keep it down. He patted her on the back.

"You okay?"

"I think so. Just after I finish coughing up this lung."

He gave her a playful shoulder check. She lost her balance momentarily. She breathed in, cleared her lungs and took another drag.

"Feels good, eh?"

She saw the hotel in the distance. *Can I finish it before then?* She took another drag, controlled the rate of her inhaling and felt the kick of the cigarette make her feel even lighter. It was as if gravity had lost some of its pull. A good shot of something would go down really well right now. She managed the last puff and threw the butt into the cigarette tray outside the hotel.

The attendant opened the door. Tall guy. Probably a university student working to pay the bills. Abby thanked him, then followed Jake to the lobby. They took the elevator. Got into their room. Hit the sheets. After, Jake took out two glasses.

He opened the bottle he had picked up. A 40 of rum. He poured them both a shot and downed his in one gulp. She wasn't as courageous. She let it touch her lips. Too strong. This was not going to go down well. She took half of it, grimaced in an effort to brace against what was coming and swallowed. It felt like someone had doused her in gasoline, lit a match and set her on fire. *Can somebody please put out these flames?* She opened her mouth and breathed in. The effect of the cigarette combined with the rum made her feel like she was on the bow of ship. Up and down. Starboard to port. He went to the phone and ordered her up a red and a white wine.

She tried to stand up on the bed and then lost her balance. Time seemed to speed up. One moment she was standing, the next she was face down against her pillow. Okay, let's have a time out. She breathed in. Felt reality return. That wasn't so bad. She sat up, collapsed into his arms.

"So," she said, already wondering what the wine would taste like, "what's this money-making idea you have?"

"It's kind of crazy."

Without really wanting to, she reached out and took her glass. She let the rum touch her lips. "I like crazy with you, Jake."

"Okay—"

Someone knocked on the door. She was prepared this time. No panic. The alcohol in her system helped with that. It wasn't her parents anyways. It was the wine supply. Jake opened the door. Cracked open the red wine first. Poured her a glass. She gulped it down like grape juice. The alcohol warmed her from head to toe, causing her to feel more and more woozy.

"We can make a lot of money," he said.

"Sounds good to me," she said as Jake refilled her glass. "How much is a lot?"

"At least a hundred."

"A hundred bucks a day?"

"An hour."

Abby sat up. For a lightweight girl who had consumed that much alcohol she suddenly managed to pull herself together. A shocked expression came over her face. Gold mine. Screw all that panning in the shallow waters. We hit pay dirt.

"You mean it?"

"A thousand a day isn't a problem."

"No way," she said, more to herself than to him. Her mind started doing the mental math. She stared up at the ceiling. A grand a day. Three hundred sixty-five days a year. No. No way. Was that thirty-six grand a year? She sucked in some more oxygen to figure out the math better. Three million? No. Come on. Three hundred sixty-five days times a grand a day. Big wheels keep on turning. How much? Wait. That's three hundred sixty-five grand a year? No … Yeah. Yeah it is.

"Doing what?" she asked, looking back at Jake.

"It works. I swear. I've heard that it gets done all the time. People are getting rich."

"How?"

Jake pulled out his phone. He logged onto a website. Showed Abby pictures of girls. All kinds of kinky poses. Some of them not so kinky.

Each with a slogan underneath. For a good time. One night only. Worth every penny. Hot. Young. Whatever you want.

"These ugly girls are making tons of money."

"Having sex?"

"Yup. Glorified porn stars. But they're smart. They take in a few screened guys each night for thirty, fifty, a hundred, depending on what the guy wants and how long."

Abby looked at the pictures. Scrolled through them. The list was endless. She turned over onto her back.

"These girls are making that kind of money?"

They waited in silence. Abby's mind was turning. Did lawyers even make that kind of money? A few hours a night for dough like that? The entire day would be free. Shopping, fast cars, hockey games, nice hotels. Come on. It couldn't be that easy. Could it? The alcohol must be talking.

She was sure of it.

"I think you would get way more," he added.

She hit him with the pillow. He smiled. Tickled her. She squealed and rolled over.

"Yeah, I could totally get more than those whores," she joked. She drank from her glass, sucking in the last drops. Jake refilled it.

"How much you figure you could get?

"I don't know. I don't know what those skanks make."

Jake looked through the list. He showed her the amounts. "You could totally beat them."

"No, I couldn't," Abby said, suddenly feeling like she was in a beauty pageant, being lined up, rated and compared against other girls.

"You? You're gorgeous. If these girls are making that kind of money, how much would you make?"

"I don't know."

"Want to find out?"

"I'm not going up on that site!" she said, throwing a pillow at him.

"We could take a side picture. Nothing too revealing. Just enough. Show your gorgeous body. Your great hair."

"That's dumb."

"It's just for fun. Let's see."

"Jake?"

She finished her glass. That was more than enough. She stretched her face in a vain attempt at keeping her eyes focused. But the booze was doing its job, and her world was starting to spin again. She thought about Jake's idea. Anonymity. *No one will be able to recognize me.*

"I don't know."

"Come on, baby. I love you. You're amazing. You're the most beautiful woman in the world."

"What if they don't like me?"

"Then we get rip roaring drunk and tell the world that guys who surf the net for girls have no idea what a hot woman looks like."

She blushed.

"What do you say?"

She thought. *What's the harm?*

"As long as there's no way you can tell that it's me."

"For sure."

She turned to the side. Pushed her hair down in the direction of his cellphone. Tilted her head. Jake took a bunch of shots. They lay back against the bed, looking through the pictures and deleting the ones that showed too much of her face. They kept the ones showing more of the rest of her. Finally, they agreed on one.

"This is insane," she said.

He posted the picture. "No one will know. Besides, it will be fun to find out. That's all. If you don't want to do anything more, no pressure."

He put the phone down. They got busy with other things. And as she went off to sleep, as her tossing ship in the sea went in all directions, before she faded off, she wondered, *How much will I get? How many offers will come in?*

How much am I worth?

chapter eleven

A summons to the justice minister's office was never a good thing, least of all for someone like Joy, who hadn't exactly complied with the requests of his department. She had made Brennan and Ferris look foolish after they reported back to their boss that they had managed to get the member from Kildonan-St. Paul back in line. No problem. She had her delinquent case moved up the party line.

Round two of the fight saw Joy squaring off against other party officials. They did their part as best they could to get Joy back into party shape. If members such as Joy had a hard time remembering that their job first and foremost was to toe the party line, they would be encouraged to do so. This consisted of making promises to the delinquent member. It could also involve getting other members to put pressure on the black sheep of the family—not unlike a political form of shunning. Then came the threats of not supporting a member should they wish to run again. And last, any chance of a promotion for the member in question could be put in jeopardy and the member demoted. In Joy's case that included being yanked back in seating at the House of Commons. It was the political equivalent to having your tickets down at glass level replaced with seats in the last row in the upper deck.

But none of this had any effect on Joy. She had no interest in becoming a minister. She didn't care about being pushed back. You actually get a better view the farther up you sit. And there was zero—absolutely zero—

chance of anybody getting rid of a highly educated, duly elected female member of Parliament.

In the first round against Brennan and Ferris, she had landed a punishing blow to the opposition—what a strange thing to consider, seeing how they were all in the same party. In round two, after the bill was officially introduced, Brennan and Ferris came out slugging, but Joy was equal to the task and didn't go down.

Now came round three. And as she walked down the hall to the minister of justice's office she wondered what was waiting in that room for her. She had directly disobeyed the party line. And she showed no signs of backing down.

She opened the door. Joy put on her trademark smile to greet the polisci grad working at the front desk.

"Good morning. How are you?" Joy asked.

The woman adjusted her sombre expression. She had been briefed on what this meeting would be about. And she had not expected Joy to act in a manner in keeping with her name. At least, not given the circumstances.

"I'll let them know you're here," she said.

"Okay," Joy replied with an even bigger smile.

The assistant opened one of the large wooden double doors to the conference room, said something, and then turned to Joy, raising her eyebrows to indicate that the firing squad was loaded and ready for her to take her place.

Joy entered. The justice minister sat in the middle on the opposite side of the wooden conference table. He was flanked by Ferris and Brennan on one side and two women on the other. *My goodness, five of you? What's the matter? Are you concerned this is going to get violent? Or did you make the wrong assumption that you were going to somehow bully me with your numbers?*

They all shook hands. The justice minister introduced Sarah and Christine. More names to commit to memory. They sat down. Joy was tempted to look at her watch. How long would it take before things got ugly?

They spared each other the obligatory niceties. No one was under any illusion about the purpose of the meeting.

"Joy, we have a ..." He paused. That surprised Joy. Given the amount of time the justice minister had to prepare for this meeting, it seemed odd that he wouldn't have his opening argument ready to rock and roll. "We have a disagreement that we are hoping to resolve."

"Great," Joy said. "Vote for my bill, and everything is resolved. Easy, isn't it?"

Arthur—not *Arty*—smiled. The others on that side of the table followed his lead. They nodded in unison as if trained to do so.

"I wish it were that simple," he said, trying to be congenial.

But Joy would not give him that luxury. "It *is* that simple."

"Joy, you're an educated person. You understand that this is not about MPs having their pet projects."

"Thank you so much for noticing my qualifications. Forgive me if I tell you that, given all of *your* education and qualifications, how odd it is that you can't see what needs to be done."

Ferris was equal to the fight. At least that's what he thought. "You lied to me—"

The justice minister stepped in. "Okay, okay. Stop it. Both of you." He ran a hand through his hair. *Why doesn't she just fall in line?*

"Joy, there's an expectation, as you know, that a private member's bill will not, I repeat, will not address the Criminal Code of Canada."

"Why?"

"Because that's the direction we've taken."

"Why?"

"Because we can't do everything."

"And the result is that innocent girls get raped. That doesn't bother you as a justice minister?"

"That's unfair."

"Unfair? What's happening to our Canadian girls is unfair. Get that through your legalistic brain." Joy spoke louder. With more force. More conviction. "And I don't care about your policies. I don't care about your agenda. We do what's right. You know why? Because it's right. And as for you and your protocol—"

"You are way out of line, Smith," the minister said, pointing his index finger at her. "Human trafficking is not on the government's agenda."

"Then put it on the agenda," Joy fired back. Her voice echoed in the room. It hurt the ears of the others in the room to hear it.

"You're trying to amend the Criminal Code of Canada. That is no trivial thing."

"Neither is a Canadian girl's life." Without noticing, she steeled her back, as if getting ready for an attack. "You're weak, you know that? Spineless. The whole lot of you."

This was getting way out of hand. And neither side showed any signs of taking a much-needed break. Even if it was this early in the conversation.

"Nobody is arguing the value of a girl's life, Joy. Or any life for that matter. Get that through that impossible head of yours. You're on a crusade that does not have the support of the government. We can tackle this some other time."

"Oh, that's so generous of you. Thanks for putting the lives of Canadian girls on your list of things to do. They will feel so honoured and relieved that they got pencilled into your precious calendar."

"Stop with the tone, Joy."

"Stop with your rank inability to see the obvious. How do people like you function in jobs like this?"

"Enough." The room went quiet. Though it had all the indications that it would explode again. "We're not getting anywhere."

An idea came to Joy. Was she fighting to get the bill through under her name? Or was she fighting to get the bill through, no matter who got the credit? A lot can happen in a split second. In that moment Joy did a ton of soul-searching. And found a possible path forward.

"Take the bill," she said. Her voice was so quiet, it was hard to believe she was the same person who had gone toe to toe with them a few thoughts before.

"What?" one of the girls asked. Christine. Sarah. Which was which again?

"You can have it." Joy said. "Take credit for it. Sponsor the bill yourself. The supporting information for the bill is truly incredible work. Don't take my word for it. Legal counsel that the prime minister himself is very familiar with have done a lot of work on this bill. This is not just some pet project. This thing is the real deal. I'll hand the whole thing over to you."

Arthur took in a breath. Thinking he needed more convincing, Joy continued.

"A report calls for Canada to make a number of changes, including to amend the Criminal Code to provide a mandatory minimum penalty for child trafficking."

"Come on, Joy. There's a report for everything under the sun, and you and I both know it. For every think tank that supports something, there's one against it."

"That doesn't make this irrelevant."

"Fair enough." It was a good move on his part. Why not admit that your opponent has a good point? "But I have to give you some sobering information."

Okay, here it comes. This wasn't just the *be a good soldier and fall under command* shtick. He had an ace. Maybe two. And by the way he said that, it seemed like he had an entire deck ready to throw at her.

Joy didn't answer. She watched him. Tried to discern what he was about to say.

"I've talked to people," Arthur said. "MPs. On both sides of the aisle. I did my homework, Joy. I thought to myself, maybe she's got something here. But whether or not you have something, Joy—and please don't misunderstand me; I beg you to try to listen to reason—is not the issue. It only matters if you can get it passed. Are we at least on the same page there?"

No response. None needed. Arthur continued. "All right. We're in agreement, not in general, but at least on this point. We both agree that going guns blazing as one person against a massive army is not the best approach, because you have no chance of winning."

"Get to the point."

"No one is going to support you in this."

A knife plunging into her back might have been less harmful. It wasn't that people weren't going to support her. That made no difference to her. What bothered her was that people weren't going to support the bill. They weren't going to fight human trafficking. For some, this would have been cause for defeat. Some give up when the stats are way against them.

Others become more emboldened.

The justice minister took her silence to mean defeat. "No one believes that human trafficking is happening to Canadian girls." Joy clenched her teeth. "No one buys it, Joy." She gripped the armrest. It was as if she were a boxer getting beaten in a corner, only to find that sudden surge that crushes her opponent. "You're wasting your time."

That was it.

"Wasting my time?" she said.

The justice minister nodded.

"Wasting my time?" she said louder, direct. Each syllable perfectly enunciated.

"Yup."

"I'm rescuing girls off the streets."

"That is admirable."

"Admirable? Admirable?" Her voice hit a higher register again. Like an engine starting up.

"Joy, can we please just end this?"

"Human trafficking in Canada? Absolutely. Drop this debate? No. No, we can't."

He leaned his head back. "Why are you so difficult?"

Joy stood. "Because girls in hotel rooms and apartments are being forced to have sex with multiple men every night. And they need our help."

"They have the police."

Joy thrust both hands out. "That's the whole point! Aren't you listening? The police are doing their job. You—" She was ready to blast him but held back. "They make the arrest, but there's hardly anything to keep the trafficker locked up for any real length of time."

"That's hardly proof for a bill."

"You want proof? What if I took you down to a graveside where a girl born and raised in Canada who came from a good middle-class family got sucked in by a human trafficker and, when she wanted to leave, he strangled her to death with an extension cord! Would that help you understand, Arthur?" Joy's face flushed red. "Would that help you?!"

Arthur looked visibly shaken. The blood drained from his face. A ghastly image of a young girl with a cord wrapped around her neck flashed in front of his eyes. There was a disconnect here. Had to be. How do we go from having a strangled girl on the one hand and a slew of MPs denying it's happening on the other hand?

He felt lightheaded. Like he had had too much to smoke and drink all at once. He sat there, so quiet. Joy refused to interrupt his silence. Going down the rabbit hole of human trafficking is a terrifying experience. It strips you of the fake comfort you think you have in the world around you. Worse yet, it tears away the false covering of naïveté that protects those you love. Then, finally, "Is this without prejudice?"

He used a legal term. Made sense. When in doubt, retreat to what you know best. *Without prejudice* means that both parties agree not to use what is about to be said against each other. It's like a conversation outside a conversation. A cone of silence. Where people can just speak freely without fear that their words can come back to haunt them. It's what reporters call *off the record.*

"Yes," Joy said, recomposed.

"All right. In your own words. No legalese. No media sound bites. Just tell me what you think is happening."

That crack of daylight. This was it. *Don't be long-winded. Don't be a salesperson. Just ... just tell him what's on your heart.*

Joy thought a moment. She wanted to share about her son Edward. But she feared it would bring back too many memories and cloud out the hard facts.

"When people hear the term *human trafficking,* they immediately think of foreign girls tricked into coming here under the guise of working as a nanny or whatever, only to be forced into massage parlours and servicing men out of apartments or hotels. And that does happen. But the hidden secret, the hidden shame in our country, is that girls who are born and raised right here in Canada are being trafficked. It's happening to girls all across Canada. From all walks of life. From major cities to small towns. Kids coming from great families and kids coming from wrecked families. Coast to coast. It's also happening on our reserves. No girl in Canada is immune from the threat of human trafficking."

Joy stopped. Waited. The group across from her looked like the veil had come off their eyes. Whether they would retreat back to what they held for certain before this meeting was anybody's guess.

She thought of her son Edward. His wife was Ojibway, and her mind trailed off a moment to the many stories of trafficking on the reserves. Then she thought of parents across Canada who had come to her pleading for help.

"I can't even begin to count the number of parents w
crying with me about how shocked they are that this has I
their upstanding family from a good community. It's always someone
else's family, right? A foreign girl coming in. But that's not the whole
story. Canadian girls. Trafficked right under our noses."

"How?" Arthur asked. "How does it happen?"

Joy observed the expression on his face. He was open. No government
agenda. No *toe the line* mantra in those dark eyes of his. Bags under them,
though. Long days. Short nights. Par for the course.

"Human trafficking stories are all different, and yet they're the same,"
she said. "There are many different entry points. But in the end, it all
comes down to someone, usually a man, controlling a poor girl who wants
to leave, but she's so terrified and confused that all she can do is continue
in her horrific life."

"How does it happen? How do they get sucked in?"

"Let's go over the top five ways. This is a generalization, but we have
to talk in generalities or we get lost in the details. First is the runaway
pickup. A girl doesn't like it at home. Or she's being abused at home. Or
her caregiver is a drug addict. Whatever the reason, she leaves home,
thinking she can make it on her own. Traffickers watch the bus stations,
the airports, the malls. Any girl on the street is approached within 24
hours. She's offered a place to sleep, offered food in exchange for a few
favours. She gives in. They tell her she has to sell her body or they'll kill
her."

The group of five fell silent. The weight of truth pressing down on
them.

"Next is the guerrilla method. Snatch and grab. The girl does not
get lied to; she's just taken. Outside a mall. From a park. A home.
Grabbed, thrown into a vehicle. Usually drugged. Then beaten to a pulp.
Conditioned, you know. And they sell her to men five, six, ten times a
day."

Sarah and Christine looked sick. They'd been through many other
issues before. But not this. Nothing could prepare them for this.

"Third are renegades. These are girls who initially choose to do
prostitution. They want make some money. What's the harm, right?
Eventually, no matter how tough they are, many of them—not all, but the

majority for sure—end up wanting the protection of a pimp, or they give in to the constant pressure. It's all a lie. Pimps are traffickers. Plain and simple. They get her onto drugs. And keep most, if not all, of the money she makes."

Ferris took notes. She admired him for that. Admired all five of them, really. They'd shown a lot of interest. Humility. Maybe they weren't as off as she thought.

"Four is when a female friend introduces a girl to the world of trafficking. They show her how to get a guy. How to turn tricks. How to make money. Sounds great, but they're really grooming her. Eventually they introduce her to their trafficker, and the trafficker gives her drugs. Forces her to have sex. You get the drill? Starts differently. The entry point is different. But the end result is all the same. A girl is promised a dream. The girl believes it. But it's all a lie."

Joy stopped. They knew she wasn't done. They felt the unbearable burden of evil. Too much all at once. It's easier when it's framed in legalese. The fancy words keep it at head level. But this. This just ripped into their souls.

"But the most common method is the lover-boy method. Sometimes it happens in person—a man approaches a girl at a mall, a community club, or even a school or church. But more often it's happening online. These guys are talented in manipulation. They get onto social media, and they fish. They try to start friendships with dozens of girls. And they target all kinds of them. Lower class, middle class, upper class. I know you'll have a hard time believing this, but money doesn't protect anything. All religions. All skin colours. Doesn't matter.

"These guys hunt for girls who for a brief time might be having a bit of trouble at home. Or not. Maybe home life is great. Maybe the girl just likes the attention. Anyhow, she bites. She figures it's another contact among her many. No big deal. He tells her how gorgeous she is. How wonderful she is. And she loves to hear these words. Who wouldn't? Every girl wants to hear them. And he's in no hurry. But he's very crafty. He waits until they are good friends, and he invites her out. He rarely, if ever, comes to her home. In fact, he plants seeds of doubt in her mind about her parents. Her dad, especially. He tries to get her away from her home. He showers her with gifts of jewelry, clothes and other nice stuff.

He pushes material possessions on her so she's tricked int
is in love. The more physical representations she has of his
the more she buys in.

"Sure, he'll tell her he loves her. Over and over again. And when
he thinks she's hooked, when he thinks she's turned her back on sound
reason and has given her heart to him, he sells her on her dream. A nice
house. Cars. A family. Whatever he discovers that she wants. He gets her
to believe he can make her dreams come true. She's looking for love, and
he's willing to use that against her.

"So he invites her on a little trip. Out of town. Not too far. Nothing
unreasonable. Then he says they can have a great life together. But, here's
the catch. He tells her they need a lot of money so they can have their
dream together. If they get a lot, they can have a great life. And by that
time, she's so drawn in to his love—she wants to believe in this dream so
badly—that she agrees to do what he wants. It's all lies, but she can't tell
the difference. She thinks she's in love.

"He takes a picture of her. Maybe he blackmails her. But more than
likely he will just say she can make money selling her body. Just a few
times. Nothing much. And who cares? It's just sex. Not love. By this time
he's had sex with her so many times that she's emotionally convinced of
his love for her. So she agrees. She starts turning tricks—servicing men.
Serving johns. And the money rolls in. He hangs on to it, of course.

"But now he has to keep her going. How does he do that? Keeps
pumping the dream game. But if she wises up and wants to stop, he either
gets her hooked on drugs or threatens to kill her or her family if she
leaves. No handcuffs needed. It's total slavery by mental and emotional
means. So she's trapped. Sure, she can run. She can run and risk being
killed. So she stays in her nightmare. After all, being a sex slave is better
than death, isn't it?"

Ferris stopped writing. He put down his pen. Didn't have the energy
to hold it. *Jesus Christ in heaven. What did I just hear?*

"How big is it? What's the extent of the problem?" the justice minister
asked.

"Arthur, you start in Vancouver Island, and you make your way all
the way to Newfoundland. Everywhere your foot stops—within one
kilometre there will be a girl held against her will."

"Impossible."

"It's not impossible."

"A crime this big—a crime so massive—right under our noses, and nobody knows about it?"

"Very few. But the group of people who are in the know about this crime has just grown by five members today. Am I right?"

Was she telling the truth, or was she looking at a few cases with such passion that she was projecting the whole thing to be bigger than it really was? The justice minister didn't know. He scratched his head. What to say?

"I'm having a hard time with this, Joy."

"No. The girl with the extension cord had a hard time with it. Your issue is that you're just not seeing the facts."

"So you have an endless stream of low-lifes supposedly wanting to have time with these girls?"

"Low-lifes? Men who pay for sex are pathetic people. You got that right. But the guys who use girls—the johns—they're not bottom-income dwellers."

"They have to have money to feed their habit," Brennan said.

"Johns fuel the whole industry. They're the reason traffickers do what they do. Traffickers don't care about the girls. They care about the money. The girls are a means to an end. Drugs you can only sell once. A gun you can only sell once. But a girl? You can sell the same girl five, ten times to different johns each night. Canadian men. Lining up. One after another. Their money is a main reason our Canadian girls are enslaved," Joy said.

"So who are these guys? Who are these johns?" She leaned forward. The group was still. Brennan and Sarah hadn't moved in a long while. They had become like statues. Like Han Solo frozen in carbonate. The weight of truth bearing down on them and on the others.

"You'd be surprised who a typical john might be."

chapter twelve

David Peterson skated across centre ice. Pulling back his stick he slapped the puck along the boards around to the net. Dump and chase was normally his last resort. But he had come on first after a line change and had no teammates to pass to. That's what he convinced himself of anyway. A few years back he would have carried it in. He skated in after it.

When he was in his twenties, hockey felt so much faster. His blades would cut into the ice with that trademark grinding sound of a forward giving it all he had. Now in his thirties, that sound faded somewhat. He didn't want to admit that he had lost a step against the younger guys out on the ice late on a Monday night at a Mississauga arena. Still, he was grateful it was a no-hit league. It scared him to think of what would happen if he were suddenly transported into the reality of full-contact hockey.

The opposing team's defender picked up the puck and broke out of the zone by skating right out in front of his net. It was a move largely frowned upon years before ("never in front of your net" his coaches would say), but with the tighter and tighter checking it became almost a staple move for some teams. The opposing forward blew past David. Every week it seemed they were getting faster. The forward took a shot on net. Dave's goalie flashed his glove and got enough of the puck to send it off the glass into the corner. His teammate went in after it and fired the puck up the boards. Dave took his position on the half boards between the goal line and the blue line. The puck jumped over his stick towards the blue line. The opposing team's defender pinched in to make a play. He missed the puck. It cleared the zone. Dave skated past the defender and raced after it.

The other defender skated to centre ice, swivelled his hips perfectly and skated backwards. Dave pushed the puck forward for his teammate who raced down the left side. Dave powered down the middle. It felt just like Gretzky and Lemieux bearing down on that Russian defenceman late in the third and last game of the 1987 Canada Cup. His teammate crossed the opposing team's blue line. Passed it back to Dave. Dave fired it top right corner. It cleared just over the goalie's glove into the net.

Dave threw up his hands. His teammate cheered. Which was good. Because at this level, there were no fans in the stands. A horn sounded. Their hour of paid ice time was up. The Zamboni stood ready to clean the ice. The teams left for their changing rooms.

Dave took off his jersey and shoulder pads, unlaced his skates and sat back. He tried to recover. Most of the rest of his team had cleared out. To his right, down the bench, a couple of players in their twenties had managed to take off their helmets and gloves. They huddled over a phone, lost in their own little world. Dave thought perhaps they were playing a video game. Maybe checking up on the NHL scores. But their muffled laugh—the kind Dave figured would be a lot louder if he wasn't in the room—caused him to think they were looking at something else. Both worked in construction. Single. Energy to burn. Money too. One of them, dark hair, built like a tank, glanced over at Dave. The guy looked down the bench to see that it was clear, then pushed over to Dave.

"What do you figure, Dave?" he said, showing him the screen. A big grin on his face.

Pictures of scantily clad girls filled the screen. One-line summaries accompanied them. Dave looked at the faces. At first glance they seemed cute and young. But on further observation they looked more sultry than happy.

"I think you guys gotta find real girlfriends."

"What, you don't like any of them?" the red-haired player who had passed him the puck on the goal joked.

"Pictures don't do it for me," Dave replied.

The other two laughed. This time much louder. Then they became quiet. Dave felt a disconnect between him and them. Somebody wasn't understanding something.

"No kidding," Red said, turning to the tank and pointing to one of the girls. "Seventy bucks? Not bad."

"Give it a try," Tank said. "See if you can get her tonight."

Red typed into his phone. The guys waited. A ring tone signalled a message had come back to them. Red laughed. "We're in!"

The guys raced to get their gear off and fired it into their hockey bags as fast as they could.

"You guys in a hurry?"

"Gotta get there in 15 minutes," Red said.

"For what?"

The guys laughed. Red stopped. Looked at him. *Is Dave joking or he is this naive?*

"You serious?"

"About what?" Dave asked.

They two players glanced at each other as they finished taking off their equipment.

"We're going to hook up with a girl."

Yeah. A disconnect. For sure.

"You met someone online?"

Red showed him his screen again.

Dave saw the image of a girl. Her byline read, *"Eighteen years old. Hot. One night only."* Dave looked closer at the girl. No way she was 18. No way.

"She's even on the way home," Red said.

Dave glanced up at the website. "You know this girl?"

Tank laughed. "No, but we're going to know her for about half an hour," he said.

"What is this?" Dave asked.

The guys picked up their hockey bags and sticks. Red shook his head. "You pay your money, have some fun, help with college or whatever she needs the money for, and that's it."

"You've done this before?"

"After every game."

That was a lot of games. They'd been together as a team for a few years. Sometimes you don't know people as well as you think you do.

"A lot of girls do this?

"Thousands," Tank said. "Check out the site."

"I'm married."

"Yeah, great," Red replied, heading to the door. "Awesome goal by the way. Surprised you could keep up on that play," he said, laughing on his way out.

"Just be thankful I was the one shooting," Dave said, giving it back to him. "You would have rifled it over the net."

Red laughed. "Whatever. See you, Dave."

The door closed.

The drive to his Mississauga home felt longer than usual. Was tonight's game more tiring than others? Had it been a particularly intense day at the office? He glanced at the time as he pulled into his garage. Eleven o'clock. He opened the garage door, thinking his wife and son to be asleep. He closed it as quietly as he could. Heard the soft steps of their border collie. She poked her head around the corner. Dave smiled. "Hey Checker," he whispered. Bent down. Scruffed her neck. His son, Nathan, joked that because she was half black and half white she looked like a checkerboard. When Nathan was a little boy he wondered if she would stay that pattern her whole life or if one colour might win out more over time. Dave checked her water supply, gave her a hug and brought her back to her bed. He took the stairs up and was about to grab a shower when he saw a crack of light from Nathan's room. He gave a quiet knock.

"Yeah," a voice inside whispered.

Dave opened the door. Model airplanes from all time periods lined the shelves. Hockey posters plastered the walls. A white lamp illuminated the desk where Nathan typed at a laptop. He looked up and smiled. The kind of kid parents hope their daughter will end up with.

"Long night," Dave said.

"Paper on comparing two Victorian books," he said, trying to sound bored, but his dedication proved otherwise.

"Which ones?"

"*Dr. Jekyll and Mr. Hyde* being compared—and contrasted as well, mind you—with *The Picture of Dorian Grey.* How was hockey?"

"I scored. Just like the way Mario Lemieux did in '87." Nathan gave a blank look. "Canada Cup." Still blank.

"Yeah," Nathan said. "It's Sidney Crosby, Jonathan Toews and Connor McDavid these days."

Dave smiled. "Good books?"

"Compelling. Make you think about life. Whether our actions are connected to our character. Consequences of choices. That sort of stuff."

"Keep up the good work. Get a good sleep."

"Good night, Dad."

Dave showered. He got into bed, being careful not to wake Hope. He resisted the temptation to kiss her on her soft brown hair. Her slender body barely took up any space. He rested his head against his pillow and closed his eyes. He could have thought about hockey. His work. His son. His wife. Checker even. But a different thought crept into his mind. It stayed there. Like when a coin falls between the seats in a car, and try as you might you just can't get that thing out. In the deep of the night, when he should have been drifting off to sleep, he thought about that website the guys showed him in the locker room. He thought about the girls. It couldn't be that easy to get one.

Could it?

The whole lie was starting to stretch out past what was reasonable.

Abby's shtick about going right from the cabin to school was a bit much. She caught herself looking at her reflection in the hotel bathroom mirror. Was she really getting ready to jettison her family? The pounding in her heart of the affection she felt for Jake was unmistakable. Before meeting him, her greatest passion was soccer. Playing it. Watching it. But now, she felt more secure in his love than anything else. Still, she found herself thinking.

What are you doing? Are you really ready for this?

Of course. He loves me.

Loves you? Really? You're in Montreal. You live in the GTA. What kind of a guy keeps a girl from finishing school?

Who cares? I hate school. I can do it by correspondence anyways.

Listen to yourself. This guy doesn't love you.

Yes, he does. Look at everything he's done for me. Takes me to the best places. Buys me the best stuff. Listens to me talk for hours. Tells me I'm gorgeous. Who else does that for me?

She knew that, sooner or later, she was going to have to tell her mom she was running away with Jake. But not now. That could come later.

The door opened. "Look at this." Jake showed her his cellphone screen.

She looked at the sort-of picture he had taken of her. Not much to look at, even if she did admit so herself. At the bottom she saw 66 comments. All men. Simple questions. When? Where? Tonight? What will she do? How much? A lot of the comments were vulgar.

"That's crazy," she said.

"You rock, babe. See. I told you."

The numbers didn't lie. She had figured one guy might respond. Maybe two. But this many? More demand than supply? That means only one thing.

"We'll be rolling in dough in no time," he said.

Dave checked the time on his phone. An hour and a half to get from his office in a class B building on Bay Street to the airport. No problem. He could make it. Dave made it a priority to meet with his clients face-to-face at least once a year. Most of them never saw the inside of his office. He saw no point in paying big bucks for an office few people would notice. Besides, the Bay Street address on his business card and website did enough. Many of his clients lived in the GTA. Others were as far away as Vancouver. Some in Calgary. A few in Winnipeg. A handful in Halifax. One on P.E.I.

Today was Montreal.

He grabbed his phone and checked to make sure the electronic ticket he had verified earlier this morning was still there. He got into his car and drove off.

Making his way through security, Dave walked to his gate at Pearson. He ordered a mocha latte and found a place to stand at the charging table, even though seats were available. He would be sitting enough on the plane.

He cycled through his emails, deleting anything remotely irrelevant first. Then he went through the critical ones. He had long before disciplined himself to go through each important email in a systematic fashion, resisting the urge to skip complicated queries and steadying his mind until he had solved the issue. When he had caught up, he checked the NHL standings. Would it be the Leafs' year? Finally? But as he looked at the stats, he felt the same nagging he had when he went to bed the night before.

Check out the site.

He pushed the thought out of his mind. He had work to do.

He exited the airport and met his first client at her clinic in Montreal. A radiologist in her mid-thirties who had switched over to him a year before. She had said she didn't like the returns or the service from her previous financial planner. No problem. The stock market had seen good years ever since she switched, so it was anybody's guess if it was just the market or also Dave's skills that added value to her portfolio. They discussed strategy. He was normally a good listener. Normally had a relaxed approach. But this time he found it hard to concentrate. Like he was late for something, in spite of his schedule being perfectly planned out.

He had meetings throughout the afternoon. Supper with a major client. Drinks afterwards with another client. Late check-in at a five-star hotel. When you travel, you get a great hotel. No exception. That was his rule. Putting his feet up on the suite's sofa, he worked on summarizing the conversations he had that day with each client. A 24-hour turnaround was another rule of his. He glanced at the time in the corner: 1:02 a.m. Next meeting would be in six hours. He rubbed his eyes.

Come on. One look at the site. Just to see if you remembered the web address correctly.

He worked on the last summary. Hit send.

You have to at least be curious.

He didn't sleep well the night before. He wondered why. Normally it wasn't a problem. Dave turned off his notebook.

Just take one look. Then forget about it and go to bed.

He got changed. Plugged in his phone. Chastised himself for not texting Hope during the day. He always sent her a message when he landed. Today it had totally slipped his mind.

What's the problem with looking? It's just something different. That's all. You want to be aware of what's happening out there. Don't you? I mean, you did look awfully silly in front of those younger guys. If so many others are doing it, aren't you curious how it actually works?

He checked a stock summary on his phone. Glanced at his browser. Put the phone on the table. Downed a shot of rum from the mini-bar. Hope always hated it when he drank before bed.

What was the name of that site again?

He picked up his phone and moved it to the bedstand. But it felt like it was attached to him.

Come on. Come on. Come on. Just look and be done with it.

No. I have to get to bed.

One look. Who cares? What difference does it make?

Good night.

One look. One look. One look.

He reached into the mini-bar. One more shot. Vodka this time. That should do it.

Dave. Dave. He's our man. If he can't do it—

I have to get to bed.

One look, Dave. Then hit the hay.

Fine. Fine. Fine. Then leave me alone.

Dave grabbed his phone. It was 2 a.m. He typed in the web address, which took him to a totally unrelated site. Had he remembered it wrong? He looked at the letters in the address. Changed one of them. His mistake. Waited for it to load.

Bingo.

A brief but powerful rush of electricity ran through him as he looked through the first page of girls. He scrolled down. More girls. Scrolled more. Still more girls.

This is crazy. No way. No way there's this many.

He touched the location button. Entered in Montreal.

A fresh crop of girls came up. Different skin colours. Different poses. Different slogans. He looked at the faces of the girls. Strange that they all seemed to have a similar look in their eyes. He couldn't quite place what it was.

The girls were stunning. He read the write-ups. If his teammates were right, and he had no reason to suspect they weren't, these girls were making a lot of money. Good for them. Escaping university without a student loan, especially in the current housing market, was not a bad way to get started.

He gave the page one last flip, thinking he was done for the night. But one girl caught his attention more than the others. He found it interesting that he could have stronger feelings for this girl over all the others without knowing anything about her. What her interests were. What she hoped to be when she got older. Without even knowing so much as her name.

This girl had a mysterious and captivating presence. The picture was more of a side shot revealing her blonde hair. He couldn't see her face well. He glanced at the time—2:30.

Put this thing down.

He fluffed his pillow.

Cute, eh?

What's cute? You can't even see her face.

Would you like to?

Give me a break. I have work to do.

You have a full day ahead of you tomorrow.

That's right.

But not a full night. Let me remember the calendar. Last appointment is at their house for 6 p.m. but you have to be gone by 6:30 because they have company coming over. Last flight leaving Montreal is 9 p.m. That means—

That means I finish my work, get on a plane, go to my house and get some much-needed rest.

Just saying. You know. She is in Montreal, after all. And it looks like you'll have enough time. What do you think?

Dave closed his eyes.

The image of the blonde-haired girl followed after him.

chapter thirteen

The call would be coming any moment now.

Joy looked at a picture of her and her husband, Bart, on her desk. She wondered what the verdict might be and thought of how life has the potential to change so quickly.

Alone in her office she took mental stock of the week so far. So many opposed her. Some had shown interest. She tried her best to convince herself that they just needed more time, needed to have the facts work into their minds so they could process them and come to what should have be an obvious conclusion. Or maybe they were just flat out against her bill. She had expected opposition. She believed anyone starting out in any venture was wise not to fall into the trap of thinking it to be easy. Still, the heaviness of battle weighed on her.

Rescuing girls from the grips of trafficking gave her inspiration to continue. In the face of horrific stories and the terrifying acts committed against these girls by Canadian citizens, Joy sensed the purpose that comes to people for fighting a good fight.

But the process of trying to get the bill through proved to be an increasingly discouraging battle. And what bothered her was that she was feeling this struggle so early on in the bill's process. How much tougher would it get? *Stay the course. Keep with it. Greater is he who is in you.*

Long days, late nights and many confrontations in meetings are manageable when you feel a part of an army heading in the same direction. This bill, however, felt different. She felt that not only was she fighting a battle without much help but she had to convince people there was even a war going on.

She touched the picture. Looked into his eyes. She thought back to last time she had seen Bart. It was supposed to be just another ordinary, routine trip back to Winnipeg. She remembered how quiet the Hill felt that day.

For a complex that was filled with the bustle of people during the work week, Parliament Hill on that Friday afternoon became contrastingly quiet. It was as if a hush had fallen over the buildings in an effort to recoup from the week's activities and to draw strength for the coming Monday morning. The stillness was a welcome change for those still present. Members of Parliament normally flew home to their ridings each weekend. Joy had booked a flight out in the late afternoon to finish a meeting with a member who wanted to know more about human trafficking. Compared to the uphill battle she had been facing, it was a relief someone wanted to know more.

She had stood up from her chair, hoping a trip home would clear the discouragement from her mind.

She boarded her flight to Winnipeg. Sat back in her seat. Looked out the window. Starting a journey always brings so much optimism. But the real battle is the one you don't anticipate. The obstacles you don't think of. You know they'll be there, but the ones you don't expect weigh the hardest.

The plane took off. She watched Ottawa fade beneath her. But the battle stayed right with her.

The drive from Winnipeg's James Armstrong Richardson Airport took Joy through industrial businesses that eventually gave way to residential areas. It was nice to be in Ottawa. Nice to be back in Winnipeg. Nice to be back with the people who had supported her. Her route down Henderson Highway led Joy to the north side of Winnipeg and the beginning of her Kildonan-St. Paul riding. In broad terms, the riding encompassed West Kildonan and North Kildonan in Winnipeg, which are separated by the Red River. The riding extended outside of Winnipeg after the border of the Perimeter Highway to include the municipalities of East St. Paul and West St. Paul, which are also separated by the Red River.

It was this river that flooded in 1997, causing Manitoba's flood of the century. The building blocks to the flood were laid in place on April 5 of that year. A snowstorm dropped nearly half a metre of snow in the Red River Valley. Schools and highways were closed. That was a problem. But not compared with the devastation to come. Spring runoff levels more than doubled, and many regions went under water. It resulted in half a billion dollars in damage and caused 28,000 people to evacuate their homes. It was like a time bomb ready to go off.

Joy glanced out her window. The Red River seemed different than both the Ottawa River and the Rideau Canal that feeds into it, near the Hill. The water here had a calming effect on her. Maybe it would in Ottawa, too. She never had time there to take it in.

Kildonan-St. Paul had the perfect combination of city and country life. Her riding office on Henderson Highway was located centrally relative to the population density in the riding. She and Bart lived in the north part of the riding.

Joy pulled into the gravel driveway. She saw Bart standing beside the lawn tractor, looking out at the lawn he had just finishing cutting. He waved. She smiled. But the smile was short-lived. Concern came over her, the way it does for people when they intuitively sense something is not right. She stepped out of the car. They hugged. He looked tired. But not the not-enough-sleep kind of tired. The other kind.

"I don't like how you look," Joy said.

Bart, towering above her, an athlete and normally the picture of perfect health, smiled. "I feel fine."

"You need to see a doctor."

"Joy, you just got home. Let's sit down and have supper."

"I'm not going back to Ottawa until you make an appointment to see a doctor."

"All right," he said accommodating what had to be an overreaction on her part.

But her intuition only grew stronger. Being away for a week sometimes gives a person a chance to notice even small gradual changes in another person they would otherwise miss if they were always around them. They went in and had supper. He was a great listening ear for her. By evening she felt the pressure of the week disappear, only to have it replaced with her concern for her husband.

Back at her office in Ottawa, Joy gazed at the picture of her and Bart and wondered what was in store for them. Her phone rang. It was Bart. He had gone to the doctor for tests, as she had asked. Then, more tests were done. It was all confirmed. So was her intuition.

"I have large B cell aggressive lymphoma," he said.

Joy felt a surge of worry pound through her body. Her mind tried to pretend she hadn't just heard those words. But she forced herself to accept the facts. Her heart bled for her husband. She didn't know, not then, what the words *large B cell* meant. It was the words *aggressive* and *lymphoma* that kept ringing in her ears. *How aggressive? Are we talking that this is treatable, or are we down to the time remaining?*

They would know more in a week. More test results would come in. She found it difficult to remain strong for him on the phone. He had always been there for her. A gentle giant of kindness. A gregarious person who naturally attracted people to himself. He had supported her, was thrilled for her, and encouraged her in her service as a member of the Legislative Assembly of Manitoba. Then supported her all the more in her run for office in Ottawa and her subsequent victory and service as an MP. And now, all this distance away, she wanted to be there for him. They prayed together on the phone. Told each other they loved one another.

She hung up. Touched the bridge of her nose. Closed her eyes to absorb the impact.

A knock at her door. She did well to hide the crushing news. Karen reminded her about a meeting she needed to attend. She had not been looking forward to this one. A member of Parliament wanted to find another way to get her to take the bill down. She went to his office. Sat down. He pushed her to take it down. She didn't have the energy, not now, to fight back. Didn't have the quick word exchange and firepower she had earlier in other meetings. She listened. Steeled her resolve.

Do whatever you want. I'm not taking my bill down. Threaten me all you want. Threats only work when you have something you fear losing. I have nothing for you to take. I have girls being raped in the streets of Canada.

A husband who has death knocking at his door. And I'm fighting against people like you who should know better.

Joy sat down in her chair behind her desk and picked up the phone. The windows in her office let in bright sunshine, which she didn't notice. She called Bart. He answered, and they felt the uncertainty couples feel when they wonder what the path ahead will bring. He confirmed the diagnosis. But the prognosis—about what might be in the future—was still up in the air.

"I'm quitting politics," Joy said. The finality of the tone surprised even her to hear it out loud. She'd spent time thinking her decision through inside the confines of her own mind. But saying it like this suddenly made it real.

Bart didn't react. It seemed to Joy he had known this was coming. She continued.

"I'm quitting politics to look after you," she said, needing to hear it out loud again for her own sake.

"You can't do that, Joy," he said.

"Of course I can."

"And who would that help?"

"You, for starters."

"And the girls? Who's going to take up their cause when you're gone? Who's going to go to bat for them?" Bart asked, a former baseball player himself.

"I'll find someone else," she said, unable to convince either of them it would be possible.

"You have to continue this fight."

"Bart," she began, but, surprising for a politician, she suddenly found herself without words.

"Did you expect that somehow me being sick would let you off the hook?" Bart asked. "Give you an excuse to pull yourself out of the game?"

He had a point. Maybe.

Joy did her best to hold back tears. "I don't know what to do," she whispered.

"Don't worry," he said. "God will show you a way."

"Why are we talking about me?" she said, laughing in the midst of pain. "You're the one with cancer." She smiled, but then it faded. Despite the sunlight, everything in her office felt dark.

"You have to push forward, Joy," he said. "Canada can't afford to lose this battle."

chapter fourteen

It was down to the final arguments. Abby's last bit of negotiating with herself. Was the money really this easy? And even if so, was this the purpose of sex? The whole thing seemed odd. She walked back in from the hotel room balcony. The view of Montreal gave her too much to look at, cramming more information into an already overcrowded mind.

Abby sat down on the bed. How strange that at some point tonight—or at least *perhaps* tonight; she hadn't totally decided if she would go through with this—someone she had never met before would be on this same bed with her. Maybe there would be even more than one stranger.

This is weird. Or is that even the right word for it?

I would use the word different, *Abby. It's a new experience.*

I could just go and get a job somewhere.

You could. You could struggle behind a till or at a restaurant. You'll make slightly more this way. Like ten times as much.

That's a lot of cash.

And Jake's a good guy. You have a future together. You'll have your own car, a big house. No easy feat in this market these days. No more having to suck up to the girls in school. Who needs them anyways?

She hadn't thought about her friends in days. Couldn't understand now why she had ever wanted their approval so badly.

Jake opened the door. "Hey, champ," he said.

Abby had not played on a championship team before. Technically, she wasn't a champ anywhere else. But she was here. With him. And that boosted her confidence.

"You're sure about this?" she asked.

His put his arm around her. "You ever play hockey?"

"Sure," she said.

"You ever feel nervous before a game?"

"I think this is a little different than a hockey game, Jake," she replied, feeling annoyed with him.

She felt bad for connecting his name with a negative emotion, especially considering all the good things he had done for her. He responded in a soothing voice, understanding. Always the gentleman.

"Hey, you're right. I'm sorry. Let's talk this through."

"I feel confused."

He drew her back onto the bed, leaning against the headboard. His arms felt good around her.

"What do you feel confused about?"

"How do I know I'm going to be safe?"

"I'm going to be in the next room. I already paid for it. And I'm going to check every guy out before he enters, okay? No sleazebags. Just nice guys."

"It just feels weird doing it with a guy I don't even know."

"It's just sex, baby. It's not love. It's not what we have." He squeezed her and rocked her back and forth. "These are good guys. They want some action, and they have a lot of dough."

"And if they ask why I'm doing it?"

"They probably won't care. If they do, tell them it's money for college."

She couldn't come up with anything to counter this logic. He was right. It wasn't a big deal. Just turn a few tricks for some guys. Besides, it wasn't like this was the first time for her. It would be the first time with a stranger—yes, that still felt odd—but Jake was right. This wasn't love. It was money. And if Jake was even half right in his predictions, this would bring in a whole truckload.

Time to make a decision.

"We can try it for one night," she said.

"Deal. If you don't like it, we won't do it again. It's worth a shot."

She shrugged her shoulders. One night. If it didn't go well, they would head back to Toronto. She would make up some excuse to her parents about where she went. And she could find a different path to happiness with Jake.

Dave was in a fog the whole day. He had a hard time concentrating. Not that his clients could pick up on it, though. He was sharp on his feet and outgoing, which helped to mask his distraction. He checked his phone in between meetings and raced through his emails. He kept her picture minimized for easy access and was careful not to show his phone to his clients. A picture of a girl like that would be a little awkward to explain, especially to the husband-and-sweet-wife clients.

He left at 6:30 as scheduled and got into his rented car. Drove down the street. Found a parking lot.

Go or no go?

He looked at her picture.

My goodness. What if Hope finds out?

How could she possibly? You're in Montreal.

What if someone sees me going into the apartment or hotel or wherever this is?

Really? You're worried about that? You're on business. Easy excuse. Just say you were meeting a client.

At their hotel at seven?

What happened to your imagination? Tell her you were watching the game with some guys in a luxury room. But whatever you say, don't say "her" room. Don't let that slip out.

Dave thought about Hope. They used to talk all the time, often late into the nights. Those talks had been replaced with his working late hours. His doing. Not hers. Traffic was dead-stopped at rush hour, so he decided he was better off coming home later instead of wasting time on the road. Often he was tied up in meetings so he couldn't get away any earlier. Plus, he didn't want to bring work home and preferred to stay in the office later instead. He planned to make it up to her on weekends, but soon the weeks turned into months, which turned into years, the way time goes unless you figure out some way to intervene. And he didn't remember the last time they'd had a meaningful conversation.

There's no harm in contacting the girl and setting up a time. You can always back out later if you change your mind.

I hate not following through on commitments.

She's probably already taken. So there's no harm either way. 'Course then again if you don't act now you're not going to get her.

Dave wrote a message. His fingers seemed to move on their own. "Interested. Time tonight?"

He hit send. Had he actually done that? Did he just initiate contact to meet a girl? He felt shock, fear and excitement surge through him all at the same time. He didn't know which was stronger. It was like that sinking feeling when police lights appear in the rear-view mirror. And at the same time, he felt like his numbers just got drawn for a lottery or that he had scored the deciding goal in the championship game with only a few seconds left in the third.

Done. He had tried. He shook his head, staring at his unanswered message. She was already taken. Time to go back to the hotel and—

His phone buzzed. That police light feeling intensified. He looked down. A simple message. The time. The place. The amount for services. Abbreviations were given. He could make out most of them. That fog came back over him. It wouldn't have surprised him one bit if this were a dream. But in spite of the little sleep he had and the day filled with meetings, he suddenly felt a jolt of energy.

Another message. "Confirm???"

Dave typed in the letter *Y.*

He hit send.

Putting the car in gear, he drove in the direction of the hotel whose name he'd been given.

He knew where it was.

"He's on his way," Jake said. "I won't let him through until I see him and get the money."

Abby's pulse throbbed in her throat. She was too nervous to answer. What was there to say? Jake kissed her on the forehead. "I love you, Abby.

We have the start of something real. You're amazing. And you're going to do great, okay?"

She nodded as if on instinct, like there was some mechanism inside her that responded the moment he spoke.

She waited on the bed. He sat in the chair. How was she supposed to look happy when she was nervous, scared, and—

It's going to be fun. Have a good time. You're building your dream.

She glanced out the balcony window. Then at the door. Jake got up and stood there, looking at his phone. She could fake being sick. Lock herself in the bathroom.

Relax. If you don't like it, you move on. Nothing ventured, nothing—

But her logic did little to calm her nerves. That pounding in her ears only grew louder and louder.

Until it was the only thing she heard.

chapter fifteen

It was down to the waiting. Her decision had been made. Now all that was left was listening to the pounding in her throat keep time until the eventual knock at the door.

When she was younger she used to sit in apprehension in the doctor's office for her annual checkup. She experienced an eerie calm, knowing that the needle prick was coming but wishing all the same that the door wouldn't open. When it would, a painful shot of adrenalin would rip through her body. But the doctor was blessed with a happy disposition, and when it was all over she would leave, wondering why she had been so worried in the first place. Sitting here now at the end of her bed, she felt the same way as in that doctor's office and wondered if the end result would be the same.

What do I know about this guy? Nothing. I know nothing.

It will be fine. It's an adventure.

What if he's gross and I don't want to be with him?

So what? You don't like tests at school either, but you do really well at them, so what's the difference? You get it over with, and you're richer for it.

Back and forth she argued with herself, becoming more and more afraid as she was left alone with her thoughts.

What if …

What if what?

This guy found me online. He could be anybody.

Jake's going to check him out. Remember?

Is Jake a perfect judge of character?

He picked you, didn't he?

But this is different.

How so? Jake found you online. He connected with this guy online, too.

But what if this guy's a psychopath? What if this guy's my worst nightmare? What if he turns violent? What if Jake hears me scream but can't get here in time. What if he—

You're worrying too much.

Or maybe I'm not worrying enough. There's no telling what might happen.

He's going to be a regular guy. They all will. They hook up with you. You both move on.

I don't know. What am I doing?

You're taking control of your life.

Was that what this was? If so, it came with a lot of anxiety.

She hoped it would disappear.

Dave parked on the street. He felt he needed to be close in case he had to make a quick exit. He looked at the hotel sign. He'd driven past here for years on his trips but had never been inside. He found it interesting how a building he had seen so many times and held no relevancy for him previously suddenly became the focus of all his attention. He glanced at the clock in the car. Digital. He missed those analogue clocks with the arms rotating around. Somehow, even though the two different styles showed the same information, Dave often felt there was more time remaining with the analog watches.

It was go time. Do or die. Now or never.

I could just leave and forget this whole thing.

You could. But you did make an appointment. You know how ticked off you get when people blow you off last minute. Especially when it was in their power to honour their commitment.

This is different. If I cancel, nobody cares.

No problem. You want to go? Go. Nobody is forcing anybody here.

Maybe this isn't such a good idea.

Maybe. Or maybe it is. I mean, something in that picture caught your attention. She's pretty cute, right? At least from what you saw.

Yeah, true. But pictures can be deceiving.

No kidding. Sometimes you see a girl from one angle—

He checked the clock. One minute had passed. He should be up there by now. Or at least on his way.

I don't know.

Look, you go up there. Check her out. If you don't want her, you leave. That way you've kept your end of the bargain by following through on the money you promised, she gets the money she expected, and everyone leaves happy.

He glanced at her picture again.

Upstairs in the room, Abby experienced the sum total of all complex chemical reactions the body experiences when filled with anxiety and nervousness. She didn't want to look at the time. Even doctors aren't always on time, are they? But they do show up. Rarely early. Sometimes right on time. Sometimes late. But they do show up. That knock was coming. If she had been through this before, she might have had the courage to stand out on the balcony and take in a breath of fresh air before getting started. If she had, and if she had looked down, she would have seen a rental car down below.

And a nervous customer trying to make up his mind.

Dave opened the car door, stepped out and crossed the street. It occurred to him that he hadn't even looked to see if cars were coming. He trusted that his subconscious had done the looking for him. That his peripheral version had somehow communicated to him that it was okay to get up and go. Still, it spooked him to think he hadn't looked both ways. Hadn't made that mistake as far back as he could remember. As far back as when his mom taught him about crossing the street and right from wrong.

He adjusted his suit jacket the way he often did when heading into a business meeting. How are you supposed to look natural when this is the first time you're doing something like this?

Dave entered through the lobby door. If there was a doorman, he was too focused to notice. He pulled out his cellphone as if he were checking the time, trying to give the impression he was heading into an important meeting. Which was true, in a way.

He hit the up button in the lobby and waited for an elevator. The doors opened to an elevator beside the one he was standing in front of. He moved over, and as he stepped in, so did a family. The kids were wrapped in towels, their hair soaked. A waft of pool chlorine filled the small space. Dave shifted his feet uncomfortably, hoping they wouldn't end up on the same floor. He hit the button. The mother pressed hers. He felt a slight drop in blood pressure.

Different floors.

The elevator stopped at their floor. They got out. He slid to the side so as to get them out of view earlier. The doors closed.

The ride to his stop seemed to take a lifetime. The doors opened. A sinking feeling developed in his stomach. He stepped out as though a magnet was drawing him forward.

How does this work exactly? What happens? What if she isn't what I expect? What if she's crazy? Aren't there stories of hookers on crack who totally lose it and go ape on their johns? What if she gives me a drink and it's laced with something … Forget it, forget it, forget it. Just keep walking.

In his haste or confusion, he wasn't sure which, he walked past her room. Catching his mistake, he turned back. He wondered how he looked, then realized it didn't matter. He knocked on the door.

Bang. A jolt of electricity shot through both Abby and Dave. For Abby, the sound was magnified a thousand times in her mind. Like a jet engine had just started. Part of her wanted to be on that plane. Part of her wanted to stay right here.

On the other side of the door, Dave took in a deep breath. He heard the lock unbolt. The handle turn. This was it. The point of no return. He was going to see a girl. For money.

The door opened. Dave looked at Jake. A clean-cut recent high school graduate wasn't what Dave was expecting to see. Weren't these guys all supposed to be wearing chains and smoking pot? Whatever. Dave handed him the bills. He'd counted them and recounted them so many times. Still, he felt unsure the amount was correct. Jake flipped through them and nodded.

Jake walked out.

Dave walked in.

The door closed.

Abby stood up from the bed. Her heart beat so loudly she was sure he would be able to see it pounding from the doorway. She relaxed somewhat when she saw the businessman standing there. He wore a ring on his left hand that he had evidently forgotten to take off. Or did married guys even bother with that?

How was she supposed to act? Play a role? Be herself? Small talk? No small talk?

He doesn't look like a serial killer. What a minute. What do serial killers look like? Maybe he's like the guy from Dr. Jekyll and Mr. Hyde. *All nice on the outside, but the opposite on the inside.*

Just relax. You're making this way bigger than it needs to be.

She held her breath. This was it. Money had exchanged hands. Time to keep her end of the bargain.

When it ended, Abby heard the door close as Dave left. She got up from the bed and walked to the bathroom, locking the door behind her, turning on the fan but leaving the light off. No doubt Jake would be in the room right away. She was right. No sooner had her first customer left than the door opened. Jake knocked on the bathroom door.

"Everything okay?"

"Fine," she lied. "Just going to grab a shower."

"You sure you're okay?" he asked again.

Why wouldn't I be?

"Yup."

She sat on the toilet cover. Buried her face in her hands. *What just happened? I didn't just do that. I don't even know who that was. Why do I feel so dirty?*

Part of her wanted to cheer. More of her wanted to scream.

She stood up. Faced the mirror. It was too dark to see her reflection, and for this she was grateful. It gave her comfort to have the illusion of being able to look at herself without having to make eye contact. She backed away and turned on the shower water.

Well done, whore. You are going to make a ton of money.

What? I'm not a whore.

You're going to make so much dough. Remember the Leviathan ride? You're headed for the time of your life.

I'm not a whore. Jake and I are building a life together.

You're going to have everything you ever wanted. Not bad to be so young and be in control of your future.

I am not a whore.

Sorry? Wow. Wait. Let's not get ahead of ourselves here. If you take money and have sex with someone, that classifies you as a whore. Working girl. Whatever. It's just an expression. But you are what you are now.

That's so unfair.

Unfair? Who cares about unfair? It's accurate.

She washed her hair five times, but it still felt unclean. Jake knocked on the door a couple more times. She said she'd be out in a minute but thought she would stay in there forever. In the dark.

Abby covered her face again. Trying to keep out whatever light the dark was letting in.

Not so bad, eh?

What have I done?

She began to cry. She wasn't exactly sure why.

Somehow this isn't right. You shouldn't feel this way after doing it, should you?

It's just an emotional reaction after all the pressure you've been under.

This is worse. I've done something wrong here.

Wrong? You made money. You took a step forward with Jake. He loves you, and you proved you love him. You were totally stressed out beforehand. Man, you should have seen yourself. But now it's over. And this is how your body is telling you that you made it. You faced a challenge, and you made it.

Did I?

She stepped out of the bathroom wearing a hotel robe.

"How're you doing?" Jake asked, giving her a hug.

She didn't lift her arms. She felt awkward, like she was both here and someplace else at the same time. Jake handed her a glass of wine. As if on autopilot, she took the glass and began to drink. She felt it go down her throat and release a warming sensation in her body. She finished the glass in one shot. That helped.

Jake poured her a second glass. She finished that one as well. Spaced it out in three gulps. The wine helped to quiet the voices in her head and drive out her conflicting emotions. Though she wondered if, in her attempt to find some peace and quiet, all she managed to do was numb everything for the time being.

She walked out to the balcony. Looked out at the evening toward nothing in particular.

"There's another guy who can come tonight," Jake said. "He can be here in 15 minutes."

She didn't reply. The alcohol was making its way through her, lulling her into a docile, complacent state. Jake began typing. It seemed he wasn't looking for a reply from her. Not looking for her agreement. Whatever. Leviathan, right? We're all strapped in now.

Let's see where it leads.

chapter sixteen

Dave drove to the airport, trying to figure out if he had in fact just done what he had just done. He checked the rear-view mirror a couple of times to see if somehow his appearance had changed, as stupid as that sounded even in his own mind.

Do I look guilty? Did something happen to my eyes to make what I did recognizable? Or maybe it's worse than that. Maybe, maybe other people can recognize it in me but I can't tell it myself?

You look fine. Just get on the plane and forget this ever happened.

Forget it? Nobody forgets fun times.

I'm blocking this whole thing out. It never happened.

Good luck. Your wife will see it all over you when you walk in.

No way.

What, you think women can't tell? How stupid can you be?

It was a mistake.

You got that right. You're a total idiot. What kind of a fool jeopardizes his marriage like this? You have clients who have gone through divorces. You know how expensive they are. Get ready.

She won't find out. She's not going to divorce me.

People have split over far less.

Dave tried his best to shut it out of his mind, but his conscience continued to shout at him. If only there was some way to stamp that thing out.

He washed his face in the airport bathroom. Looked in the mirror. He didn't look guilty, did he? He couldn't leave this behind fast enough.

Hey, we can come up with a whole new expression. What happens in Montreal stays in Montreal. It'll sound better with the accent en francais. What do you think? A bit of a rip-off of Las Vegas, I know, but it could work. At least for you.

Go away.

She'll see it all over your face. She'll file in the morning.

———

It was a strange time to have a meeting. MPs worked crazy hours. Fourteen-hour days were the norm. Meetings. Helping constituents. Question period. Every MP knew if they wanted to meet with another MP they could do so during the day. Which was why it was so odd that this MP wanted to meet with Joy late in the evening when everyone else had gone.

Joy sat down with Thomas in her office. She didn't know him all that well. Had been in meetings with him. Seen him at functions. Liked him. Liked his charisma. Some people just have that *joie de vivre*—that joy of living.

"Thank you for coming to see me," Joy said. "Sure is late in the day."

Translation: Something is wrong. Nobody comes this late unless there's a problem they don't want discussed out in the open.

"Thanks for your time, Joy," he said. He wore a black suit with an off-white shirt. His short blond hair was not able to hide his tired eyes.

They talked about the trivial everyday things the way MPs do when they are starting a conversation. Joy listened. She felt small talk was important because if you show you are willing to care for someone in the mundane things of life, it demonstrates you are willing to care for them in the deeper issues. She saw small talk as a testing ground where people see if you are worth going to the next level. When she thought he was ready, she said, "So, how can I help you?"

Thomas shifted in his chair. He smiled in a nervous way. Strange for such a congenial guy to be this out of place.

"You're getting a lot of heat for your private member's bill," he said. "The human trafficking one," he added, as if she needed reminding.

"Nothing worthwhile is easy."

"It's a lot to ask, isn't it?"

"To get human traffickers to stop torturing our Canadian girls?"

"To go against party lines and then hope the rest of the House will give you a majority vote."

She paused. Ice water ran through her veins. "If you've come here to dissuade me, you should know I've already stared down the party and the Justice Department."

"You think that's wise?"

"To free girls who are being enslaved? Yes, I do."

"To jeopardize your future political endeavours, I mean."

"If I drop the bill, girls die. But I would get a promotion. Is that what you're saying?"

He shifted again. This wasn't going as planned. "No. No, I'm not saying that at all."

"You're not making any sense," Joy said with a laugh. Her smile put him at ease but also served as a veiled warning that she knew there was something deeper he was after.

"Let me try again."

He looked at the door to make sure it was shut. To convince himself as best he could that there was no one else on the other side of that door listening in. Come to think of it, could her room be bugged?

"There are a lot of bills that could be put through."

"Like changing constituency names? Big, critical bills like that?"

"You're walking a lonely journey," he said.

She watched him. Studied him. Listened past the words. Read his demeanour. Something was very, very wrong here. "Thomas," she said. Then waited for effect. "Why don't you tell me the real reason you're here?"

The blood drained from his face. He no longer felt like an equal. This wasn't about two MPs in a room anymore. She seemed like the principal and he, the student.

He closed his eyes. Was he really going to say this out loud? He whispered it.

"Can I ask you to reconsider doing this bill?"

"Why?"

"Please."

"Why?"

"Joy, I'm asking this as a favour."

"A favour. What kind of favour?"

The puzzle components started coming together for her. She had the corners and the edges figured out. It hinted at a picture she didn't like.

"I'm in trouble," he said.

"What kind of trouble?"

He couldn't look her in the eye. How did it come to this?

"I'm ... I'm seeing girls."

The longer you work in politics, the less surprises you. But this one caught her off guard. Joy felt such disappointment in him. Surprise, yes. But mostly disappointment.

"You?" she said, more to help her accept what she had just heard.

"I need a favour."

She couldn't believe it. Of all people. Of all the MPs in Canada. This guy.

"A favour?" she asked. "You need a favour from me? How about you do a favour for me, Thomas? Can you help me understand how someone like you pays young girls to have sex? Girls who are being held against their will, who have been deceived, who are psychologically enslaved, and yet you go on living with such happiness? I really need you to explain that to me."

"It's more complicated than that."

"Really? Enlighten me."

"Joy, I'm scared."

You're scared? Can I tell you what scares me? Guys like you scare me. If you each had signs on your faces that said I have sex with trafficked girls *I could identify you. But men like you are more insidious. You commit these horrific crimes against people, and yet no one can tell. Not even me. I am at the very core of fighting human trafficking, and I can't identify you, the enemy. That scares me.*

"It's odd you mention being scared," Joy said. "When I think about human trafficking and I think about people being scared, you'll forgive me if a member of Parliament like you who earns a six-figure salary, has a wife and children, has two, maybe three places to call home—if someone like you is not the first person I think of when I think of fear." She paused. A flash of so many girls she had rescued passed in front of her mind in an instant. "When I think of fear, I think of the girls you abuse. Girls who are terrified of being killed by their traffickers. Is any of this connecting with you?"

It was. He was making that painful journey from being interested in his own safety to understanding he was directly involved in ruining the safety of others.

"Joy, the woman who sets me up with these girls—"

"A madam," Joy said, in an effort to get him to learn the lingo. While many traffickers were men, there were also many women who coerced young girls into sex servitude.

"She heard about your bill."

"Good. Word's getting around."

"She says if I vote for the bill she is going to expose me." He pressed his lips together. "I will stop. I promise. But I can't take the humiliation of her outing me."

Joy waited until she was sure she had his attention.

"I want you to hear me very carefully." Her eyes burned into him. He shifted again, like he was getting ready to hear a guilty verdict. He would rather have had Superman fire his laser vision at him than to have to stare into Joy's gaze. "You are going to vote for this bill. And can I tell you why?"

He didn't want to respond. He had placed his one request. Had asked her to save his skin at the expense of so many Canadian girls. It didn't work. And it wasn't until he was sitting there with Joy that he realized the utter arrogance, stupidity and evil of his request. He didn't want to hear what she had to say next.

"You are going to vote for my bill for two reasons," she said. "Number one. It's the right thing to do. And number two, as an extra measure of encouragement for you—if you do not vote for my bill, you don't have to worry about your madam outing you. I will out you myself. I will expose you right to the core," she said. "You're so sick it doesn't even occur to you how much you are damaging those girls."

He waited in the silence. No movement. No need to shift in his chair anymore.

"You have to stop," she said. "And you are going to vote for this."

He stood.

"Did you hear me?" Joy asked.

He looked so beaten down she wondered if he had the courage to say anything at all. Thomas showed himself out in silence.

Joy closed her eyes. *Dear God in heaven. Am I fighting against everyone on this bill?*

————

Dave pulled into his garage. He hoped his wife was sleeping. Maybe there was a 24-hour grace period where the guilt wears off. *Stop it! Stop thinking this way. Just forget it ever happened.* He entered his home. Faithful Checker walked up to Dave, then stopped, as if her intuition told her something was out of the ordinary.

"Hey Check," he said. The hockey-crazed family often shortened her name.

"How was your trip?"

Dave nearly screamed. He turned around. Hope stood in her white silk pyjamas. Her gentle, trusting demeanour emanating from her. His pulse hurt as a painful burst pushed through his body. *Can she tell? Can she tell? Can she tell?*

"Good. Lots of meetings."

You're telling me. Got an extra one in this time, didn't you?

She came up and wrapped her arms around him.

I'm sorry. I'm sorry. I'm sorry. He wanted to say it. Wanted to get it off his chest. Wanted to go back to what they had. But the truth would destroy her. She would crumple to the ground and melt into water if he told her. He couldn't do that to her. He hugged her back. Sort of.

"I'm going to bed," he said. "Really tired. Sorry."

"Sorry?" she asked smiling. "It's been a busy trip. You have nothing to be sorry about."

You got that right. She faithfully waited for you to come home, while you were—

As they went upstairs, Dave looked down at Check. Could the dog tell? Check tilted her head. Gave a slight whimper, then went back to her bed.

Dave took a shower. Avoided looking in the mirror. Climbed into bed next to Hope. The day couldn't end soon enough.

Hey, you want to play a riddle?

No riddles.

Come on. One riddle. You're smart. See if you can get it.

No. I want to go to sleep.

Here goes. What does an eagle in the sky, a snake on a rock, a ship in the sea and you with that girl all have in common?

I don't care. I want to put this out of my mind.

Come on. Give it a try.

He had heard this somewhere before. Where, he couldn't remember.

Eagle. Snake. Ship. Me. I don't know. I'm tired.

Try it again. You'll get it.

I don't know. Can we stop?

Don't give up. Here's a clue. Don't think of the eagle while it's in the sky or that snake while it's on the rock or the ship on the sea or you while you are with the girl. Think of them afterwards.

You win. I give up.

Really?

Yes, really.

You disappoint me, Dave. Okay. Here it is. None of you leave a trace.

Interesting.

After the eagle has flown through the sky there's no proof it was there. If you weren't around to see the snake on the rock a few minutes ago, you would have no reason to believe it had been there. A ship leaves a wake while it passes through the sea. But afterwards, it's just the sea again. The same with you, my dear friend. The same with you. Get it?

Yeah, I get it. Now forget it.

You see your wife? Sleeping there beside you? No clue. Not a hot clue. You're as innocent as a snake on a rock. You can look at that sea and know that you left no trace. See? She doesn't suspect a thing.

Fine. It's done.

It means you can do it as many times as you want and she will be none the wiser.

That's not the point.

That's entirely the point.

It's over.

Okay. Okay. No problem. You're the boss. But just one last thought, okay? … Hello, Earth to Dave. Come in, Dave.

Yeah, what?

It was fun, wasn't it? Even if you never do it again. It was fun. N'est-ce pas?

Sure. Okay.

And she was cute, wasn't she? I mean, you know how to pick 'em. She was cute, wasn't she?

I'm going to sleep.

But she was cute, though. Wasn't she, Dave?

Dave breathed out. He was home. Could he just edit this part of his life out?

Or maybe not. Maybe he didn't need to cut this out. Maybe just compartmentalize it. Like putting it in a high school locker inside his mind with a combination only he knew. He thought back to her. The girl. That's all he knew her as. No names exchanged. First time in his life he hadn't given his name to a person he met.

Yeah, Dave thought. *She was really cute.*

chapter seventeen

When it was all over for the evening, Abby began to process what all had happened. They came in one after the other. Sometimes as much as half an hour apart. Sometimes right after one another. None of them were as decent as the first guy in the suit. There had been an older guy who gave her the creeps, smiling at her like he owned her. A gross, greasy-haired guy who was into weird sex. Another guy she thought she recognized as a professional athlete. A police officer. A teacher. Crazy how much people revealed about themselves. Like she cared.

How many had it been tonight? Six. No. Seven. She wondered about the actual count, then felt a strange sense of being out of control. She had to remember how many there had been—much the way people stranded on an island or held prisoner in a remote jail scratch a mark for each day they are in exile. There's something about keeping track of the passage of time that maintains sanity. Would that work for keeping track of the number of men she had been with?

A pilot was the last to go at 2:30. She celebrated by escaping into a full bottle of wine. Now that her shift was over, she could go all out. Locking herself in the bathroom, she took her familiar spot on the closed toilet seat. *What are you doing? What are you doing? What are you doing?*

This all seemed like a bad party. Jake was right. What she did with these guys tonight wasn't love. Not even close. None of the guys, not a single one, asked her age. Her makeup made her look older. Eighteen for sure. She was really scared once. Her thin frame opposite that big guy. She closed her eyes and pretended she was on the Leviathan. One of the differences between this and the ride was that thrill rides are engineered. That's not a total guarantee. Accidents still happen. But there was no engineer or psychologist or any other referee to guarantee the conduct of these guys, apart from Jake's omnipotent skills in character assessment.

Jake knocked on the door. *Please God, not another one. Not tonight. I just can't.* She told him she was fine, hoping that by saying so she would be able to convince herself of the same. Everything hurt. Her mind was spinning. She wanted to race out into the Montreal night. She wanted to collapse in bed. She wanted to down another bottle of wine. She wanted the cleansing feeling of pure French spring water. She wanted to invite a dozen more guys. She wanted to remain chaste the rest of her life. She wanted to run off with Jake. She wanted to bolt out of here and go home. Her mind was a spinning mix of everything. Her desires warred with each other, effectively cancelling each other out and leaving her in limbo, halfway between whatever world she was in and whatever world she was entering.

Stop and think. You can turn this thing around. It's not too late to go back.

Go back? Now? After I've come this far?

Think of what's happened. Is this what you want?

I have Jake. I don't need anything else. He loves me.

When you were young is this what you wanted?

Times change. We all have to grow up.

You don't even remember the number of guys you've seen tonight. Doesn't that tell you something?

Seven. I think. And it's a job like any other. Does anyone remember how many burgers they've flipped? How many lawns they've mowed? How many pizzas they've delivered?

This is different.

You got that right. Like ten times more money different.

Do you like this? You like the way you feel now?

Every job feels different at first. If I work like this I can earn as much money—

"Abby?"

How to respond? To run or to embrace? Is this the start or the end? The ascent into bliss or the descent into hell?

"Abbarama?" he said, joking.

Just grab another drink and put this out of my mind.

Out of your mind? Is that what you want?

"Abracadabra!" he said. "That's a cool name. What do you say?"

Part of her wished the incantation would make her disappear.

She opened the door. Their eyes met. He handed her a glass of wine. How many glasses had it been tonight? She didn't take it. She was about to lie down on the bed, then decided against it. She didn't want to touch the bed that six, seven, eight—whatever—number of guys had been on. Abby walked to the balcony, the only place she hadn't been in the last few hours.

The evening air cleared her mind, like the wind blowing away clouds, giving her some objectivity. Instead of still living in it, she could live outside of it.

They leaned against the railing. She looked down. Not out. Was this going to be worth it?

"I don't know, Jake," she said, straddling that line between looking for reassurance and expressing doubt.

"You did amazing, babe. I love you so much. We're going to do it."

"How? By lying on my back and every other position, doing stuff I never even dreamed of?"

"You didn't get hurt, did you?"

Abby didn't say anything.

"Abby?"

"No."

That wasn't true. She half-hoped he would have realized that. But he didn't pick up on the lie.

"You see. I told you I would take care of you." He pulled her towards him. "You stay with me, and you can have it all."

"I don't like being with those guys. I like being with you, Jake."

"And you are with me. Don't ever leave me, baby. Those guys are just cash. They're giving us our dream."

The night air grew cold. Even in his embrace Abby felt an uncomfortable chill. She waited, hoping it would pass. Instead, she began to shiver.

She wondered if it was better to stay out here freezing with him or to go back inside to that room filled with memories of what had just happened.

She opened the door and went back in. The sight of the bed made her sick.

"I can't do it anymore, Jake. I just can't."

She looked up at him. Studied his eyes. Wondered what would be coming next.

"It's all right, baby," he said.

"You sure?"

"You gotta want it. If you want out, you got out."

He reached into the back of his jeans. Abby took a step back. A sudden fear came over her about what he might be hiding back there.

"You want out?" he asked.

She took another step back. The back of her legs hit the bed. That bothered her. She didn't want to touch it again.

"Abby? Abracadabra?"

He seemed different. Same body. Different person. How did his eyes change like that?

"You sure you want out?"

His hand seemed to be grabbing something. She swallowed.

It's a knife. He's going to slit my throat so fast that this is all going to be over before I even know what's happened.

Woah. Hold on. Get a grip on the imagination, will you? This is Jake you're talking about.

He pulled out his hand. Fast. Like he was drawing a gun. Abby cowered backwards, lifting up her hands in a panic. A fluttering sound flew past her left ear.

"Abby! You sure are jittery."

She turned around. Was this real?

Scattered over the bed she saw dozens of twenties. Red fifties. And the beauty of them all. The brown one hundred dollar bill. Just like the bill Jake had used to pay for her at the fair.

She gasped and got onto the bed to count them, forgetting all about not wanting to be on it again. How much was there?

"Are you serious? This is how much we made?"

"Nope," he said, tossing four more fifties in the pile. "This too."

She touched the bills. Felt the soft paper. But it was more than paper. Much more. This was the reward. A few hours of work. And an incredible payday.

"You make more money than a lawyer," he said. "You'd have to finish high school and go to university forever, and even then you wouldn't make this much. Who's better now, baby?"

She gasped. Scooped the money into her hands. Put it into a neat stack. Flipped through it like it were a deck of cards.

"Who's your daddy?" he said.

She turned to kiss him. "You are, baby."

He took the money from her hands.

"Tomorrow we're celebrating." They embraced. Fell back on the bed.

She woke up at noon the next day. Jake was passed out beside her. They'd finished a bottle of whatever that was. She staggered to the bathroom. Looked at her reflection. No change. Well, no real change. Red in the eyes. Bags under them. Nothing a pair of sunglasses couldn't fix.

She went to the bed to find her phone. Not there. She had plugged it in the night before, before number one showed up, and had had no reason to check it since.

Did one of the guys from last night steal it? She rifled through her jeans. Shirt. Purse. Emptied it out in a panic. It surprised her how uncontrolled she became. *Where is it? Where is it?!*

She was about to jar Jake awake when she saw his jeans on the floor. She went to the back pocket. Breathed a sigh of relief. Smart thinking. Better he have it than leave it out in the open for the johns to see.

She sat down at the desk. Voicemails galore from her mother. Texts, too. Kedisha sent one. All variations of *Where are you?*

No point in hiding it anymore. She poured herself a drink from the mini-bar. Drinking this early? No matter. She was going to need it to write the text to her mother. No *Hi Mom* to start. Just right into the message.

"*I met a really great guy. He loves me. I don't expect you to understand. But it's amazing. I'll call in a couple days.*"

Abby's mother heard her phone beep. She had it clutched in her hand like a life preserver in a storm. She saw Abby's name in bold and breathed a sigh of relief that a text had come in from her. It was all fine. Just some dumb teenage misunderstanding. She would give her daughter a talking to later. But that could all wait. She was safe. She had a response. And she felt the comfort parents feel when the currency of communication is still in circulation.

At least that's what Abby's mother thought initially.

She presumed she'd receive some dumb excuse. A crazy adventure Abby was having somewhere. But the words she read put a knife into her heart. Her mind immediately put up a protective barrier. Like it could reject the reality of the words and figure out some way to back this train up and create a different result. *This is not saying what I just read.*

But reality can be cruel. Her knees grew weak. She slumped down from the kitchen island to the ground. She read it over again.

The message didn't make any sense coming from her daughter. *Have I been that blind?* Two completely opposite people. There was the Abby who was home last week. And now there was this Abby. Or worse, maybe it was the same Abby all along, only she had been too removed to really know her. She hit the call button.

Abby saw her mother's name flash on the phone's screen as it vibrated. No point in answering. Just give it some time. In a week there would be so much money. In a month, no telling. She would figure this out as she went.

Your mother is calling, and you're avoiding her. Does that tell you anything?

All that will happen is I'll go back to what I had.

Yeah. Schooling. A good friend. Soccer. You love soccer.

With this kind of money I can get front-row tickets to any game I want. Who's the winner now? Taking that call from my mom would mean my future with Jake goes poof.

Abby put her phone down. Stood up. That was a mistake. Her little body was still hungover. She went back to bed and pulled the covers over her head.

Abby's mother was frantic. She called her husband. Called the police. "No, I don't know where she is … Yes, it's a problem … No, I have no idea who she's with ... Then put out a missing person's bulletin! ... What do you mean you can't get a cop on it? ... Do your job!"

Lots of cursing.

"I'm trying to calm down! I've told you the facts. You know what I know ... Okay. Okay. Thank you. Yes, you can call me here. I'm sorry. I'm sorry. I'm so stressed ... All right ... Abby left home Friday ... Please. All right. I'm sorry ... Okay. Yes, I have a friend I can call ... Yes, you can have the officer come over tonight ... Thank you for your help. Please help me. Please help me ... Thank you."

She slumped back to the ground, tears streaming down her face. When all the calls were made she texted a friend to come over. She emailed her boss and said she wasn't coming in today.

I'm not coming in today because I am a total failure as a mother. My daughter would rather be out with some guy I don't even know, in some place somewhere in the world, doing who knows what, and I may never see her again.

Even though a black leather chair was right beside her in the living room she only found it possible to stay crumpled on the ground. It was as if someone had stuck a massive needle inside of her and sucked the life right out of her.

She stared at Abby's message again.

If only she could reach out and pull Abby back in.

chapter eighteen

Despite the negative face-to-face meetings surrounding the bill, Joy received emails and signs that maybe, just maybe, a groundswell of support was taking shape. A Conservative MP sent her an email that read, "Thank you for the leadership and persistence you have given to this whole human trafficking nightmare. You have my complete support on your private member's bill to amend the Criminal Code, and I will do what I can do."

Contrary to the notion that there would be no support from across the aisle, she did receive backing from various MPs, including an email from a Liberal MP that read, "Not only can you count on my support; should you wish to increase the mandatory minimum for these types of crimes even further, I would be supportive."

One of the strategies Joel came up with that helped, especially from a messaging and image perspective, was getting MPs from each party to "jointly second" Bill C-268 after it had been introduced. Joel researched and identified an MP in each of the Liberal and NDP parties who might be interested. Liberal MP Boris Wrzesnewskyj had a sister who headed up an NGO that helped victims of sex trafficking in Ukraine. NDP MP Peter Stoffer had previously introduced a private member's bill on child pornography. Joy and Joel approached them individually, and both immediately agreed to second the bill. This allowed Joy and Joel to put out a press release indicating to people that the bill was supported across parties. They hoped this would help break down the partisan walls.

Joel also developed an outreach media strategy. It included emails to supporters explaining how they could help spread the word about the bill and encourage their MP to vote for it. He started a social media page for the bill that soon attracted 5,000 followers. Joy emailed every MP and responded to all of their questions. She connected with the party leadership, asking for an exception to the party line that there be no justice private members' bills.

It was difficult to tell where she was in the race. Was she gaining ground or falling behind? It's dangerous to let a few positive emails make you think you're getting ahead. Equally dangerous to let a few nasty visits make you think you'll lose. The whole thing was a mystery. Politics is like that. You never know until the vote is taken where people really stand. The political graveyard is filled with people who were sure they were going to win. And the House of Commons has more than a few MPs who, when honest with themselves, will admit they are surprised to be there. The smart politicians manage to stay both optimistic and realistic.

She called Bart. In his trademark genuineness he asked her questions about how the bill was going, what she needed and how he could pray for her. Even in his illness—his life sentence perhaps—his focus remained on her. It seemed to Joy that the burden he felt for her in her fight against human trafficking was greater than the crippling weight of his own cancer.

It felt good to hear his voice. It was if he were right beside her, encouraging and inspiring her. Some men exude love without saying a word. To her, the geographic distance between them wasn't the length of a flight. It was zero. It was as if the concept of space didn't exist at all. Perhaps it becomes that way when people care more about the other person than they do about themselves. Each seemed to know what it felt like to be the other person, and in so doing they managed to escape the common myth of separation by distance.

She hung up. Rested her elbows on her table. Buried her face in her hands. Her tank had run dry. She lived with a constant fear of what would happen to Bart. Was he getting better? Was he getting worse? His condition occupied her mind. Conscious most of the time. Subconscious all the time. She felt a steady drip of worry entering her bloodstream. Pounding headaches. Seeing every conversation through the film of her husband's suffering right in front of her. She took in a breath.

That's it. I'm done.

She wanted to untie her skates. Leave the rink. The fight was gone.

I've never felt so exhausted in all my life. I just can't go on anymore, God. I've done the best I can. But I'm putting it all in your hands now. Your will be done.

She looked at her screen of emails. If only she could take a poll right now among all MPs. Where did she stand?

A knock at the door. Joel looked in.

"You have a visitor."

There were no appointments booked. It was late in the day. The way Joel said it conveyed that it was someone involved in human trafficking. She could always sense it in his voice. See it in his eyes. Some people have a mechanism that prevents them from feeling someone else's pain. Others know that healing comes from absorbing someone else's devastation. You have to be both strong and weak to pull that off.

Joel walked away and returned to bring in the visitor. Joy had expected to see a young girl. A survivor of human trafficking, perhaps. Instead she saw a woman in her forties. Her face beaten down from a hurricane of grief. Like her soul had been emptied out, and all that was left was skin and bones being controlled remotely by someone. Even the slightest movements seemed to cause her immense pain.

"You're Joy Smith?" she asked, as if the task of remembering the confirmation she got from Joel a few moments before was too much for her. Seeing Joy face-to-face made her want reassurance that her journey had brought her to the right place.

Joy gave a slight smile. Looking into the woman's eyes, she sensed that her pain that had reached a place so deep that words alone could not mend it.

"Won't you sit down?" Joy said, sitting in one of the armchairs and offering her one opposite her so they would have nothing between them. Quite different from when the party bagmen paid her a visit.

It seemed to Joy that it took all the woman's effort and concentration to sit. Her face looked devoid of life, like someone had done a masterful job in creating a wax statue of her—duplicating everything except her humanity. She rested her elbows on her knees, drawing Joy's attention to her jeans, which looked like they had been slept in. She covered her face. Blondish strands of hair fell down.

Joy waited, refusing to interrupt the woman's grief.

"I'm sorry," the woman said. She began to cry uncontrollably. She'd made it this far. What was there left to do? Where on God's green earth was there left to go? Why did he not create a button that people can push when the pain threshold goes past maximum so everything can be reset to good again?

Joy handed her a box of tissues. Put her arms around her. Then poured her a cup of tea, placing it on the stand beside her.

The woman pleaded and begged with her own sanity to make this all go away. But facts were facts. Reality was what it was. Want it or not.

"My daughter's been taken," she said. She lifted her head, eyes closed, and covered her mouth with both hands. Maybe that would prevent her from saying any more and giving credence to the reality that had ripped her soul from her body.

"She fell in love with some guy and ran off with him. But—" There was always a *but* in human trafficking. I thought he loved me *but*. He treated me so well *but*. We tried to teach her right from wrong *but*.

"But someone said they thought they saw a picture of her on—" It was a whole new world for her, and she couldn't understand it all. "They saw a picture of her on a site where men—"

She gasped. It was all too much.

"She sent me a message saying she's in love ..." She tried to recall the exact words Abby used. Having read it so many times, she thought she would have had it burned into memory by now. Either way, the fact was that her daughter had been deceived. And what hurt her the most was that it was only a matter of time before her daughter figured it out.

"Thank you for trusting me to come and tell me this," Joy said. "And I'm going to help you in whatever way I can. What's your name?"

Had the stress been that intense? She hadn't even remembered to introduce herself.

"I'm sorry," she said again, feeling the misplaced guilt that accompanies people suffering from unbearable pain. "My name is Talia Summers," she said. "My daughter, Abby, is gone."

THE TRUE STORY OF CANADIAN HUMAN TRAFFICKING

Talia covered her eyes again. "At this point I would have been grateful if it had only been running off with a guy. It would have been better than … than …"

She looked down at the floor. "We phoned everyone. Friends. Friends of friends. Posted her picture everywhere. Went to the police. Private investigators. Someone found a picture online that listed her in Montreal. Police tried to respond to her ad. But there was no response. It was like that guy could smell someone was on to him."

Talia rubbed her temples to help fight off a headache that so many painkillers had failed at touching. Like a boxer being beaten mercilessly, she gave up the ability to defend herself. She exhaled and felt the frailty mothers feel when the circumstances of life are too crushing to bear.

No one had ever told her that grief is so similar to fear. She glanced back to make sure the door was closed, thinking perhaps her daughter's trafficker was on the other side of it.

"What's going to happen to her?" she asked. "Why didn't I see the warning signs? Why didn't I see them?"

"It's not your fault."

"It's absolutely my fault. I'm responsible for her. Are you a mother?" Joy nodded. "Then you know what I mean."

"These men are devious. They pretend to love them. They sell them on the dream."

"And it's my job to warn her about those kinds of guys. I didn't. I failed. I failed."

"Which police officer did you speak to?" Joy asked. Talia gave the name. Joy recognized it. Talia sent Abby's picture to Joy, who then sent it out to her network of contacts.

"I'm going to Montreal. I can get there in a few hours," Talia said. "Thank you for your help." She tried to hold back tears. Then released them. "I read about you in the news," Talia said. "I never knew that human trafficking happened to our girls." She looked up. "I hope your bill gets through," she said, clinging to that weak rope that was still keeping her attached to whatever semblance of hope she still thought she had left.

"Talia, the police are looking. You can't do anything tonight. It's not right for you to be on the road."

"Would you stay still if your daughter was out there?"

"I would," Joy said. "If a night's rest meant I would be more effective in the morning."

Talia considered the advice. Nodded. Joy called a hotel for her. "Call the officer the moment you get to Montreal."

"Am I going to get her back, Joy?" she asked. "Or is she gone for good?"

Joy could have told her what she wanted to hear. But lies and truisms do more harm in the long run.

"Everyone is looking for her." Joy hugged her. "Phone me before you leave."

"I will," Talia said.

Joy walked with Talia to her car. She got in. They waved goodbye. Joy watched as Talia drove off, hoping she would get at least some rest to help her cope with her incredible anguish.

Joy went home to her apartment and sat down at her kitchen table. Talia and Abby weighed heavy on her mind. She made herself a cup of tea in a bright red mug. Somewhere out there Abby was following some guy, believing she was in love with him.

And it had left an unbelievable and growing wake of destruction.

chapter nineteen

For a life that was supposed to be easy, Abby found herself busy every waking second of the day. There was always stuff to do. Buy clothes. Buy makeup. Get hair done. Eat. Sleep. Sort of. And then work. Lots and lots of work. She saw at least seven men a night, sometimes at many as twelve. She started around eight and went until the early morning. When the last customer had gone, which was always long after she was drained and done herself, she would guzzle a bottle of wine. That worked well for the first few days. She was able to wake up in the morning and put the night behind her. But now, a full week in, she found that the alcohol trick wasn't doing it for her. Wasn't helping her relax.

It all felt like one long day. Pieced together. Like an endless roller coaster. Fun at first, but the thrill eventually begins to wear off.

Jake moved them around from hotel to hotel. Changed her online pictures. Her appearance. If she was honest with herself, she'd have to admit she didn't even know the address of the hotel she was now in. All she could tell was that it was different. Not as nice. No bathrobes. Bed was smaller. It had a balcony but not nearly as beautiful a view. No mini bar. Not that it mattered. Jake kept her filled up.

Abby woke up groggy the morning after the most gruelling night of the week. She kept her eyes shut, hoping to go back to sleep. In those first few seconds her mind and body tried to figure out if she was rested or not. She felt as if weights had been dumped on top of her and chains had been wrapped around her shoulders and hips, pulling her down against the mattress. Her calves, ankles, and feet felt full of poison. She wanted to stab them to release the incredible stinging.

Why am I waking up if I'm so exhausted?

Did she have enough to drink last night? How many glasses had she consumed? Was it the typical total bottle of wine, or did she forget and just go to bed? No, no, she had the bottle. Rosé wine. Went down like flavoured water. That should have been enough to knock her out. Ten hours for sure. So how long had it been? Got to bed at, what, 3 a.m.?

She forced her eyes open. Blurry. Everything hurt. She stretched her legs out on the bed, massaging her calves. *What's wrong with me?* Her eyes finally focused. She stared at the clock on the night table.

7:06.

A.m. or p.m.?

Wait. What if it's not morning? What if I slept through? Has to be p.m. If it were a.m. that would mean I only slept ... She tried to do the math that normally came so easy to her. *That would be four lousy hours? Go back to sleep.* She had managed a combined total of seven hours of sleep in the last two days. That should be enough to knock a young girl out for the count.

Instead, she felt both exhausted and hyper at the same time.

It's p.m., you idiot! Get out of bed. You've been sleeping all day.

It can't be. Just let me rest.

Get going! The guys are going to be here any minute, and you're not ready.

Jake keeps me on schedule. If I was late he would have told me by now.

Prove to him that you can keep up. That you can hold up your end of the bargain.

She got up, shivering even though she felt warm. Her mind seemed numb. Like she was out of her body somehow. As if she were on a movie set. Like none of this was real. Or worse, that it was real but she wasn't.

She put her finger on the night table. Just to be sure. Part of her felt like collapsing to the ground in sheer exhaustion. The other part felt like she had been pumped full of two pots of coffee. Shaking. Jittery. Vigilant for no apparent reason.

You have to stay awake. Stay awake. Who's in the bathroom? Who has a key to this room? Who else can get in? Watch the door.

Would you relax? My goodness! You're so stressed out.
You have to watch every movement. The next guy. He might—
Time for some air.

She forced open the balcony door after it stuck on her first try. She took in the chill of the morning air and felt the cool breeze against her skin, standing out there in a skimpy spaghetti strap shirt and her soccer shorts. The concrete felt cold against her bare feet. Traffic flowed below her, people making their everyday trips to their everyday destinations. Silly people. No idea how to make a real living.

Glancing at Jake lying on the bed, she felt both an urge to crawl in beside him and a desire to stay as far away from that bed as possible. She looked over at the bottle on the ground beside the desk. It was way too early for that. She felt sick even looking at it yet found an unexplainable need for it. Like she would go into an absolute panic fit if she discovered the bottle were empty.

Without realizing it, she grabbed the balcony railing tighter than usual. Her forearm muscles tensed to the point of beginning to shake.

Get a hold of yourself. Just breathe. My goodness!
Take a moment and think. You're out in the cold. Shaking.
"Baby?"

Abby recoiled in shock. It was as if she and her friends were in the basement, and they had just seen a scary part in a horror movie that none of them wanted to see but watched just to prove to themselves they could do it.

"You sure are jumpy this morning," he said. "You're not thinking of going over the edge, are you?" he said with a laugh. "It's cold, baby. It's not good for you."

"I just wanted some fresh air."

"I know. But you should really ask." He stretched out his hand. She thought it was a chivalrous move at first, expecting it be palm up, waiting for her to accept his invitation. Instead, he reached out, palm down, to grab her. He put his hand around her trembling wrist. He pulled her in, closed the door and gave her a hug. Should she collapse or start to shake uncontrollably? She didn't know which to do. Or if she even had a choice.

"I know what's best, baby. You gotta trust me."

"I do, Jake. I trust you. I'm just feeling so off."

"I can fix that."

He put two pills in her hand and gave her the bottle of wine.

"What are these?"

He looked at her with his calm, easy stare. "They'll help you rest."

"Promise?"

He nodded. She threw the pills into her mouth. Took a slug of the wine bottle. A few moments later she felt lightheaded. Her vision became blurry. Oh, that felt good. The itching in her calves left. The jittery caffeine feeling disappeared. The chains dropped off. Gravity didn't seem to apply to her anymore. Was she on the moon? She felt her body falling forwards; then she collapsed into bed. Finally, relaxation.

The scene was not so peaceful back in Markham. Talia sat at the kitchen table, her face an ashen grey, her eyes staring out at nothing in particular. She and her husband had driven to Montreal. Showed Abby's picture in hotels. Went to the airport. Bus station. Came up empty. Travelled back to Toronto. Drove through various suburbs. Posted images on social media. Phoned and phoned and phoned.

She tried to push that 24-hour rule out of her mind. Most kids— the ones that get found—get found quickly. Within that one-day window. Misunderstandings. Kids who got confused and went to a friend's overnight. Then sense kicks in, and they are found. But for Abby, it had been way longer than a day. And the fear and pain over what might be happening to her were putting Talia's mind in such a state of grief that it held her captive—as if those chains holding Abby had now been placed on Talia as well.

She put her elbows on the table and buried her face in her hands, trying to prop up her heavy head. Years earlier, Talia often thought about the dangers of bringing a newborn child into this godforsaken world. All the evil. All the disgusting horror of what happens when a garden turns into a desert. But optimism won out. And they brought her in. Raised her. Watched her play soccer. Lots and lots of soccer. She sure could run. Soccer was followed by a trip to the ice cream store. She usually got a double scoop, with half of it ending up on the ground. No matter, there was always time for a second cone. They read her stories at night.

Then came the teenage years. And they all started drifting. Ironically, she and her husband got the furthest away. How that happened was anybody's guess. So gradual. Like resting on a floating mattress near the shore and then you realize the current has dragged you way out. He got busy with work. Didn't have any more time for Abby's games. Little time for family movie nights. He rolled the dice, hoping that one big vacation per year could mend months of absenteeism. He was great when he was around, though.

Exhaustion rolled into her like morning fog. It overcame her. And yet, she felt the need to stay awake for her daughter. Like a soldier standing guard. Maybe it would help. Maybe it would make a difference.

She needed whatever hope she could find.

She called Joy. Hearing the sound of her voice helped. Helped to speak with someone who knew about the pain. Joy explained how the RCMP and local police were doing everything they could to find Abby. But it wasn't enough to bring Abby back.

Evil just had too many places to hide.

Abby felt herself flying through the air. Wind raced past her, and the sun beat on her face. It should have been euphoria. The feeling of freedom. But something felt out of place. Something she couldn't immediately identify. A chill ran down her body. She wasn't flying after all. She was falling. She looked down. The water raced towards her. Her body began to shake.

"Abby." She opened her eyes.

Jake shook her shoulders. "Time to get up."

She felt rested. Looked at the clock. Five o'clock.

"First guy's going to be here in a few hours. Grab a shower. Get dressed. Let's go shopping."

"Okay."

She got out of bed. Her feet felt better. She looked on the table, then reached down and searched through her jeans.

"Where's my phone?"

"Time for a shower, Abby."

"I want to listen to music. Where is it?"

He smiled. It seemed like a regular smile. Like when they first met.

So why did it feel so different?

"You'll take forever if you listen to music. Come on, baby, get ready."

She grinned. "You want to join me?"

He paused. The hesitation hurt. "Later, babe."

"Can you say 'Abby'?"

"Abby," he said with a laugh. "Get going."

Abby came out of the bathroom dressed in ripped jeans, a black T-shirt and a grey hoodie. She smelled a hamburger and fries and saw a meal waiting for her under a silver lid. She sat down at the desk. As starved as she was, she suddenly lost her appetite. Her heart began to pound.

"Come on, Abby. Eat."

I know I'm supposed to eat, you idiot. Something's wrong.

Woah. Hang on. Idiot? Since when do you get off calling him—

You're right. You're right. I just … I'm not feeling myself. Something—

"I'm stressing out."

"The food will help," he said. He poured her a glass of water from the bathroom and put it beside her. She didn't drink it.

"Abby, you need to eat."

He's right. You haven't eaten all day.

I just don't want to.

Do what he tells you. Use your head. You need to eat. He's just looking out for you.

She bit into the burger. Squeezed a pack of ketchup onto it and forced herself to keep going.

"Taste good?" he asked. She nodded mechanically. Anything tastes good when you're famished. When she finished, she reached for the water and downed it one shot. Jake smiled. "Feel better?"

"No."

"What's wrong, Abracadabra?"

What if the first guy tonight has a knife? What if one gets rough? What if it gets even weirder than last night? I'm tired of hurting all the time.

Jake read her expression. "Put this under your tongue," he said.

"What is it?"

"Trust me."

"What is it?

"Just take it. Open your mouth."

"Jake, what—"

"Open up."

She did. She felt a small piece of paper under her tongue. Nothing happened. She waited. Jake tossed her phone to her. She turned on music. Sat against the chair. She didn't go the bed. She'd be there enough tonight.

A while later she saw Jake stand up and drink a shot of rum. His figure was blurred, like the way the Flash superhero runs with that image of him trailing behind. She blinked.

"You okay?" Jake asked.

Abby saw a rainbow forming over his head. Felt herself in an altered state. Like she was still there and not there at the same time.

"I'm great. And you look really funny."

"I do, eh? What can I say? I'm in love with a beautiful girl."

"Yeah, Jakey. We're in love, right?"

He kissed her. "I never loved anyone the way I love you."

"I love what we're doing. We're making a life for ourselves. A great life."

"Amazing."

She smiled. "We're going to go places we never ever dreamed of."

"Hey, I got an idea. We're off to an amazing start," he said. He opened a backpack. Pulled out a whack of money. So much he needed two hands to carry it.

"You robbed a bank. You're really bad. You're going to jail. My Jakey is going to jail."

"I didn't rob a bank."

She leaned forward. Pouted out her lips. "Yes … you … did."

"Guess where all this dough came from? From you, baby."

"No. Really?"

"Look how much you made."

"We're going to be rich in no time."

"I have this crazy idea."

Abby threw her head back and let out a hysterical yelp. Jake rushed over to put his hand over her.

"Abby! Sshhhhh. I have this crazy idea. We should get out of Montreal."

She whispered and mouthed the words so big she stretched her lips to the limit. "Why? We are doing so *bon dans la ville* ... *le ville* ... which is it? Ville de Montreal, *mon ami*, Jake."

Jake's phone beeped. He glanced at it.

"He'll be here in a couple of minutes. Ready, baby?"

"Bring 'em on in, Jakey. I want them all in here now. Big money."

"No, no. One at a time."

"Ahhh. No fun."

"Here's what's fun. I say we get out of Montreal. We go out to Halifax. Then we make a trip across Canada. What do you say?"

Abby placed both hands on either side of her face. "You mean it, Jake?" She giggled. "That would be so romantic."

Jake texted the guy back. He sat Abby down on the bed. Then he went to the door.

"You still got rainbows, Jakey." She scrunched her nose at him.

"What do you say? Coast to coast across this amazing country."

"You got it, Jake."

"I love you, baby," he said. "This is going to be a trip of a lifetime."

chapter twenty

In spite of the sheer volume of people on Parliament Hill, a person can find themselves strangely alone. Not in terms of having others around them. But in terms of ideals. Of missions.

Of purpose.

Joy sat at her desk, trying hard to remind herself of the support that had been coming in for her bill. MPs. Signatures from constituents. Positive media stories. But in the face of such evil, even encouragement seemed nothing more than the morning frost that burns off with the heat of the day. Fellow Winnipegger Steve Bell's music played quietly in the background. How many times had she heard his songs? The familiar melodies were comforting, especially after meeting with survivors, while on the Hill, while travelling. She especially appreciated his music at times like this, late in the evening while she and Joel cranked out more notices, worked on more angles and spread the truth as best they knew how.

She stopped typing. Thought. Took off her glasses.

"It doesn't seem to matter what I tell some people, they just ..." She shook her head. "They just don't seem to get it."

She looked at the Wilberforce quote. "You may choose to look the other way but you can never say again that you did not know." In times like these, she took inspiration from his fortitude. His willingness to persevere when the battle seemed like an eternal uphill climb.

Joel sat across from her with his laptop. He glanced over at her. His eyes adjusted. How many hours had he logged on this computer today, and how many since he started with Joy?

"You're concerned we won't be able to convince those with clout in the parties?"

"I know that some MPs are visiting trafficked girls. They're begging me to stop this bill to save their filthy reputations. Other MPs have so much going on that they can't find a way to fit the safety of Canadian girls into their agenda."

"But you have made breakthroughs, Joy."

She had. She knew she had. They had. Together. But was the groundswell enough? Would there be enough momentum, like the wave at playoff games, to carry this bill through?

"How can some people not see this?" Joy asked. "And how can anyone in their right mind possibly be opposed to this?"

She put her glasses back on. Shook her head. Went back to responding to a question a director at a NGO had about how to help restore a rescued victim of human trafficking.

Joel thought about the questions Joy had just asked. Thought back to the conversations Joy had had when people had changed their minds about human trafficking. What had he heard? What had worked? How had someone's opinion been changed?

"The conversation with the justice minister."

"Which time?" Joy said, smiling.

"When they all ganged up on you."

"There've been a few of those," she said with a laugh.

"The time when you left that meeting, you said you saw a change in him."

Joy hit send. Joel had a point. The justice minister did have a change in heart. He asked questions about how girls were trafficked. The methods by which they were deceived. And he wasn't placating. Something had impacted him.

"You're right," Joy said, sensing the connection people have when they are on the verge of discovering a better path forward.

"What changed his mind?" Joel asked.

Joy thought back to the meeting. It got heated in there. He blasted her. She blasted him back. It got so loud. Each firing arguments at the other. Then the mood changed. What had she said?

"When I told him about a girl ..." She paused. Drew strength for what she would say next. "When I told him about the girl who had been strangled."

How would she ever get those images out of her mind? They don't leave. They never go. And maybe they aren't supposed to.

"What if the reason they aren't on board is because they don't understand?"

Joy filtered her thoughts through all the mess of arguments she had been through. "Once he heard about the girl's story, he changed his mind."

"In that moment, in his mind, this stopped being a theoretical debate. He now had to face the fact that a real Canadian girl died. So," Joel said, "how do we spread that understanding to others?"

Joy narrowed her eyes. She let herself feel encouragement from the lyrics of Bell's "Burning Ember" playing in the background.

Somehow I knew
I would be new in your glowing

Judge for yourself if a fire isn't safe
When cities fall before her face
Yet a flower can endure the course of a storm
When bowing to the tempest's rage

"I have an idea," she said.

The view of an open field from the living room in the safe house north of Toronto stretched out as far as Joy could see. She thought it would be the exact view a girl recovering from trafficking would love to see, giving her a sense of wide open space. No restrictions. No four-walled hotel room prison sentence. It took some girls months to even look out the window and take in the beauty—to come out of their unbearable nightmare and see something other than the memories of where they had been.

She spoke with Alexandra, the woman who looked after the home and lived there as part of her commitment to seeing girls get back on the straight and narrow. Alexandra survived being trafficked in her teens and now dedicated her time to loving and mentoring other survivors.

Joy heard steps behind her. She turned. The girl standing there had cut her red hair. Her green eyes were filled with uncertainty. She had been delivered from the immediate terror of being trafficked, and now came the hard work of figuring out exactly who she was and what she would do with the rest of her life.

"Hi, Mrs. Smith," she said.

"Hi, Samantha." Joy gave her a hug. Alexandra excused herself. Samantha sat down on the red couch, looking like she felt at home. Joy sat down in an easy chair. "You look wonderful."

"You think so?"

"I love your hair especially."

Samantha had come so far since that day in the Ottawa Hospital emergency department where the two of them first met. She glanced out the window. "Thank you for always taking my calls."

"I love hearing from you, Samantha."

"I always feel guilty calling," she said, not breaking her gaze out the window. "You're so busy and all."

There it was. That ongoing feeling of guilt. Shame. Not being worth someone else's time.

"Samantha, it means a lot to me that you call me."

"I'll bet. All the work you have to do, and then you have to put up with me." She swore about herself. How useless she was.

"I know you don't feel it, but I see a lot of change in you."

Samantha stood. It didn't surprise Joy. "This is a mistake," Samantha said. "I shouldn't be wasting your time. See ya." She began to walk out of the room.

"Suit yourself. But I'm going to sit right here in my chair for the next hour either way. And as much as I love the view, I'd rather spend the time with you. If you want."

Joy turned to meet her eyes. Those soft green windows that so desperately wanted to be loved.

Samantha considered, then sat back down. "Thanks," she whispered, beginning to cry. Joy saw that as a good sign. The ability, and willingness, to show emotion was a key sign of healing. Most girls went through their fair share of cursing and anger. And Alexandra had to patiently endure so much of it while helping girls like Samantha get to the next stage. "You really believe it? You see change in me?"

"Of course. You think I'm going to drive all the way out here and lie to you?"

Samantha cracked a smile. And that little sliver of laughter gave Joy a glimpse into a fun, unique personality.

"Are you doing well here, Samantha?"

She nodded. "I have an edge over the other girls, though," she said.

"How so?"

"My trafficker is dead. I don't have to worry about him coming after me. For the other girls here, even though this place is secret, they still have the idea their trafficker is going to come around. With a knife. Gun. Extension cord. You know."

"We're pushing as hard as we can to get this law in place."

Samantha went back to looking out the window, staying still as if her memories had frozen her in place. "You believed me, Mrs. Smith," she finally said. She turned to look at her. Not as a politician. Not as a lawmaker. But as a mother. "If there's anything I can ever do for you, you just let me know."

Another good sign. Being willing to help someone else.

"Funny you should ask."

Samantha studied Joy's eyes, wondering if Joy actually considered her someone who could provide help.

"We're having trouble convincing some people about the bill."

"To put these creeps behind bars?" Samantha asked, adding a slew of expletives.

"This is a hard favour for me to ask," Joy said. "And I want you to know there's no pressure, okay?"

"What is it?" Samantha asked with the directness people have when they have been through tragedy and want to get to the point.

"I think it would help if a few survivors of human trafficking came to Ottawa. Shared their stories about what really happened."

"In front of a group of people?"

"Key decision makers."

Samantha swore and exhaled. "You were right about it being a hard favour to ask."

"You think about it as long as you want."

Back to the window. To the view. To the freedom to escape.

"You think they'll listen?"

"I think they'll have to."

"I don't know, Mrs. Smith. I don't even have my life back together. I'm in no shape to be telling other people what happened to me."

"I understand completely."

"And yet you drove out here convinced I was ready. Right?"

"That's right. But it's your life. You're going to be the one who would have her name recorded. You're the one who'll have to talk in front of all those people."

"Wouldn't it be something if I recognized one of the guys in the room?" she asked, shaking her head. Joy believed that was entirely possible. "You think my testimony will help?"

"I do."

"It would be so humiliating."

"Or courageous."

"What?"

"One day I'm going to convince you that you're a hero."

Samantha let those words wash over her. Slowly but surely, those truths were replacing the lies that were pushed into her all those years.

"I want to help you, Mrs. Smith. I do. But to go in front of all those people … I'm scared of what they might think of me. That they won't believe my story. That they won't be like you."

"I understand, Samantha. There are a lot of good people on the Hill. But even some of the good ones need convincing too."

Clouds cleared away from the sun, letting a burst of light into the home, illuminating Samantha's red hair.

"If they're so good," Samantha asked, "why do they need to be convinced of the obvious?"

chapter twenty-one

Abby collapsed into bed at 3 a.m., then woke up every hour until finally giving up on sleep at 7. She sat up and stared out the window. Her body screamed at her for rest. She wanted to obey. Wanted to give her body what it wanted. What it needed. But her mind would not shut off. If she had felt a massive caffeine jolt before, she was now experiencing an unrelenting panic.

Keep your eyes open! Get up! Get up! You can't afford to be asleep. You have no idea who's going to walk through that door.

Just shut up and let me sleep. I'm done for the night.

But the moment she put her head back down again, her mind began to scream at her to keep vigilant. To keep watch. To be aware.

If you stay awake you at least have a fighting chance if one of those creeps tries something really sick. If you're asleep, you've lost the edge. You can't protect yourself. And he can just come in and do whatever he wants.

I'm already dragging myself around. Unless I'm drugged up, I can't even function. I feel like a robot. I need to sleep. Please just let me go to sleep.

But her mind and body could not come to an agreement, and in the end she found herself looking out at Montreal, feeling a constant state of exhaustion.

Jake got up. They took separate showers and headed down to the Mustang at nine. He pulled the top over. Cold weather ahead.

Abby stared out the window as they took the Trans-Canada Highway out of Montreal. She felt so different leaving than she had arriving.

Shouldn't that tell you something?

It doesn't mean anything.

You smiled when you guys drove into Montreal. Are you happy now?

I just need a good breakfast and a decent sleep.

And then, what, you're going to live in a nice castle with servants and get pulled around in a horse-drawn carriage?

This is real life. It's tough. I have to fight for love. I have to believe in it. I have to believe—

In him? Is that what you were going to say next?

I just have to figure out how to handle the evenings better.

Better? What you're doing is not normal. How can you be expected to handle it better?

I have the perfect plan.

Really? You can escape.

I don't want to leave Jake.

And you won't have to. It's quite easy. We just make two of you.

What? How?

You as Abby the wonderful girl. And then you as the girl with the guys you see at night.

How do I do that?

You've already started. Pound yourself full of drugs. That way the real you can stay you, and you can create a second person. So if something goes wrong, you can assign it to the other Abby. And if something is good, like Jake and the money, you assign that to you.

Can that really work?

She didn't want to have this conversation. She felt the drug of sleep coming upon her and wished there was a way to overdose on that one. She watched the scenery as urban life give way to rural. She leaned her head against her seat and felt herself begin to drift off. The leather smell was gone.

Or maybe she had gotten used to it.

As if on cue, she woke up an hour later. The engine still humming. The Quebec rural farmland countryside still going by. And Abby still feeling more exhausted waking up than when she went to sleep.

"Time for something to eat," he said as more of a statement than a question.

She nodded.

"You're looking a little tired."

"Sorry. Yeah, a little."

A little? You're going to collapse.

Stopping at a drive-through in Drummondville, they picked up breakfast consisting of wraps, orange juice and coffee, not that she needed any more stimulation. They got back on the Trans-Canada. He turned on music. Justin Bieber blared out the speakers singing "One Less Lonely Girl."

"Can I have my phone?" she asked.

"You don't need your phone, baby. Okay?"

She shrugged her shoulders. "Okay."

An hour and a half later they stopped for gas near the Quebec City turnoff. She looked up at the green sign. She had learned about Quebec in history class. Saw pictures of the horse-drawn carriages. Thought they would be so romantic. What had her French teacher called them again? *Calèche.*

Go ahead. Ask him. The city is right there. The rides take an hour or two. You know how many thousands of dollars you've made. See if he'll take you.

"Want to go to Quebec City?" It took all her courage to ask. "They have those horse-drawn carriages."

Jake looked at his phone. "Sounds like a plan."

See.

He drove them through the city and parked the car. Taking his hand, she walked with him on the sidewalk. They crossed over a cobblestone street. She smelled a pizzeria on the corner preparing for the lunch rush. The architecture of the buildings changed from modern to historic. The change was so apparent that Abby turned around to make sure they hadn't passed through a fantastical gate taking them into a new world. She heard the neighing of a horse. Turning a corner, they saw a beautiful black carriage with a rider and horse. She smiled. They stepped into the *calèche.* Experienced Old Quebec. The citadel. The Château Frontenac. She leaned back in his arms.

Who says I can't be drawn around in a horse and carriage?

Dave looked out at the Toronto skyline. The late afternoon sun began to show a hint of an orange glow, differentiating it from the bright yellow of the day and signalling that the end of daylight was near. He had finished all his meetings. He was blessed with good clients and enjoyed their conversations. His secretary said good night. He heard the clicking of her pumps against the tile floor on the way out. Another couple of hours and he would be fighting much lighter traffic.

You know that website had girls in Toronto, too.

Not interested.

Sure you are. You're just worried you might get caught.

I'm married.

You were married when you saw the blonde in Montreal. Come on. You can get a girl on the way home from work.

Dave ignored the voice. Tried to focus on his work. His mind drifted back and forth between reviewing his clients' portfolios and wondering what the girls in Toronto looked like. An hour's work stretched into three because his thoughts kept wandering.

One little look. Just for curiosity's sake.

Hope would kill me.

She would. If she found out.

Even if she never figured it out, I would still know it's a lie. I couldn't live with myself.

Easy. The girls you see are just a fling. Something for fun. So when you leave, you shut that part of your world out. That way you can be the real you with Hope and at work. And you can be another guy with the girls.

Seems complicated.

Or brilliant. Just saying.

I don't think so.

One look.

No.

One look. One look. One look.

Fine. Fine. If it will get you to shut up.

Dave got on the site. Just one look to drown out the voices in his head. He glanced at the girls.

Lots to choose from. Just don't pick anyone too close to home. Might be a connection.

One caught his eye.

What are you doing? Stop this.

Something pulled him out of his chair. He grabbed his suit jacket. Locked up. Took the elevator down to the parking garage. He could have gone straight home to his wife and son, but they didn't expect him back for at least two hours. A haze came over him. Like he was still all there but had entered another reality.

He pulled out his phone. Sent a message.

If the reception is poor down here and the message doesn't go out, I'll go home.

But he got a response. It was like the guy on the other end had been just sitting there waiting for him. Fisherman and fish. Dave didn't want to think about who was who.

He received the address. Drove out of the garage. Decided on a route. There would be a ton of traffic on the way there. No matter.

It would be worth it.

———

Jake booked them into a hotel. Abby hinted at the Frontenac. But he picked one outside Old Quebec. She got ready at eight. Took her first hit of acid just before her first john. Worked through until three. Woke up every hour and tried to go back to sleep. By seven the next morning she was even more of a basket case than the day before.

They were in a new city. But it was same old, same old.

They got into the Mustang. Next destination: Halifax.

After following the Trans-Canada along the east side of the St. Lawrence up to Rivière-du-Loup, they turned southeast to Edmunston near the U.S. border near Maine. After passing through Fredericton and Moncton, they headed down to Nova Scotia.

"Want to go to Cavendish?" Abby asked. "Anne of Green Gables."

She'd read the book three times.

"I have a surprise for you in Halifax."

They left the Trans-Canada at Truro and drove down to Halifax. He checked them into a decent hotel. Nothing to write home about. Not that she would.

He walked them down to the waterfront. They found a restaurant with a rustic wood exterior and red-and-white checkered tablecloths. He ordered them each a beer. When they arrived, Abby surprised even herself when she drank half her bottle in one go. Wine, yes, but beer? She usually sipped at it, like when they were at Canada's Wonderland, letting the coolness wash over her. But now it didn't refresh her like she remembered.

"Want to go touch the ocean?" she asked.

Jake shook his head. Abby stood up. She glanced back at Jake, looking for permission. There was an uncomfortable pause. He nodded.

She drank the rest of her beer. Put the bottle down and walked out.

Abby walked along the wooden planks. She imagined what it might have been like for immigrants to land here on the large ships. Wondered if perhaps an ancestor of hers had walked exactly the same path.

She took a ladder down a few rungs to the water level. Reaching down, she put her finger in the water. Brought it to her tongue. Tasted the salt. It was stronger than she expected. A bitter aftertaste. She was sure she was imagining it, but her stomach felt upset. Must be the beer. Salt doesn't make you sick like that. She climbed back up and stood on the wood boards of the Harbourwalk.

Something felt off. She glanced out at the water. She wanted to take a picture, but Jake had her phone. Still. She turned around.

Saw Jake standing there. Watching her.

Her pulse quickened. That was odd. Why was she feeling scared?

"Hey, Aberama. Food's here! You're going to love it!"

They returned to the restaurant and sat down to a lobster supper. Even though she had ordered lobster many times before, she followed Jake's lead on how to eat one. She grabbed hold of her lobster. Took the body in one hand and the tail in the other. She twisted them in opposite directions, making a cracking and crunching sound. She broke the tail off and rolled it on its side. Pushing down on it with both hands, she heard the shell crack. She inserted her thumb into the flipper end of the tail and pushed the meat out the other. She dipped it in butter sauce and ate it, getting rid of the salty aftertaste from the ocean.

Next, she twisted off a claw at the joint, making another series of cracking sounds, and finished eating. Then they each had a couple more beers.

She looked down at the checkered cloth. It reminded her of a checkerboard. The setting sun caught her eye and served notice that it would be time soon. Time for husbands, single men, older, younger, all shapes, all sizes—and an increasing number of guys with strange, even scary, ideas of what they thought was fun—to show up at her door.

She glanced down at the mess of broken red pieces on her plate. A few minutes before they had been a complete creature. Now it was smashed to smithereens.

"I'm not sure this is such a good idea," she said.

"Our plan is working, Abby."

"Is it?"

"You'd better believe it. You want to see the money?"

"Not really."

"I'm going to find us an apartment. We're nearly there. Only a little bit more. Can you do that, Abby?"

She touched the red shell of the lobster. A hit of LSD would go good right about now. Get some rainbow around that lobster. Maybe try something stronger. She was going to need it tonight.

And she figured she would need it every night moving forward.

You don't want this, and you know it.

He loves me. Just grin and bear it. Look how far I've come. I don't want to waste all the work I've already done, do I?

She nodded her head. "Okay," she said, standing up.

She could take one for the team.

But for how much longer?

chapter twenty-two

The water felt cool against her hands. Abby splashed it against her face. She didn't have the guts to look in the mirror. She felt horrible, and there was no point in having her reflection reinforce that. It had been a light night. Relatively speaking. But it felt like much heavier.

Five guys total. Three of them were university students who came to visit her for some fun. Two were experienced, and they dragged in their buddy as a novice. Big joke, right? Funny. Ha ha. Spend time with a young girl who's making money to pay for college. Maybe we'll see her in class next semester and she can thank us for helping her afford post-secondary education.

Jake let them in one at a time. The novice got rough and left her with a bleeding lip. The guys left before Jake found out about it. It made Abby curious about what he would have done had he caught the guy.

The fourth guy was a judge. The fifth was a grandfather who told her he had grandkids her age.

This isn't working.

Not working? Have you seen how much money has come in?

I've seen some of it, but I don't have a dime of it for myself.

Jake's looking after it. You guys are going to have a big house and—

Blah. Blah. Blah. No house is worth this.

It's a way to make money, and then you put all this behind you and go live your dream.

Provided I live that long.

Oh, give me a break. It's not like this is a death sentence.

Abby dried off her face and lay down on the living room floor. Her stomach ached. She touched her lip. The outside felt all right. The inside had been cut against her teeth.

Take some time off. Go home. Re-evaluate. He'll understand. Tell him you're homesick. Or tell him you want to see Anne of Green Gables in Cavendish on your own. Tell him you want a couple of days to clear your head. Just you by yourself.

How long could she handle doing this? A month? A couple of months? Maybe more? Maybe she was on a learning curve, and once she got over it, everything would get easier. Abby thought through the mental math. Cost for a house, a car, and enough money in the bank. Thought about how much they—she—brought in each night. She rechecked her math. How long to achieve their dream? She did the numbers a third time. Yup.

Five years.

Not so bad if you're doing a job you love. Even one you don't love. Not so good if at this early stage you have serious doubts about being able to stick it out.

Jake came in with a fast-food breakfast. He put it on the tiny kitchen table. The small apartment featured a living area furnished with one chair, a bedroom with only a bed, a bathroom and a kitchen without a dishwasher. It paled in comparison to that gorgeous Montreal hotel.

He sat down in a fold-up chair and pointed to the other one. She sat, and he put a breakfast burrito in front of her. The curtains were still drawn. She preferred it that way. The sunlight gave her a splitting headache. She dropped her forehead onto her arms resting on the table. She didn't know what caused her to be more afraid. Thinking about last night or what she was about to say. No point in sugar-coating it. Just come out and say it.

"I need to take a break."

She didn't need to look up. She heard him stop eating.

"Abby, we've talked about this. I love you, baby. You love me. Let's go down to the water. Spend the day there."

"I'm reeling. I'm spinning. If I don't have drugs, I can't get through the night. If I don't down a bottle at the end, I can't get to sleep. And even then I keep waking up. I'm a zombie. I love you, Jake. I just need—"

"There's no stopping."

The room went silent. She felt the sting of tears forming behind her eyes and was powerless to hold them back. The air felt thinner. Her lungs laboured to take in oxygen. She felt delirious. Panicked. Like she was under water and couldn't get to the surface.

"I have to get out."

Abby stood and attempted to head for the door. But in her disorientation she went the wrong way and banged into the kitchen counter.

"Abby, sit down." Jake grabbed her by the shoulders and pulled her back.

Tears streamed down her face. Her knees gave out, and she grabbed on to Jake to keep from falling. "Jake, please. Please! I need help. I need to go." She began to sob uncontrollably. A combination of fear, exhaustion and confusion.

"Get a hold of yourself, Abby."

She sat down. Sucked in air in short, erratic gasps. Swallowed. Waited for herself to calm down.

"I have to get out for a while."

She stood from her chair again and walked to the door, getting the direction right this time. It caught Jake by surprise. He got up and pulled her back by her shoulder, turning her towards him. She pushed him away. He clenched his right fist, swung at her and punched her across the cheek.

Abby felt her head snap backwards. It came with such force that her feet left the ground. She flew back and crashed against the wall.

She rolled over onto her side. Covered her head with her hands. Expecting another blow. Her arms began to twitch, like she was a malfunctioning robot. The violent jerking motions made their way into her body and her legs so that she was a complete nervous wreck.

I'm dying. I'm dying. I'm dying.

"Abby, get up."

Dear God, don't let him hit me with a chair. Don't let him choke me.

She tried to breathe but found her throat clogged. She coughed. She looked at her hands. At her shirt. They were covered in blood. It reminded her of when she was playing soccer and collided with that opponent. It had sent her to the ground and gave her a bloody nose. That hurt terribly.

But it was nothing like this.

She coughed again, trying to clear her throat from all the blood coming down from her nose. She lifted her head and tried to take in air through her mouth. Everything throbbed. Her brain screamed for more oxygen. She sucked in air as best she could, hoping for that moment when her body would tell her that, in spite of the trauma, the worst of it was over and she was going into repair mode.

She felt a tissue drop on her. Jake bent down. Abby cowered in fear.

"I beg you, don't touch me, Jake. I'm sorry. I'm sorry. Please."

"Hold this under your nose."

She did as she was told. She tried to keep her eyes open, wanting to be ready in case the next blow came. But her eyes had teared up so much that she couldn't see properly.

"Abby, I just want what's best for us. Okay?"

She blinked. Eventually the water cleared. She half sat, half lay down on the ground. Got her breath back. Managed to focus on Jake's eyes. What happened to them?

"You are not going anywhere, do you understand me?" he said. "You are staying right here. In this apartment. No phone. You got that? If you try to go to the police, you are going to get it ten times worse. Don't make me do that. You do whatever I tell you to do. Got that?"

Just let me lie here. Just let me be.

"Abby, I need you to respond. Nod your head that you agree. If not, I have to find ways to make you understand, right? You agreed to this. So you're going to stay here. No cops. No leaving."

Abby forced her head to nod.

"Very good." Jake stood. He opened the door a crack. Checked that no one was in the hall. Went out. Locked the door.

She sat up and placed both hands on the floor. But it did nothing to help her dizzy feeling. She felt like she wasn't sitting on the ground anymore but on a ship. She lay back down on her side. That seemed to help. Short, quick breaths. A song by Nickelback kept spinning in her mind.

I was waiting on a different story …
These five words in my head
Scream "Are we having fun yet?"

She opened the curtains at various time during the day. Not because she wanted the sunlight to further aggravate her headache but because she wanted to have a sense of the time. The microwave didn't have a clock. Neither did the stove. The sun had gone down. It was way past eight by now.

So where were all the johns?

She had cleaned her face. He had caught her on the cheek and the nose. Both showed bruising. It hurt to touch them.

A key slid into the front door lock. She felt her pulse quicken. The door opened. She looked up from the kitchen table. She had wrapped ice in a tea towel to press against the bruising. She took it down.

There was no food in Jake's hands.

He didn't sit. Didn't say hello. Didn't ask how she was. He just seemed so matter of fact about the whole thing. Looked just like the guy she had met at that restaurant on their first date. Same expression.

"Abby, I think you need to take a break."

Thank God in heaven.

"If you do what I say, everything will be fine. We just need to stick with the plan."

"Can I have something to eat?" she asked.

Jake gave her LSD. She turned her head to the side, but he forced it into her mouth. In a few minutes she began to feel the effects. She felt quiet. Like she was shrinking.

"Time to get some rest, baby."

Abby felt herself drifting off into a different world. "Thanks, Jakey."

"We have a future together."

"I know. We're going to make it."

Jake left the apartment. Abby tried to get some rest, but sleep was elusive. The more she thought about it, the worse it became.

He's no good. Certainly now you can see that?

He has some rough edges.

Some? Can you name me one good thing about him?

He's with me.

His presence scares you.

I can change him. I know what we had. We're just figuring things out.

He's using you.

We're in this together. He loves me. Besides, it's my fault. I shouldn't have threatened to leave him like that. It's going to be better. You'll see.

Jake didn't bring her any food the next day. But he did bring her drugs. Some wine, too, but no hard stuff. She seemed not to take to it too well. He kept her high the entire day. She passed out in the evening. Same thing the day after and the day after that. She stayed alone in that room. Fine when she was high. But terrified and in pain when the drugs wore off and she was faced with that terrible place called reality.

He came back for her on the fifth morning. When she heard the lock turning in the door, she hurried to him, a bewildered, desperate look in her glazed-over eyes.

"Jake, what have you got for me?"

"No breakfast—"

"You know what I mean. Come on. Please, Jake."

Jake reached inside his pocket. Closed the door. Gave her a pill and put it under her tongue. He opened a bottle of wine for her. She drank it straight. The drug started kicking in.

"Thanks, Jakey." Her mood switched. She became docile and pliable.

"You're special, Abby."

"You think so?"

"You're an amazing girl."

"Okay."

"We're a team. And teammates stick together. Got it?"

"Sure thing."

"And what I say goes."

"For sure. You can trust me, Jake."

"Tonight we're starting up again."

"You can count on me, Jake."

Jake left. Abby lay down on the ground. Looked up at the ceiling, which morphed into a kaleidoscope of colours.

When the effects wore off, she got up and splashed cool water on her face. How many days had she gone without food? And where was Jake? Where were the drugs?!

Nice guy you found.

I know how to make this work. I'm going to do what Jake wants, and he'll love me in return. You may not like that. But I do. I don't care about the guys I have to see. They're losers. They're pathetic wannabes who are handing over their money so—

So Jake can take it and use it for himself.

Stop lying! I don't want to hear from you again. I have someone who loves me. And I'm not turning that down.

Jake opened the door. New clothes for Abby. Jeans. Shirt. And a bag of takeout. She chewed into her hamburger, her entire being focused on each bite. When she was finished, she snorted a line of cocaine.

There we go. Back to normal.

"Ready?" he asked.

"I'm sorry about how I acted, Jake," she said.

"That's all in the past. We're moving forward, right?"

She nodded, feeling the tiredness that came with her body processing food again. But, at the very least, she had her energy restored.

She was going to need it.

chapter twenty-three

Joy arrived early in the House of Commons. Sat down in her seat. Glanced around the chamber. Thought of the many important decisions that had been made here throughout the years. Thought of the decision that would be made on her bill.

Today would begin the second reading. She would speak. The bill would be debated by various members from each party. Each member would be allowed to speak only once, except for Joy, who would open and also respond to questions. Then at a second hour of debate at a later date, MPs would debate again, Joy would close the debate and the MPs would vote. If it passed it would get referred to committee and then go to the third reading.

Recently, she had spent the day in an Ottawa courtroom listening to a case of a trafficked girl whose trafficker got off with a light sentence. She used that story in her meetings with MPs. She also garnered public support, working evenings and weekends with her staff and volunteers to get the word out. She had done everything she could. But you can practise all you want. In the end, you have to put that skate on the ice and face whatever opposition may come.

And hope you're prepared enough to win.

Other members entered. So did the Speaker of the House. As was the custom before every sitting, the Speaker of the House read out a prayer. And as was the custom, all those in attendance rose to their feet.

"Almighty God, we give thanks for the great blessings which have been bestowed on Canada and its citizens, including the gifts of freedom, opportunity, and peace that we enjoy. We pray for our sovereign, Queen Elizabeth, and the governor general. Guide us in our deliberations as members of Parliament, and strengthen us in our awareness of our duties and responsibilities as members. Grant us wisdom, knowledge, and understanding to preserve the blessings of this country for the benefit of all and to make good laws and wise decisions. Amen."

The prayer was followed by a customary moment of silence. Joy prayed silently.

Dear God, today is a big day for this bill. It's been a long journey and there's still a long way to go. But you've been with me each step of the way. Thank you for your presence. Please help this bill to go through. Help it to pass this reading. Help the members present to understand its importance. Help me to respond kindly to people. As you are well aware, I'm not so good with controlling my thoughts about people who disagree with me. But help me to be considerate of everyone. I leave the result in your hands. In Jesus' name, amen.

Thoughts of her son Edward filled her mind. She remembered the conversation she had with him all those years ago. He used to come over all the time. Tell stories about his work as a police officer. Then he transferred to the Internet Child Exploitation Unit. He didn't come over so much anymore. He became more distant. Secluded. Finally, he did come over. Joy spoke with him in the kitchen. He looked different. How does a person age so much in such a short amount of time?

They made small talk until Joy came out and asked him, as only a mother can, what was wrong. He became quiet.

"There are so many youth in Canada that are being trafficked," he said. His eyes had looked out as if gazing at events he had seen in the past. "You catch the traffickers, but the majority receive short sentences. They go right back out there and do it all over again." The ravages of facing an evil world had their effect on Edward. "There needs be a law that keeps the traffickers in jail."

As she watched him leave that evening, she wished she could do more to help him. She thought of what he had said. *There needs to be a law that keeps the traffickers in jail.* His words drove her to begin her fight against human trafficking. They continued to echo in her mind.

Right up until today.

The Speaker of the House gave instructions for the doors to be opened. Guests and the public entered. Television coverage began. Joel took his seat up in the gallery. Joy was called on first. She stood.

"Madam Speaker, today I am pleased to speak to my Private Member's Bill C-268, An Act to Amend the Criminal Code. A minimum sentence for offences involving trafficking of persons under the age of 18 years.

"I ask members to take a moment to imagine a 15-year-old Canadian girl, who lives not far from the nation's capital, who sat in court recently telling of the horror she endured from the man who trafficked and sold her for sex for two and a half years. A man who made in excess of $360,000 off this innocent young victim by threatening her, beating her, and forcing her to have sex with strangers.

"As a result, this man was able to buy himself a BMW and an expensive house in Niagara Falls. Even though he was eventually caught and convicted, he spent less time in jail than he did exploiting this young girl and destroying her life. He told her that if she got out of line, he would beat her. He would threaten to kidnap her brother or harm her parents. I would like to read a statement she made.

"'I am constantly looking over my shoulder, afraid that either my trafficker or his friends are going to come after me for putting him in jail. I don't feel safe at home. He knows where I live and what my family looks like and where they live. I have nightmares about him. I have low self-esteem. Feel like I am only good for one thing ... sex. I don't see why someone, a man, would be interested in me and try to get to know me, because I feel unworthy, dirty, tainted, nothing.'

"Traffickers prefer young people like this girl because they are impressionable, easy to control and easy to intimidate."

Joy took a moment to glance around the chamber. *What are they thinking? Are they in favour? Are we moving towards victory or sliding towards defeat?*

"Section 279.01 of the Criminal Code carries a maximum term of imprisonment of 14 years and up to life imprisonment if the victim is kidnapped, subject to aggravated assault or aggravated sexual assault, or killed during the commission of the offence. So some will argue the amendment I am proposing is unnecessary. They will suggest that individuals convicted of trafficking in Canada already face up to 14 years, even life in certain circumstances, and therefore there is no need for mandatory minimums."

Joy and her team had drafted this segment into her opening speech because they knew of members who would oppose the bill for this very reason. Knocking on each and every MP's door was an arduous task. But persistence pays off. If you can't win your enemy over in the research stage, at least you will know their point of dissension. That way you can prepare a counterargument long in advance.

"Let me be clear. This view is naive and ignorant of the reality of human trafficking convictions in Canada. Over the past year Peel Regional Police and Montreal Police Service have rescued the first child victims of sex trafficking in Canada and secured convictions against their traffickers. The man I mentioned earlier was convicted last June of trafficking a 15-year-old girl. He sexually exploited her daily for over two years. For the offence of human trafficking, he received only three years and was credited 13 months for the pretrial time he served.

"This past November in Montreal, a man was convicted of human trafficking. He was sentenced to two years' imprisonment for trafficking a 17-year-old girl and selling her for sex. He served only a single week in prison after being convicted because he was given a two-for-one credit for his one year of pretrial custody.

"In light of the incredulous sentences these men received, I cannot imagine what one would have to do to receive a full 14 years. These are our Canadian children.

"I want to take this opportunity to commend the wonderful police officers in the Peel and Montreal police forces for their dedication in combatting this horrific crime. I can tell members they are shocked at the exceedingly inadequate sentences that have been handed down by sentencing judges in Canada's first set of convictions for human trafficking involving children. Bill C-268 arose directly from consultations with these officers and victims' organizations across Canada who are concerned about the safety of our children. These convictions set an alarming precedent for all future cases involving trafficking of children. With almost a dozen similar cases before Canadian courts today involving the trafficking of minors, it is imperative that Parliament send a clear message that the trafficking of minors will not be tolerated."

Joy read support letters from major stakeholders in the fight against child trafficking, including a note from Canadian Police Association president Charles Momy, which said, "The United Nations has identified human trafficking as a serious concern, and Canada is not an exception. This is a very real crime in this country. We applaud the member for Kildonan-St. Paul for raising this issue in the House of Commons and welcome this bill as a means for Parliament to address this problem in Canada."

Grand Chief Ron Evans of the Manitoba Assembly of Chiefs offered his support as well: "On behalf of First Nation's people, I am pleased to support Bill C268. Both the U.S. and Canadian government reports have shown that Aboriginal women and children are at greater risk of becoming victims of human trafficking than any other group in Canada. Bill C-268 is one step forward for the First Nation's women and children of Canada."

"The trafficking of children is not a Conservative, Liberal, Bloc, or NDP issue," Joy continued. "I have worked diligently to gain support from all parties for this bill. In the past our parties worked together to pass legislation put forward by the honourable member for Mount Royal to bring in Canada's first human trafficking offences. It is vital that all Canadians and the international community witness all members of Canada's Parliament standing unified against this horrific abuse of human rights. We must act to end the trafficking of children here in Canada and abroad. We can, and we will."

Paul Szabo, a Liberal MP from Mississauga South, indicated he would be speaking later to the bill. But for the information of the House, he wanted to first inquire about the wording of the clause Joy was proposing to be added to the Criminal Code. "Could the member indicate who developed the language? Is it modelled on some other jurisdictional language? Is there some assurance that we have it right?"

"It has been a two-year process on this bill," Joy said to the Speaker of the House. In Parliament, members do not address each other directly. Instead they refer to a member by their riding, not by their name, and address questions and answers to the Speaker of the House. "I have been waiting for the opportunity to present this bill here in Parliament. There are precedents with the same wording in the United States and Australia that are very tight. Those two countries have mandatory minimum sentences for child trafficking. They have been used as a model. In addition, Professor Perrin, who is very well versed in human trafficking, is one of the lawyers who has been a part of the process."

Steven Fletcher spoke next. Steven was the first quadriplegic to become a member of Parliament. After graduating with a degree in geological engineering from the University of Manitoba, Steven hit a moose in Northern Manitoba while travelling on work-related business. He was told he would have to remain in an institution the rest of his life. He later joked that he didn't think the doctors ever thought the institution would be Parliament.

"Madam Speaker, I commend the member for Kildonan-St. Paul for bringing forward this bill. It is something she has been very passionate about since before she was elected. I also know the member is the mother of a large number of children and has a unique perspective because one of her children is in the police service. Could the member explain the impact the bill would have not only on the victims but also on their families?"

"Madam Speaker," Joy said. "I am the mother of six wonderful children, and yes, my eldest son is a member of the RCMP. He is my role model. He was in the ICE unit, and I saw his hair turn grey in less than two years because of everything involved in rescuing child victims.

"Mandatory minimums will give hope to the families who have had children who were taken. For example, a girl related to a police officer in Edmonton was taken. The daughter of a teacher was taken. Those families have in their hearts the fact that we, as parliamentarians, need to say very strongly that we will not stand for child trafficking on Canadian soil."

The Speaker recognized Paul Szabo.

"Madam Speaker, I feel very close to the member in terms of how she feels about championing this issue. She knows there will be some detractors from it, but I sense from her speaking that she is ready to defend the bill that she has presented to us through all stages of its legislative process."

You got that right, Joy thought.

"Private members' bills sometimes are successful when they are targeted and focused, and I think this one is. I have seen some bills that try to do a little too much, provide a little too many tentacles out there, where somebody could find one reason why they might not support it. I think this one is clean."

Szabo's comment was aimed at preventing potential dissenters from voting against the bill because of some minor disagreement with one of the items. Totally for or totally against were the only options. In the event dissenters did not like components of the bill, it could be debated in the committee stage, which came after the second reading, provided a majority in the second reading voted in favour.

"As a member of Parliament from the region of Peel, I do know how the Peel Regional Police worked with the Montreal police services on the case that was referred to. There will probably be some detractors to this bill, and they will probably talk about mandatory sentencing. When we look at the clause that is being proposed here, there are so many different elements that might be reflective of this offence, but they are subject to interpretation. However, I am sure we will get a chance at committee to vent these kinds of questions, and I know the member will be well prepared to deal with them."

Szabo hoped his comment could help the bill get pushed down the line to the committee stage. Even if opponents voted in favour of the bill now at second reading, they would still have a chance to vote against the bill in third reading. In other words, don't vote against the bill now. Give it a chance.

"I thank the member for the bill. I will be supporting Bill C-268, and I will be recommending that my colleagues support it."

So far, so good.

Conservative MP Lois Brown stood. Joy and Joel held their breath. What was the government's official position going to be?

"If this bill is referred to committee for study, I hope that the committee will consider the bill by looking as well at how the existing Criminal Code penalties addressing child victims are working."

Joy tried to evaluate the comment, thinking that so much of what a person says is subject to interpretation. She took Lois's comment as positive. But however her words were received, it was clear to Joy that she was being encouraged to show that existing laws were aimed to fight human trafficking.

Next came the Bloc. If Joy's research and attempts to speak with members from this party were any indication, this was going to be a statement in opposition to the bill.

Claude DeBellefeuille addressed the Speaker. "Although we are well aware of the worldwide scourge that is human trafficking, the Bloc Québécois cannot support this bill," she said.

Big surprise there, Claude. Big surprise.

"In 2005, the Bloc Québécois voted in support of Bill C-49. Creating an offence to specifically condemn human trafficking was necessary, and we willingly co-operated to see it passed. Bill C-268, however, we believe is a step in the wrong direction. By automatically imposing a minimum sentence of five years on anyone convicted of the trafficking of persons under 18, the government is not solving anything. Many experts have established that minimum sentences have variable effects on prison populations and no discernible effects on crime rates."

It's in moments like these when protocols are so important. How else do you keep from interrupting your opponent?

That's not the issue, Claude. Let's take the story of the girl in Montreal. Her trafficker goes to jail for one year. I'm proposing a minimum of five years. That means if we had this bill passed already, he would have stayed in jail for four years longer. That would give the survivor that much more time to get her life back together without him breathing down her neck.

"Minimum sentences can encourage plea bargaining by lawyers wanting to have their clients charged with offences that do not have minimum sentences."

That's why you don't plea bargain with human traffickers.

"We oppose mandatory minimums because we believe judges should be free to decide."

Wrong again. No matter how you look at it, a trafficker who tortures a girl getting one lousy year in prison is no solution. And help me understand why a judge would only give one year to a trafficker. Be thankful I'm only asking for five. I wanted it to be life but already toned it down because I would get push back for a Supreme Court appeal if I put a bill forward with the 97 year—yes, 97 year—minimum sentence I was hoping for. I wish the sentence would be life for every human trafficker. I wish it were—

"We are having a hard time understanding the logic behind Bill C-268."

I'm sure you are.

"On the one hand, they say that they want to prevent serious offences involving the trafficking of minors by imposing minimum sentences, but on the other, they are not changing sentences for offenders who use extreme violence in committing the crime."

Okay. Fair point. We'll address that. Thank you for raising this.

"We believe the most effective approach is prevention."

No kidding, Claude. That's obvious. But this is a private member's bill—

"We believe the bill's approach is harmful and ineffective, and we are concerned it will do nothing to improve the safety of citizens."

Claude, can I ask you to speak to a victim of human trafficking? You cite all kinds of experts in your response. But have you spoken to the true experts? Have you spoken to the victims? Have you taken the time to understand their side? … Maybe you have. I don't know. I shouldn't jump to conclusions. Dear God, please help me. I'm just saying, Claude, that when every victim—every single one—supports this bill, can you understand why you seem out of place to me right now?

Peter Stoffer spoke next.

"I appreciated the fact that the member for Kildonan-St. Paul came to my office. We had a heart-to-heart discussion on this issue. I pledged her my personal support for the bill. I would encourage the honourable member to open up the discussion to get at the root of the problem of why children are so susceptible to this. What expertise do the mostly men—but there are women who are traffickers as well—have to exploit these vulnerable children? What is the role of the family and the provinces and everyone else?"

Shelly Glover, Conservative, spoke in favour. "I spent four years investigating sexual and physical abuse of children as a detective in the Winnipeg Police Service Child Abuse Unit. With this in mind, I know first-hand that strong responses are required to address this horrific crime of exploitation and abuse."

The break between sessions gave Joy and her team a chance to respond to the items raised during the first hour of debate. Four and a half weeks later, she rose and addressed the concerns raised by Claude De-Bellefeuille first.

"I want to thank the honourable member for Beauharnois-Salaberry who pointed out in the first hour of debate that there is no minimum sentence for aggravated offences in a paragraph of Bill C-268. This paragraph provides for an individual to be sentenced to life imprisonment, which means that he or she will only be eligible for parole after seven years. However, should this bill go to committee, I have had an amendment drafted that would be within the scope of the bill and that would amend the paragraph to ensure there is no question that this paragraph also provides for a minimum sentence of five years."

She then moved on to respond to other concerns raised by Claude and other members.

"I understand that some members do not feel that mandatory minimums are appropriate in any case. I want to remind members that according to the Supreme Court of Canada, a mandatory minimum sentence constitutes cruel and unusual punishment only if it is *grossly disproportionate*, given the gravity of the offence or the personal circumstances of the offender.

"The long-term physical and psychological impact of human trafficking on its victims, especially children, is devastating. I have continued to call for a national action plan to combat human trafficking that would provide better coordination between the provinces, territories and federal governments to deliver effective victim services. Only two years ago, members of this House unanimously supported Motion 153, which called for a national action plan.

"I strongly believe we need to address the factors that lead to exploitation, such as poverty and marginalization. Our Aboriginal women and children are especially vulnerable due to these factors. These concerns, however, cannot be addressed through a private member's bill. I have put forward Bill C-268 to amend the Criminal Code to address the critical legal aspect of child trafficking and to bring parity between Canada's legislation and that of many other countries."

She had responded to each criticism of her bill. They had worked to craft the responses in such a way that would help those opposed to the bill to understand the error in their thinking. Joy's goal was to say it in a way that wasn't confrontational and offered opponents a respectful way of changing their minds.

"It is my hope that members of all parties will support this important legislation and soundly denounce the trafficking of children."

The two-week break gave Joy more time to garner support. When Parliament reconvened, the Speaker of the House called for a decision. This was the next big hurdle. No matter how much campaigning you do in politics, you never really know what's going to happen when it comes time to vote.

Members stood respectively when their vote was called for whether they were for or against the motion. The yea votes were counted. The nay votes were counted.

The bill passed second reading with a vote of 232 to 47. The entire Bloc Party voted against it. Except for Maria Mourani. The bill would now be referred to the Standing Committee on Justice and Human Rights.

On to the heavy part of the battle.

chapter twenty-four

He should have filled up the car before taking his wife out on a date. He normally did. In fact, Dave couldn't remember a time when he hadn't done so. But the light came on just before reaching home, and if he didn't do something now, he would run out of gas somewhere between here and the restaurant. And as cool as they make those advertisements with people on the side of the road seem, getting stranded would not go over very well. Not for Hope.

Dave filled up the tank and went in to pay. He could have used full service, but with some things in life he was a real miser. So he preferred to save the few cents a litre. Spend his money on other things.

After opening the door to the gas station he walked on the black-and-white tiled floor to the girl working behind the counter. He noticed her innocent brown eyes that to him indicated she had not yet seen major disappointment or needed to learn how to live with disaster. Dave figured she was finishing high school. Maybe first year college. He pulled out his credit card.

Pretty hot, eh, Dave? Why don't you ask her if she's pulling in some extra money on the side? You know. Paying for college. Ask her if she's available online.

Dave shook his head. It was enough to make Innocent Eyes behind the counter notice.

"Sorry?"

"Nothing," Dave said, smiling.

She smiled politely in return and handed him the machine.

You know what? Forget asking her that. Just say you'll be back later tonight and you can find a few minutes with her in the back seat of your car.

Forget it!

Okay, front seat, then. Either way is fine. How much do you think she'll ask for?

Stop it, and get out of my mind.

You could negotiate a discount with her. Or maybe not. Negotiating takes the fun out of it. Reduces the whole thing to just—

"Thanks so much," she said. He grabbed his card. "You want your receipt?"

But he was already headed out the door.

He sat down on the leather seat of his BMW. "Sorry about that," he said to Hope. It was the third time he'd apologized this evening. His eyes lingered on her black dress and hoped that burning an image of her into his mind would quiet the voice in his head.

The restaurant was her favourite. It was still in Mississauga but far enough away from their home to make it special. She loved the hardwood floor, the antique wooden chairs with a red and white pattern. She always took notice of the green antique couch when she entered. It was the same shade of green as the chairs in the House of Commons and the same shade that covered the couch Abby sat on when she was in that fancy hotel in Montreal.

The hostess wore a burgundy dress. Smart choice. Red would be too striking for this kind of an environment. She led them in.

What about her? Slip her your card. Maybe she makes business calls. Or you could have her as a client and give her your financial services in exchange for—

I'm not paying attention to you.

Then why are you responding, Dave? I'm telling you, there are girls just like her waiting for you. Finish your date with your wife, and we'll go find you one.

Dave held the chair for Hope. She sat down and looked up at her knight in shining armour.

He sat down opposite her, his back to the other patrons in the restaurant. It relieved him to sit this way. Less distraction. At least visual distraction.

If you turn around now you can still get a look of Burgundy Hostess over there as she goes back. She looks pretty good.

He resisted the urge. Forced his eyes to stare at the menu. Though his mind was imagining her.

"How's your day been?" Hope asked, wishing he had asked her the same question first. She waited the entire car ride here for him to ask.

"Good, thank you. How about you?"

Her shoulders relaxed just slightly.

"Great."

"Work going well?"

She'd been in line for a promotion. He knew. And she knew that he knew. Still, he seemed to be strangely aloof in matters that were important to her.

She touched her glass of water and felt the cold against her fingers reach into her hand.

"It's okay."

That should have been a clue. Should have been a dead giveaway. He paused. He knew something was wrong. *Okay* is the flagship code word for *there's a problem here but I'm testing you to see if you care enough to ask.*

They looked through the menu. Dave made his choice quickly, then watched his wife deciding on her selections, her eyes processing the words. Strange that those same eyes could not perceive the guilt inside his own eyes. Why couldn't she see it? Or perhaps she could see it but couldn't believe it was true, and so she disregarded any evidence that did not line up with her conviction. Had her trust in him blinded her to the truth? Or is trust supposed to be free from suspicion?

"Your promotion. I'm sorry. Did you get it?"

She smiled in her gentle way. Pressed her lips together in an attempt to show that it was all right. Gave a slight shrug of her shoulders to indicate she had been passed over.

"I'm sorry," Dave said. "They made a mistake. You're the best."

Yup. She sure is. Wait, hang on. If she's the best, why are you with all those girls?

"Thanks, David." David. Always David. To everyone else he was Dave. But she always used his full name. They looked into each other's eyes. That made him nervous. He wondered if somehow he would give enough of himself away for her to finally put the pieces together.

"Everything okay?" she asked. She'd just lost out at work, and yet her quiet, gentle demeanour showed interest in him instead. Her concern for him made him feel all the more guilty. "You seem a little distant," she said. "For a while now."

Distant? You think I'm distant? You'd better believe I'm distant. You're on earth and I'm way out on Pluto. Probably farther. We're in the same house, the same bed. But we are light years apart.

"I'm fine," he lied. Now he had to come up with an excuse. She sensed something was wrong. And he had to find a way to honour that without betraying his lies. "Just trying to make sure I'm giving you and Nathan everything you need."

"You're doing great, David. Okay?"

Can I be honest with you? I mean, really honest? I've ruined us. Okay? If I had to sum it all up in one sentence, that would be it. Me. Dave. David. Your David. I did it. I ruined us. And you know what's so bizarre? We're completely sunk, and you don't even know it. Can somebody, anybody, please explain to me how two people can live together and know each other for years, and one of them is living a total and complete lie and the other person has no clue about it? I mean, how is that possible? This is not your fault. Not one bit. But looking back, I wish to high heaven, I wish to God, beg it of him, that on that first night you would have seen it in my eyes and threatened to divorce me and hang me out to dry if I ever did it again. You know why? Can I tell you why?

"So have we made up our minds?" the waitress asked. Dave looked up and saw her mesmerizing green eyes.

When Irish eyes are smiling.

Is no one safe?

Hey, if not her, at least it gives you an idea for the next girl.

They placed their food and drink orders.

Can I tell you why, Hope? Because I can't stop. People say cocaine is addictive. People say alcohol is addictive. Why does no one ever say sex is addictive? You know how many girls I've been with? Guess. Guess how many. You know what the answer is? The answer is, I don't know. Can you imagine that? I've lost count. I am so sick. I know it's wrong. But I just manage to shove it away.

Here we are on a date. You look stunning. You're such a happy person. And all I can think about is wishing you would leave the table to go to the bathroom so I can scroll through the girls that are available tonight. You want to see how pathetic I am? You can blame alcoholics for hiding alcohol in the house. But me? I'm worse. I'm worse because I have $300 cash in my pocket to head out tonight after I drop you off. I forgot something at the office. I need to meet a friend for a drink. Play a hockey game tonight that doesn't exist. I'm sick, and I can't fix myself.

"You're too hard on yourself, David. We have a great life and lots to be thankful for."

If only you knew, Hope. If only you knew. I hate what I'm doing. And the only way I know how to get rid of the guilt is to go right back and do the thing that makes me guilty in the first place. Like drinking gasoline to quench my thirst.

"Thanks," Dave said. "I'm sorry about your promotion."

They talked about Nathan. Sports. Politics. And as David grew less interested in the conversation, he found another voice pounding away inside of him. On the one hand, he felt trapped inside a behaviour he sensed was wrong. Like there was a code inside him that told him it wasn't right to cheat on his wife. But then there was this other voice. One that had been growing louder and louder.

Their food arrived. Rice pasta with clam sauce for her. Steak and lobster for him. He tucked his napkin into his shirt, grabbed hold of the lobster's red body and twisted it so that it cracked. It scared him to think how much he enjoyed doing that.

Hope talked about a vacation idea she had for the three of them. What about Spain? No, wait. Shanghai. Never been there.

But while she was talking he felt that other voice creeping in.

It doesn't matter to me if you find out or not. You think I care? I don't. You divorce me, we split it down the middle. Take Nathan. See if I care. He'll come back to me. The boys side with the dad and the girls side with the mom. Maybe not at first, but eventually things even out. I'll work harder and make the money back. And, by the way, it is your fault. It is totally your fault. I wouldn't be going for those girls if it wasn't for you. We all get older. That's life. But would it kill you to go to the gym a couple of times a week and get some life back into those bones of yours? And do

*me a favour, okay? No dessert. That way we can get home earlier. And I
can go out and—*

"So what do you think?" she asked.

"Excellent idea," he said, having no clue what he was agreeing to.

They finished dinner. She was too full for dessert. She took one last
look around the restaurant. He pulled her chair back for her. They left
the table. She excused herself to visit the ladies' room before the trek
home. That was fine, as it gave Dave the chance he needed to check out
Burgundy Hostess.

Hope returned. They drove home in light traffic. Both of them felt
tired.

Come on, Dave. You're not that tired, are you?

I just want to go to bed.

They got home, and Check greeted them. Dave went up to talk to
Nathan, who was busy at work on his Victorian authors paper. Good kid.
But he should get out more. All fun and no play makes Nathan—

"That was a nice dinner," Hope said. "Want to catch a movie
downstairs?"

Part of him wanted to say yes. Wanted to sit next to his wife and
watch a familiar film.

"Oh, sorry," he said. "Hockey game tonight. I can cancel if you want."

"No. I know how much you love it. Have fun."

Oh, don't worry. He will.

"Thanks, Hope. Love you."

"You too."

He was smart enough to bring his hockey bag. Even remembered his
stick. Forget either of those and it would be slightly obvious to Hope that
something was afoot.

As he drove off he tried to tell himself that he loved Hope. That he
could manage living in these two different worlds. That he could keep
them separate. That he wasn't hurting anyone.

Especially not himself.

chapter twenty-five

The phone call came in the middle of a meeting with Joel, Karen and the rest of her staff. Joy leaned over to see the number on her cell.

"Hello, Samantha, how are you?" she asked.

A long pause on the line. Joy waited.

"I've been thinking about what you asked," Samantha said.

"Thank you for considering it, Samantha."

"I'm pretty scared, Mrs. Smith."

"This is your choice, Samantha. Nobody is pushing you into anything."

"You think my testimony will help?"

"I do."

Another pause.

"I wouldn't be the only one, would I?"

"There would be others," Joy said. "Would you like to meet them?"

The restaurant was full enough so you could blend in yet quiet enough that you could hear yourself think. Joy and Samantha arrived first. Table or booth? The booths had high backs. Less chance of people hearing.

They sat near the hustle of the kitchen. The clang of dishes provided enough background noise to drown out what was about to be said. The booth could comfortably sit six, one extra than what they would need.

A girl with a worn black leather jacket approached. Her dark hair hung down to her shoulders, and her eyes showed a confidence that did its best to hide deep pain.

"Hi, Mrs. Smith."

"Hello, Adrian." They hugged. Really hugged. Not the kind of obligatory hugs some people give when one person leans in and the other would have been happy enough to shake hands. This was the real deal. Samantha noticed.

"Adrian, this is Samantha."

Their eyes connected in a way only those of survivors can. Though they looked nothing alike, they saw something familiar in each other.

Adrian hugged her. Samantha felt the relaxation that comes with being with someone who understands you without having to use words. Adrian sat down. Swore. Then she said, "This is going to be one unforgettable ride if we decide to go through with this."

Desirae and Elle came together. They couldn't have been more different, and yet they couldn't have been more alike. Desirae, playfully jabbing Samantha in the shoulder, said her friends called her Desi. She had grown up on a reserve out east. Samantha would have seen her dark eyes first if it wasn't for her puffy cheeks that hinted at repeated beatings. She smiled, revealing a soul rediscovering kindness after having to retreat in self-defence for so many years. She seemed like the kind of girl you'd picture being friends with everyone. And she would have been, had it not been for a major detour after meeting the guy of her dreams.

Or nightmares, as they could all now relate.

Elle was the quietest of the bunch. Something about her gave the impression she had a secret she was carrying around. A gentle soul who was still trying to overcome a misplaced penitence. She looked more at ease as she sat down with girls who understood her. How many times had she heard the phrase *It wasn't your fault*? And how many times would she have to hear it before she believed it?

There they were. Four girls who had been crushed into oblivion. And the mother figure who never gave up on them.

And never would.

The waiter came with menus and took drink orders. No one ordered alcohol.

Adrian looked at the menu and swore. "They've got the best stuff here. Who's in for breakfast?"

"You know it's suppertime, right?" Desi said. "Like, the evening meal?"

They all laughed. It reverberated throughout the restaurant. Something they all would have thought an unimaginable scene while they were back in *the game.*

Adrian made her selection and put down her menu. Samantha and Desi followed. Elle held hers open. The comfort of choice kept her scanning over the options.

"Okay, Mrs. Smith," Adrian said. Even with her tough exterior, she seemed she would be as comfortable rocking a newborn to sleep in her arms as she would winning a street fight. "You got us all here. We're all ears. What's the deal?"

"I want you to come to Ottawa. Give your testimonies to government officials. And help me pass Bill C-268."

The booth became still. If the rest of the restaurant was making noise, they didn't notice.

"Oh, is that all?" Adrian asked, in a quiet tone revealing the mending child inside. Joy had filled them in on the phone. But giving her request in person made it feel different. Scarier.

"What was the result of the vote?" Elle asked.

"It was 232 to 47."

"Those are pretty good numbers. Why do you need us?"

The waiter returned. The girls gave their orders, not looking him in the eye. Some rules are hard to unlearn.

"Second readings can be funny things," Joy said. "Sometimes people vote in favour in the second reading because they don't want to appear to be a stick in the mud. Sometimes they haven't even had time to read the bill in detail. But then it goes to a committee that researches it and tears every piece apart. People find things to disagree with. Factions form. It's politics, girls. There are no guarantees. We lose this bill, we may never get a chance like this again. Traffickers would then continue to get light sentences, if any at all."

The word *trafficker* would forever be etched in their minds. It would always connect them to the person who committed unimaginable atrocities against them. Led them through a life that would horrify Stephen King. Unspeakable evil no one could imagine. And those who heard their stories often had trouble getting those unbearable thoughts out of their mind. People like Joy's son Edward, for example.

In the back of their minds, no matter where they went, no matter what they did, the fear of their trafficker went with them. Except for Samantha, whose trafficker was laid to rest in a coffin six feet underground. And by now, he was a lot farther down than that.

"They're not going to believe us," Samantha said, voicing the thought that had been pounding inside her mind ever since Joy spoke with her about the idea. Samantha had resolved to share her story. Resolved to stand in a room full of strangers and reveal things about her life no person should have to reveal. Resolved to be open about events she wished she could keep nailed shut. But what caused her to shrink back in humiliation was the thought that maybe, just maybe, after she opened her soul, people would laugh or, worse, shrug it off and move on to the next meeting.

Her comment caused the other three to stop.

Adrian swore again. "You better believe they're going to believe us." She cursed a blue streak that was as poetic as it was vulgar. "If they don't buy what we say I'll tear a strip off them."

Joy didn't interrupt. Mothers know when to let a girl vent.

"Your silence interests me, Mrs. Smith," Elle said. That methodical, analytical mind processing Joy's reaction.

"Mrs. Smith?" Desi asked, hoping for confirmation she feared would not come. "They'll believe us, won't they?" Joy took in a breath. "Mrs. Smith?" Half-truths and other lies were what deceived these girls in the first place. And Joy would not gloss over anything, especially not to girls who had already suffered so much at the hands of anything but the total truth.

"There's no guarantee," Joy said.

Cue Adrian. She rolled out a slew of swears. Desi let out a sigh. Elle hardly reacted. Not on the outside anyways. Whatever little flicker of hope lay in Samantha faded to an indistinguishable glow.

"We're going to tell all and risk having it thrown back in our faces?" Desi asked.

"I'm not going to lie to you. It's possible."

The mood at the table died. They sat there in silence. The food arrived. Joy thanked the waiter, then leaned forward, folding her hands to pray.

The others did the same. They'd been travelling down the road of trying to connect the apparent contradiction of the presence of the Almighty with the torture they had gone through. And had, for the most part, managed to leave that unbearable mystery as it was, choosing instead to trust that somehow there was meaning and purpose even if, for now, it was out of reach. Joy said grace. The rest said amen.

They started into their food. A quiet, solemn supper. Strange for such a talkative group to not be saying anything. Samantha wondered if they would just call it a night and forget the whole thing.

It was Adrian who brought the table back to life. "Forget the whole lot of them," she said. "What's the matter with us, girls? Look what we all lived through. We're here. We're alive. And now what—we're scared because some dumb government official might not believe us? Who cares about them? There's somebody more we should be worried about. Isn't there?"

That brought a sense of purpose back. Turned the argument in a different direction.

"I mean, who are we all doing this for? Somewhere, out there, is a girl just like us. A good kid going to school who got in with the wrong guy. She bought his pack of lies. And now she's where we were. An inch from death. So who cares what other people think of us? Let all those people laugh at me. Let them call me a whore. Let them think their lustful thoughts if they want. That's their problem." She blew out a blast of curses. Then that quiet part of her came out—the part that was willing to hold a baby, the part that was wanting to be held herself. She felt a familiar sting of tears forming behind her eyes and working their way to the front. She wiped them away.

"I'm not gonna stand by knowing I could have done something when I had the chance," she said. Paused. "Which of us ever thought we'd get a chance to be in Parliament making a change?"

The waiter cleared the plates.

"Mrs. Smith?" Adrian asked, looking for support.

"There's a mother from Toronto. I talk with her all the time. She's trying to locate her daughter, Abby, who was smooth-talked by her trafficker. Now she's in real trouble. This law goes through, and they catch that guy, she's free of him."

"For five years," Elle said.

"It's a start. I wanted more. It was a tactic. It's what I think we can get a majority to agree on. I could have gone for more. But in the end, it was my call. Rather win with something than lose with nothing."

"So four survivors and an MP are going to change the way Canada views human trafficking?" Desi asked.

Joy nodded. It was all she could manage. She loved these girls. But more than that, she admired them. Admired their courage. Admired their desire to face the potential for humiliation to help girls who were as they had once been.

"I'm in," Adrian said, her words surprisingly G-rated.

"Me too," Elle said.

"Yup," Desi said.

They looked to Samantha. The last time she saw her trafficker, he had a knife in him that had sent him on to his great eternal destruction. She was clear of her trafficker; the others weren't so fortunate. Yet how odd and unexplainable the way a dead man could have such power over her. But not today. Not anymore. He wasn't going to keep her down.

"Let's do this," Samantha said.

"Thank you, girls," Joy said.

They began to plan what they would say at the hearing.

And hoped it would be enough to convince the powers that be.

chapter twenty-six

Being dragged from city to city hardly became noticeable anymore. Halifax through New Brunswick over into la belle province, back into Ontario. The end result was always the same. Four walls and an endless supply of men. It didn't surprise her who walked in that door anymore. Didn't surprise her how old they were, what their background was or what sort of roleplaying they were into.

But what did surprise her was that not one of them—not a single one—ever asked her age.

Are you guys so far gone that it doesn't matter to you how old I am? What goes on inside those sick minds of yours? What happens to you when you go back home? Do you have a switch that you flip to turn back into whatever you call normal?

A middle school teacher left her room, his face flushing in embarrassment that he had fallen yet again. She'd see this before—some johns felt guilty afterwards, regretted parting with their hard-earned cash. He asked for his money back. That insulted Abby. He was the first customer who wanted a refund. He explained things were tight at home and he had a daughter her age taking piano lessons. Abby would have given it to him, but she told him she didn't handle the money. He left without challenging Jake for it.

Abby thought he was her last customer of the day as she sat down on the edge of her bed. *Don't come around here no more.* It should have been the best time of day. Like when you're surrounded in war, and the enemy decides to stop launching rockets while they reload and get ready for the kill. She had arguably 16 whole hours off before the terror would start again. It should have given her time to unwind. But she felt anything but relaxed. When the guys were in the room, her mind was going a million miles a minute. Analyzing everything. Is he going to slit my throat? Is he going to throw me out the window? Is he going to choke me to death? Her attention was maxed right out. Hours upon hours upon hours straight. She needed lots of drugs to keep her in that state.

But afterwards, she couldn't wind down. She didn't have a button to push to set her back to whatever normal was. Her entire being had been stressed to the limit, pushed to the red line full on for hours on end. Previously, her mind and body groaned for escape, but now she felt relieved just to have postponed death.

You're not going to die.

Most of me already has.

Abby, don't lose hope.

Lose hope? You can't lose something you never had.

The door opened. Jake entered.

Maybe he'll push me out the window. That would end it, right?

Stop thinking that way.

Her mind became even more confused. Like there was another voice fighting inside her for attention.

You're being sold a dream he's never going to deliver on.

Maybe.

Maybe? Are you that far gone? Who's more deceived? The johns or you?

I have to see this through.

Why, because you've invested so much time into this deal?

Can I let you in on a little secret? I think I've convinced myself to believe him no matter what.

Why? Why would you do that?

Because if I don't, if I don't believe that he loves me, if I don't believe he is doing this awful plan for our long-term benefit—then I'm reduced to nothing more than a common whore. And I just don't want to believe that. I have to convince myself there is hope in him. Hope is the only currency I have left.

Jake locked the door without saying goodbye, leaving her sitting on the bed. Staring off into nothing. No will to fight. No desire to disobey. A robot. A cash machine. A programmed android. She was exhausted but found herself too tired to fall asleep and too hyper to do anything else. Where was that bottle of booze? Did he forget? Even a beer? Was that asking too much? Was that in the budget?

She tried to decide if she should collapse or take a shower. In the end, the thought of all those guys on her pushed her to try to get clean. After a half hour standing under a hot stream of water, she got out but felt no different. Not on the inside anyway. She put on a pair of shorts and a dirty white shirt and found it hard to believe that with all this money flying around she didn't have new clothes every day. She ran the water in the sink. Cooled off her face. The humidity cleared. That bothered her. She liked it better when the mirror stayed fogged over so she didn't have to look at herself. Less chance of spoiling her memory of who she thought she might still be.

She felt the cool water against her skin. Time to face it. Not Jake. Not the johns. Not anybody else.

I have to face me. I have to face what I have become.

She glanced at the mirror out of the corner of her eyes, hesitating to make direct eye contact with herself.

What will I see? What if I don't look like me anymore? If I don't look at me, how can I go on pretending that I haven't changed?

She suddenly remembered the girl who changed her clothes several times before rushing out to see Jake. Was any of that innocence still there?

Even though she had looked at the mirror many times since meeting Jake, she had avoided looking into her reflection. She'd seen enough to do hair and makeup and brush her teeth. But she had avoided seeing the verdict of what was really going on in those pools of blue.

Time to face herself.

She looked up.

She looked in.

And her every disappointment was confirmed.

Her face had sunk in, giving the impression she was on a starvation diet. Her skin tone was lighter, like someone had removed the natural colour from her face. But the real crushing reality was the vacancy in her eyes, revealing an irrefutable story of a once vibrant person who now had a foreclosure sign nailed to her door.

How did I sink this low?

Low? This isn't low. This is temporary.

It doesn't feel temporary.

Abby closed her eyes, unable to stare at the truth any longer. She had had a semblance of hope that maybe, just maybe, the brightness in her eyes would still be there, looking back at her. Instead, they were the dullest shade of blue she had ever seen. How was that even possible? Is there dull blue anywhere in creation? The sky is a brilliant sheet of gorgeous blue. The ocean is an endless expanse of blue that stretches out to the horizon.

But her eyes were far from that thrilling brilliance. And it only served to remind her of how far she had fallen.

You're going to get it back, okay? Abby, you guys are making so much money.

He hates me.

That's not true.

Sure it's true. You see how far away he is from me? He thinks I'm gross.

She wanted to smash the mirror so she would never have to look at her reflection. And yet another part of her felt the need to feel judged, to feel ashamed, and so she left the bathroom with that mirror hanging there like a judge having delivered a guilty verdict.

She stared at the bed. Her mind wanted anything besides curling under the covers that had been filled with so many men. Her aching body wanted anything but the floor. Her body won out, and she fell backwards onto the bed and stared up at a plain white light bulb. Its simple glow mesmerized her, capturing all her attention.

This is my life. This it. This is all I'm worth. I'm going to do this the rest of my existence. I'm going to have to work each night, wondering which creep is the serial killer who will strangle me to death and then nonchalantly walk out after his time is up. Or maybe Jake will do it. Call it a premonition. I have this unmistakable feeling he's going to walk in with a bat one day. Or an axe. Why does a guy like him look so great on the outside? How could I not spot it?

Finally, we agree.

Too many voices. Where was that bottle to drown them out? Or the drugs that could paint a rainbow and brighten her dull blue eyes?

She tried to fall asleep. But the drug of anxiety kept pounding her awake like an alarm that kept going off the moment she dropped into a deeper state of sleep. *Don't do it. Don't let yourself fall asleep that deep. You won't hear him coming in. You won't hear him approaching. You have to stay awake. And watch the window. Watch it! He could crawl in from there—one of the guys you saw tonight who thinks he's in love with you and wants to come back and do something to you.*

She kept the light on that night, thinking that perhaps by doing so it would be enough to keep the voices away. Enough to keep her attention focused on anything else. But try as she might, she could not shake the sinking premonition that something awful was about to happen.

I can get out.

Sure. With an axe in your back.

I can find a way.

He loves you.

I'm so confused. Don't say that.

He does. You can't make it without him.

Sure I can.

Really?

She had to be honest. No. No, she didn't think she could exist without him. He owned her. He'd even made her get a tattoo in the shape of a cattle brand mark, telling her she was a cow without him. That she only had value with him.

I could find someone else. Someone good.

What? Did you really say that?

I could.

Sure. Okay, let's play this out. You've been with how many guys? You're going to find some new cute guy—impossible for you, but let's give you the benefit of the doubt—and go on a date with him. What will you say? "Hi, I'm Abby Summers, and I've whored around with about 2,000 guys. I like hockey and making money on my back. Want to be my boyfriend?"

Stop it.

No, you stop it. Start thinking. You are nothing. And you are never, ever getting out of here. Nobody out there wants you. If they did, they would have long since tried for you. But they didn't. Jake came. And you accepted. That's the part you have to get right in your mind. You chose this of your own free will. He asked, and you accepted. This life is the best you were ever going to do.

I could go back to my family.

Really? If your family loved you, they wouldn't have let this happen to you.

My mom loves me.

Your mom loved you. Past tense. Sorry. No mother could love you now.

She faded in and out of restless sleep. Eventually the sun rose, overpowering the meagre light bulb. He would be in soon. Giving her the same spiel about getting more rest. You look tired. The guys want you looking good.

Where to turn to? What to do?

Dear God, please get me out of here.

She thought about her future and saw an endless cycle of cities, hotel rooms and men who never cared, resulting in a repeat of fear and humiliation.

Abby wanted out.

But how?

How to figure out a plan of escape? How to control her fear of what might happen? How to resolve to stay out and reject the mirror's opinion of her? How to keep her eyes from betraying to Jake what she was really planning?

Up until now she only had one goal: to live to the end of the day. She did that by obeying Jake and by staying vigilant with the johns—the tricks. She did it by not showing her terrified heart to any of them. But now she had an additional goal. She had to look for opportunities, to watch for an opening where she could bolt.

And maybe. Just maybe. There would be a way out.

She could hope.

Couldn't she?

chapter twenty-seven

Bart walked out under the evening sky with the help of a walking stick. Joy watched him from the window as his tall frame made it to the end of the driveway. He pushed himself to stand outside. Under the stars. To pray for his wife. For her fight. For her to stay encouraged.

When he came in from the cold she made him tea. They sat down in the living room and talked. Even though he continued to push for her to stay in Ottawa, she still felt a sense of guilt. She wanted to be at her husband's side to help him and to be there for him instead of the other way around. They discussed the logic of it. His health versus the safety of trafficked girls. It made sense in her mind. But it did little to comfort her heart.

He went to bed first. The cancer tired him out faster and faster. They prayed together, and then he went to sleep. Joy returned to the living room. When he was there his presence comforted her. But now that he was gone, her thoughts shifted back to the bill. To her strategy.

To Ottawa.

Joy walked down the hall to Thomas's office on Parliament Hill. She gave her name to the receptionist, who had been expecting her. She led Joy into the office and closed the door. Joy sat down. Across from her, behind the desk, sat Thomas, who had come to Joy all that time ago begging her, pleading with her, to take down her bill for fear that he would be outed.

THE TRUE STORY OF CANADIAN HUMAN TRAFFICKING

She hadn't shown any mercy then, and she was just as ready now to out him if he didn't vote for her bill.

"I'm bringing survivors to the Hill," she said. "I want you to come hear their testimonies."

He wasn't interested, but not because he didn't agree with what Joy was doing. As low as the odds might be, he had an unnerving feeling that one of the survivors might be a girl he had been with. There's awkward, and then there's downright humiliation.

"You know the truth now."

"I wish I didn't," he said, looking at a picture of his family on his desk. He thought about how he got started with the girls. Just a little harmless fun. That's all it was, wasn't it? Late nights on the Hill. A little companionship. How bizarre. How did his mind ever get him to the place where it refused to see the obvious? How could he possibly have missed that the girls were being forced? That they received nothing but threats and utter degradation in return? How does a man function at such a high level of office in the nation and yet have his common sense so completely fail him?

He was too ashamed to make eye contact with someone who had to endure so much grief all because of men like him.

He asked about Bart. She told him.

"How did you get into politics?" he asked, finally meeting her gaze.

"Everyone asks that in Ottawa," Joy said. "We all want to know what got us here. Why do you think we do that?"

"Subconscious, I think."

"How so?"

"We're trying to figure out who has pure motives for being here. I think most of us do. Though clearly some of us get off track."

"You want to get back on track?"

"You haven't answered my question," he said.

"My heart broke when my son Edward told me about all the girls being trafficked. I wanted to make a difference. That's what got me started in politics. Human trafficking consumed me, really."

"I admire you, Joy."

"You shouldn't."

"You're doing a great thing. Look at all the people you have to stand up against."

"I have a good cause. But I confess I'm ruthless in the way I go about it sometimes," she said with a laugh, having that rare ability to choose to see the bright side of nearly anything. "As you well know."

"Are you ruthless or just direct?"

Joy laughed again. It filled the room. "Maybe a little of both."

He laughed too, though his was more subdued.

"We both know why you're here," he said. The room became quiet. Joy saw the hurt in his eyes. A man conflicted. Would he go for it or not? "I'm going to vote for your bill."

"Thank you."

"I don't know if it's because you threatened me or because it's the right thing to do."

"I am sorry it had to come to that. Like I said, a little ruthless."

"You don't need to apologize for my mistakes."

Joy stood and walked to the door. She was about to touch the handle when he spoke to her in a soft voice. Like he was concerned somebody would hear what he had to say. Including himself.

"I'm scared, Joy."

"Don't be," she said. "Just do the right thing no matter what. Everything else will take care of itself."

Joy walked down the hallway. So many MPs had promised to give their support to her bill. Many said they would do anything to help her. Still, there were some, maybe enough, who opposed her. Nothing was guaranteed. Not ever. She thought back to the 1995 referendum. Would Quebec separate from Canada? It seemed impossible. And yet, as the polls began to be counted that evening, they demonstrated a terrifying potential. In the end, Canada had remained intact, but by a narrow margin of a little more than one lousy percent.

It's politics.

Nothing is for certain.

And every single vote matters.

Hence this visit.

She opened the door to the MP's office. Introduced herself. Greeted the assistant with a smile. Said no when asked if she had an appointment.

"I only need five minutes."

"I can run a note in to him," the assistant said in a cold tone.

Joy was equal to the task. "You can tell him I'm not going to leave until he sees me."

The assistant repeated herself. Joy repeated herself. The assistant shook her head just enough to convey her annoyance. She poked her head into the main office room. An exchange of words. She turned back. "He'll see you."

I had a feeling he would.

Joy entered and sat down. The MP, in his fifties, wearing a nice suit, pretended to be busy with nothing.

"You haven't been returning my calls, Ian."

"You don't have an appointment."

"I don't. And I do appreciate you seeing me."

"Five minutes."

"How generous of you."

Lord, help me not to throttle him.

"I'm not supporting your bill," he said.

"Sure you will. You just haven't let me encourage you yet."

"I don't care if you're going to threaten me. I don't have anything for you to use."

"Sure I do."

"I'm not supporting your bill."

"Do you care to tell me why?"

"Because trafficking isn't happening the way you say."

"Are you willing to consider that maybe you have your facts wrong?" No response. "If I introduced you to girls who have survived human trafficking, would that help?"

He glanced at his phone, which indicated he had missed a call. He went back to his computer.

"We just disagree, Joy. Don't take it personally."

"You'll forgive me if I do take it personally when girls are being raped."

"You're way out of line, Smith."

"You're an embarrassment to Canada."

"You're off on a mission that is as meaningless as you are."

"I'm still young enough to fight, but I'm old enough not to care what you think of me."

"You're not going to push me around."

"I don't need to, Ian."

She said his name in such a cold, even tone. It annoyed him. And she knew it.

"Then we agree to disagree," he said. "Your five minutes are up."

"You have a weakness."

"Don't walk that line, Joy."

"You want to get voted in."

"Big surprise there."

"So here's my promise to you." He continued typing away at his keyboard. "You want to stop typing? Is that too much to ask?"

He looked at his phone, checking the time. Then he looked at Joy. She continued.

"If you do not support my bill, I'm going to make a trip to your riding. I will go on every radio station and TV news station, and I'm going to hold rallies in your constituency. I will let everyone know that you voted to expose their children to the horrors of human trafficking."

His face flushed. Joy interrupted him before he could start.

"And your five minutes are up," she said, standing up from her chair. "I don't care what's going on inside that decrepit mind of yours, Ian. You vote yes, or I make sure you don't get to sit in that chair next election."

Joy walked to the door, then turned around. "Thank you for taking the time to see me. I appreciate you fitting the safety of Canadian girls into your busy schedule."

She said goodbye to the moody assistant and left. On the way back to her office she stopped in to see a few MPs from various parties. Nothing long. Nothing too in-depth. Simply wanting to thank people who were supporting her. On this issue, anyway.

She returned to her office. Sat down. Wondered.

Just how close was this vote going to get?

chapter twenty-eight

He seemed nice enough in an energetic, optimistic sort of way. In his late forties with grey hair starting to show around his temples, he told jokes to Abby, trying hard to make her laugh. She obliged and made a good audience for him. She saw him as the kind of guy who always wanted to fit in but spent his life in relative isolation. No wedding ring. Abby had seen his type—and every other type—many, many times.

The geek with low self-esteem who wouldn't get it anywhere else. The husband of a terminally ill wife who had no interest in or ability to stay faithful till death do us part. The addict who doesn't want to stop. The teachers. The lawyers. The judges. The police. All of them under a spell, convinced that because it was *just sex* it wasn't cheating. All of them assuming their actions were made between two consenting adults. The lot of them trapped in an oversexualized culture that in the name of empowering women was degrading them into sex objects.

She'd considered herself increasingly proficient at figuring out a guy's type. With a high degree of accuracy, she could determine why a guy was there, what he wanted, and what his potential triggers for violence were.

Knowledge made survival that much more likely.

He grabbed a wooden chair, turned it around and sat down. Draping his arms over the back he pointed to the other chair. "Have a seat," he said. "Let's talk."

The best kind, Abby thought. *Waste your time pretending you're on a date. Feel like a girl actually likes you. When the clock strikes one hour you leave with the fake sense that a girl wanted to be with you.*

Abby sat down.

"What kind of guy do you think I am?" he asked.

His build indicated to Abby that he had once been interested in sports. The kind of guy who tries hard to keep in shape and who tries hard to play the few cards he has been dealt as best he can. But his luck had run out somewhere along the line. He saw the futility of exercising to get a girl. No matter how much he worked out, girls rejected him. His hair was cut stylishly short enough, and he wore designer jeans. She guessed he worked in sales, maybe a middle management position. She played along. Laughed at his stupid jokes. *Just keep the meter running and get him out of here.*

"You think I'm funny?" he asked.

"I do. You have a genuine sense about you," she said.

So genuine that a pathetic guy like you pays big money to see a girl like me in an apartment. Why don't guys like you just drop dead?

"That's amazing."

Abby smiled. She didn't know where this was going.

"I mean that's really amazing."

She smiled, trying to make it look genuine. What did he really want?

"I think you're faking that smile."

What to do? Admit to faking and he goes crazy, or continue on with the lie that he can absolutely see through? She eyed him with affection. Seduction usually worked.

"Can I tell you something?" he asked.

Evidently it would not work on him.

"Sure thing."

"You're going to do whatever I tell you."

His expression changed. His voice changed. It sent a terrifying chill down her back.

"What interests you?" she asked, already dreading the answer.

He looked up, staring at nothing in particular. Rubbed his chin. He reached into his side and pulled out a knife with a long blade. Abby felt sick.

"I've killed two girls before," he said.

Abby froze.

You have to come back with something now! Say something! Make it witty. Make it sharp. Don't show any fear. You show him you're scared and he will kill you right here and now. Say something! Every second you wait gives him more power. Say it now! Say it now! Say it—

"What makes you think I haven't killed before?" she said.

Brilliant. Play at his level.

"Did you enjoy it?"

The way he asked that coupled with the crazed look in his eyes caused her to believe that he was, in fact, a murderer. He let out a short, hysterical laugh. How was it that he seemed so shy but normal just a few moments ago?

"So tell me," he continued. "Was it fun for you?"

He laughed again in a high-pitched and long tone. Back and forth they went. Bantering. She managed to maintain a calm demeanour, but her heart raced. They fought a cold war of sorts, with her only weapon being the empty confidence of words. He finally left when his time was up. When the door closed, she collapsed to the ground. She wanted to lock the door, but Jake wasn't inside. Once he got in he would pound her mercilessly for locking him out. But wouldn't that be better than getting her throat slit? Men had been violent with her before. She'd suffered through weird, awful, humiliating experiences. She'd experienced all of it, so she thought. Until she met the mirror image of Jack the Ripper a few minutes before.

Jake entered. The hysterical look in her eyes made him wonder if she had taken too many drugs. Abby stood and grabbed onto him so tight that it hurt him. He pushed her back down, reached for his phone and texted the next customer.

"We have to call the cops," she said, trying to calm herself down. But her breathing only quickened. Like there was less and less oxygen with every gasp. She felt herself panicking. "We have to—"

Jake grabbed her by the hair and forced her to look at him. "I already told you, Abby. No cops. Not ever. You can't trust them. Cops are all corrupt. All a cop will do is separate you from me. Is that what you want?"

"No."

She had managed to prevent fear from invading her mind while the crazy man was in the room. But now that he was gone, it gave her a chance to absorb what had happened. And what *could* have happened. And all of it terrified her.

"Don't ever call the cops, Abby."

She swallowed. Panic began to creep its way into her body. What if he's just outside the door? What if he knifes Jake and then comes in, sits down backwards on that chair, pulls out his knife and—

"You call the cops, and I'll kill you. Those are the rules. You don't leave this apartment, and you don't talk to cops. Not ever. I know what's best for you. Now you prove to me that you love me by keeping to the rules I've laid down. Can you do that, Abby? Can you?"

Jake left her lying on the ground. She heard the familiar sound of the door locking.

She curled up in a ball in the corner. A chill ran through her. Like a precursor to the grim reaper's presence. She breathed in and out, trying to keep herself from hyperventilating. Longer and deeper breaths. That familiar feeling came over her of being exhausted but too hypervigilant to do anything about it.

Closing her eyes, she tried to find memories that would comfort her. She thought back to when she was a child. She remembered trying to talk to her father when she was five years old. He would half-listen, being more focused on the game, his work, or anything else. She felt the distance between them, saw his preoccupation. Felt the hurt when he broke eye contact with her. When she would talk and no one would listen.

Kind of like now, on the floor, in this apartment. No one to listen to her.

She sat up and pushed her back against the electric baseboard heater, staring out at the door. She imagined getting up to walk through it but couldn't make her legs move. Her gaze fell down to the chair, and her tired mind refocused.

That's when she saw it.

She edged closer. Was it really there? Or was her mind just projecting it to be there?

She crawled up to the chair. Reached out to touch it, her last confirmation that it wasn't her imagination. Sure enough.

Jake had forgotten his cellphone.

You idiot! Don't! Just go to bed.

This is your chance. Do it now.

Leave it there and go to sleep. If Jake comes in, pretend to wake up and tell him you had no idea his cellphone was there. You have to act fast. Just like when you bantered back and forth with Knife-man.

Jake will check his phone to see if I used it.

Which is why you have to call now.

Who? Who do I call?

Your mother. The police.

I can't call the police. They're all evil and corrupt.

You can't believe that.

They are. Jake said.

Fine. Fine. Cops are bad. But call your mother.

Abby hesitated. Every second she waited was a second closer to Jake coming back for his phone. But what if he came in just as she dialed? What then? What would happen to her?

I don't even know where I am.

Turning to the window she looked outside and saw apartments everywhere. This could be any place in the GTA.

But it wasn't. She strained her neck to look as far as the window would allow. This did look familiar. Or did she just want it to look familiar? No. No, this was Richmond Hill. Not far from Markham. She knew this cluster of apartments. She tried to get her bearings. Which intersection was she at?

Start calling now.

You don't want to do this. Don't make this mistake.

I want back what Jake and I had. I want the old days back.

You never had those days, Abby.

Yes! Yes we did. Don't lie. Those were great days.

But they weren't, Abby. They were fiction.

They were not. I felt loved. I felt cared for. He cared for me.

You sure thought that, didn't you?

Jake could have killed me by now. He hasn't done that.

And that's kindness in your eyes?

Absolutely.

Can you count the number of times he has beaten you?

That's not fair … We had a good life; we can get it back.

You want to spend your life with a guy who locks you in a room with men who pull knives on you? With men who torture you for fun?

The thoughts spun around in her mind like clothes in a washing machine.

She looked back at the phone. Reached out.

Touched it.

Glancing at the door, she wondered if she could sense his presence on the other side.

She picked up the phone. Her hands shook. She could see Jake's face in front of her, asking her why she was betraying him.

What was her mom's phone number? She experienced a moment of panic as she tried to recall. How long had it been? Months. Stop. Think. There. It came back to her.

She dialed her mother's cell.

Waited what felt like eternity for it to connect.

She heard it ringing.

Pick up! Pick up! Pick up!!

She was ready to scream. Ready to smash her face through the window. Ready to tear her hair out.

She glanced back at the door.

Listened to the phone.

It rang again.

chapter twenty-nine

Answer it! Answer it! Answer it!

Abby gripped the phone so tightly her fingers went numb. With her other hand she touched the window, as if doing so could somehow bring her closer to the world on the other side of it. She waited in the silence for her mother to pick up.

It rang again.

She began preparing a contingency plan. What if this call went to voicemail? She'd have to delete the call history. But wouldn't that make it more obvious? She could stick the phone in the toilet tank. Throw it out the window. Smash it up and flush it down. He would have no proof it was left here. It could have fallen out anywhere.

She felt the long pause as if she were frozen in time. Where could her mother be? Would she even keep her ringer on this late?

Another ring.

It would show up on her phone as an unknown number. So even if she heard the call, she might not answer, especially this late in the evening.

A clicking sound. Voice or voicemail? Abby held her breath.

"Hello?"

Talia's voice was unmistakable. A flood of emotion ripped through Abby. She couldn't speak. Relief, guilt and fear engulfed her.

"Hello?" her mother repeated. Abby heard the faint glimmer of hope in her mother's voice.

Say something!

"Mom?"

"Abby!" her mom gasped. "Are you okay? Where are you? I'll come and get you."

"Mom, do exactly what I tell you. Or else he will kill me."

"Just tell me where you are," Talia said, her voice shaking.

Abby looked out the window. Gave directions as best she could. North, south, left and right. It all became so confused in her mind. But Talia figured it out, writing it down after scrambling for pen and paper.

"Wait for me in the parking lot," Abby said. There are tons of apartment buildings all around but I'll see you and come down, okay?"

"I'm leaving right now. Just hang on."

"And Mom, whatever you do, don't call the police. If you do, I am dead. Do you understand me? He told me he will kill me if I ever call the police."

A one-person rescue mission? This was not what Talia had hoped for. She wanted to bolt into her car, call 911 and have an army of police cruisers flashing their lights when she arrived, with officers already bringing Abby out. Safe and sound. Unharmed.

"Okay. I'm coming, Abby. I love you."

Abby hung up.

Talia raced into the garage. Fumbled with her keys. Missed on her first attempt to jam the car key into the ignition. Finally she got it in. Started the engine. Backed out in the black night. Put the car in drive and raced off way past the speed limit.

With any luck, she'd be there in 15 minutes.

Fifteen minutes. How unfathomable to believe that her tortured daughter—out of all the places on earth where she could have been—was so very close. It tore at her to think Abby was suffering within arm's reach and that she could have easily been rescued had Talia just known the location.

Abby hung on to the phone even though the line had gone dead. Clinging to it gave her a connectedness she had not felt in a long, long time. It was as if keeping it in her hand made her feel she was already touching her mother.

She watched the parking lot. Felt her heart pounding in her chest so hard it became difficult to breathe. *Is Jake going to come in? What if I leave the room just as he is coming down the hallway?*

If she raced out now it would look really awkward if Jake showed up. She would have to time it perfectly. Her mother's car would pull into the lot. She would bolt out. Even if Jake was in the building, even if he saw her running, it would be a foot race. But would she be able to outrun him in her condition? Did she still have that midfield speed?

She thought about putting the phone back on the chair. That made sense. If he came in now and saw her holding it there would be a serious beating. No, wait. She had to get rid of it. Put the second part of her plan in action. Dump the phone and pretend she knew nothing of it. Otherwise he could check the list of calls and—

Abby stopped. A pulsing chill of fear raced up and down her spine. The kind you have when you sense somebody else is in the room with you.

Impossible. There was no way Jake was in the room. She would have heard him if he were there. She felt sick. A shiver ran down her back. She checked her reflection in the window. It looked hazy, perhaps because of the outdoors. Perhaps because of the sheer terror pounding through her body. The angle of the light didn't show who, if anyone, was standing there behind her.

Her mind raced through the possibilities. He simply could not have entered the apartment without her knowing. *He can't possibly be behind me.* Or was she so focused on her conversation with her mother that she didn't notice him entering?

For sure she would have seen him in the reflection. But could she have missed him? Maybe her attention was so much on all the buildings while giving instructions to her mother that she never took notice of another reflection in the glass.

But if he had heard her on the phone he would have cut the conversation short. He'd have beaten her senseless by now.

All of this made sense. It proved he couldn't be there. But it was still awfully difficult for Abby to override the mysterious conviction pounding in her heart.

Abby began to turn around. She leaned towards the window, trying to give herself that extra bit of separation, which would, of course, prove totally useless in such a small space. She looked behind her.

The blood drained from her face.

This was it.

She would die tonight.

His brown eyes were so full of evil. Had they always been that way right from the beginning? Had she missed it?

It didn't matter. Not now. What did matter was that she had his phone. She had broken the rule. His silence choked her. Why wasn't he beating her right now?

How to deal with this? Is there a way out? Joke around like I did with the crazy man? Would that work? Jake is evil, but he isn't insane. Or does being evil automatically make you insane? Focus. The insane game won't work. Just give him the phone back. Take a beating. And pray to God in heaven that it's a merciful beating. One that will take the last bit of my soul but leave me enough of a shell of a body to keep me alive at least another day.

"I try so hard with you, Abby," he said in a quiet tone. She would have preferred that he yell. He squinted his eyes like he was trying to analyze her behaviour to see if he could determine what her problem was. "But I just …" He shook his head. Raised his hands palm up. "I'm at a bit of a loss here, baby."

Abby bit the inside of her lip. Tears began to form. *Fight it. Fight it. Fight it. Don't go down like this. If you act like a coward, he will treat you like a coward. Is he hiding a knife?*

She stretched out her hand. Offered him the phone.

"Thanks," he said in an upbeat tone, as if it were the early days and she just handed him a drink.

"We've never watched a movie together, have we?"

"Not yet," she said. Clever move. *Yet* leads to something that can still happen in the future.

"Want to see one?"

"Sure."

He walked towards her and placed his hands on her shoulders. He drew her towards him. Here it comes. Then he turned her to face the window, pulling her back slightly to keep her out of view of anyone who might be arriving in the parking lot.

"Math wasn't always my strongest," he said. "But if a car leaves your house, drives at speeds exceeding the speed limit, and, if the traffic is light, as it should be this time of night, how long would it take a person—your mother, for example—to arrive here? I'm going to go out on a limb here and say any minute now. How about you? What do you think?"

Abby fought back tears. Her panic had passed the red line—that marker on a car engine tachometer that tells the driver severe damage will result if the speed is not immediately reduced. "I'm not sure," she whispered.

"Oh, oh, oh," Jake said. They watched headlights coming onto the parking lot. A sea of cars. But all of them just sitting there. Except for one. "Wait until she gets a little closer." The car drove around and parked in the middle of all the buildings. A woman got out.

Abby covered her mouth.

"I think we have a winner. Now this is a great movie. Abby, come on. You have to admit. Do I know how to pick 'em or do I? I think I should go into the film business."

Talia stood in the cold evening air. Her hand on the passenger side door. Waiting for her soccer-playing daughter to bolt out. There was no immediate burst through the door of any of the apartment buildings. No problem. Talia figured Abby had now seen her, raced out her apartment door and was sprinting down the hallway to the elevator. Or better yet, the stairs. Either route would lead to safety.

Instead, Abby watched her mother shivering in the cold. *I'm right here, Mom. I'm right here. Can you look up? Can you look through the darkness to see me standing here?*

Abby wanted to scream to her, but she could only manage to breathe in erratic short breaths with Jake's arms around her.

Talia worked it out in her mind. The tallest building had so many floors. It would take about so long to get down the stairs. No matter how much she forced herself to remain optimistic, she realized that Abby should have made it out by now.

If she were still alive.

Abby felt tears falling down her face. She dropped the bravery act. She wouldn't get this close again. There was her escape, standing there waiting for her.

Talia began to shake in the cold. She wanted to stay outside. Wanted to stand guard and be a good soldier for her daughter. She was parked where any person exiting any of the buildings would see her. She got into her seat and waited.

For four hours.

"Long movie," Jake said. "How long do you think she'll stay?"

Abby didn't answer. Even from this distance, her mother's face looked ashen grey. At 3 a.m. Talia was sure her daughter either was dead or had been moved on. At 4 a.m. she got out of her car. Looked around one last time, ironically making perfect eye contact for a moment with Abby. She would have seen her if Abby were standing in the light. Talia drove off.

"Abby, I want you to hear me very carefully, all right?"

"All right."

"Strictly speaking I don't think I ever told you not to call your mother. I said to stay here in your apartment. I specifically mentioned not to call the police, which you stuck to, and I admire that. I do. So I'm going to accept some of the blame. I think that's fair. Don't you?"

There was no way to answer that question. She would have preferred to have crazy Knife-man here instead. At least she could combat his lunacy.

"Abby, if you ever speak to someone again ..." Jake thought. Abby swallowed. The word *ever* implied she wasn't going to die. Not tonight. "I will tie you up and I will leave you in the middle of a field. Someplace near people. Where people can see you from a window. Someone will call 911. Do you know why?" Abby stayed quiet. One step either way off this tightrope and she was going to the bottom. "Abby?"

"No?" she whispered, hoping to be able to retract it if she picked the wrong answer.

"You're a smart girl. They wouldn't see you, Abby. You'd be way too far away. And you would be lying down. So how would they see you?"

"Not sure."

"You have to try, Abby. You're brilliant. Don't ever let anyone tell you differently. You are lying in a field, but people call 911. Why?"

She didn't want to know. Didn't want to be inside his sick mind. She raised her shoulders.

Jake leaned in beside her. Whispered in her ear.

"Because I will set you on fire."

Abby heard the roar of an inferno in her mind. Remembered how the heat of the blaze felt when she got too close while camping. She closed her eyes. And would have closed her ears if she could have.

"I will tie you up. Douse you with gasoline. Set you on fire. And leave you to burn. You will try to scream, but they won't be able to hear you. Do you know why?"

Abby couldn't move. Couldn't think. All she could do was hear his indictment.

"Because, Abby, you will be burning. And people can't scream when they burn. The people in the apartments will dial 911. But really, there's not much that can be done at that point. You'll die hearing the sirens of ambulances, knowing that they will not reach you in time." He patted her on the shoulder. "Do I make myself clear?"

She couldn't feel herself breathing. It was as if she had been holding her breath this whole time. She forced herself to nod.

He took a step away from her. An outsider looking on from a distance might have concluded that it was over. But Abby knew better. She knew what was coming.

Jake smashed his fist into her face. Her head snapped back and crashed into the wall. He beat her so badly that the shock of the pain made her feel she was about to pass out. He left her curled up in a ball, unable to make the trip to the bathroom to clean up the blood.

The following morning, he threw her a brown bag of takeout. "Get up," he said. And she would have if only she could. He watched her lying there. Shook his head. Left.

By the next day she had managed to take a shower. When she got out, he was waiting for her.

"Let's go," he said. "We're leaving Toronto. I'm tired of this town."

chapter thirty

Given the sheer number of lies Dave had told his wife, it occurred to him that if he was going to be found out, it would have happened by now. So he drew the conclusion that he was in the clear. What she didn't know wouldn't hurt her. And if she felt no reason for suspicion, it meant he must be great at covering his tracks.

But even he had to admit he hadn't been that great at hiding his other life. There was one extra night of hockey a week. That was fairly believable. Not much of a stretch there. Even though his hair didn't look damp the way it was supposed to when he came back from hockey, she neither immediately nor eventually put that together. The work trips needed an extra day because business was good.

Keeping his extra activities secret when he was out of town was easy. But what about in Leaf country? Sure, the GTA has a lot of people. But of all the places he'd been and all the girls he'd seen, had no one recognized him? Was he really that invisible out there? Not to have even one person come up to Hope and say *Hey, we saw Dave at such and such hotel*, raising her suspicions? She wouldn't have had to look very hard to figure it out. That's the problem with trust. It keeps one person believing even if the other person is a liar.

He considered himself to have done an excellent job divvying up his life between him as everyone knew him and him as only the girls knew him. He managed to separate those two worlds. Drifted back and forth between them as if they were mirror universes, with a single door of entry and exit between them to which he alone held the key.

A better system of unlimited freedom had never been invented.

Not in his mind.

He was also good at hiding the money. That was tricky. He had shelled out thousands and thousands of dollars, and it took a little finagling to make it unnoticeable. Nothing that a person well versed in finance couldn't figure out. And she wouldn't look too hard. There was still enough coming in. Again, the beauty of trust.

He'd meet other johns coming in and out of the girls' places. All types. All nationalities. He'd see familiar faces now and again. But nothing to worry about there. There was an unwritten rule about no snitching on other johns, for obvious reasons.

It all seemed to be going so well for him. He'd covered his tracks. Had seen as many girls as he wanted. Hope had no idea. It all looked so perfect.

So why did he feel so horrible about it?

He found it impossible to look at himself in the mirror. But even that was easier than looking Hope in the eye. Sure, he looked at her. But it had been a long time since he had looked into her. They had drifted apart. Still, she believed him to be something he knew he was not. That brought with it an extra heaping of guilt. No problem. He could drown that out too. He stayed even longer at work. Made more money. Bought her stuff she never asked for but appreciated all the same.

Something was eating away at him.

There's nothing wrong. It's just a little fun.

Fun that leaves you guilty? Fun that makes you lead a double life?

I can stop whenever I want to.

Great. Do it.

Fine. I will. I'll prove I can stop. I don't need to spend money on girls.

Spend money on girls? Strictly speaking you're not spending money on the girls. You're investing in them. They're making their way through college. Education costs a fortune, and they need the dough. Ten years from now they'll thank you.

As long as they don't thank me when my wife is present.

Would you get a grip on yourself? You're headed for a disaster.

It isn't that bad. It's a bit of a hang-up. Nothing I can't manage. Besides, it's not hurting anyone else.

Not even your wife? You are in such denial.

It doesn't concern her.

You ever notice what happens to you when you see the girls?

I'm happier.

Are you? Admit it. You have to become someone else when you're with those girls. It's like there's two of you.

I think you're making more of this than what's there.

Speaking of what's there, you ever notice something missing in your life?

I have everything I could possibly want.

Really? You have any friends?

Of course.

Look around. You have nobody in your life.

A total lie. I have tons of people.

You mean clients? You mean hockey players you see for an hour a week? You've made yourself into an island. Here's a question for you, Dave. If you died, could you find six pallbearers?

It should have been easy to rattle off six names. But he couldn't.

You're out of control.

I'm in total control. I've controlled it before. I stopped for a week once.

I should get you a medal.

That proves if I want to give it up I can.

But not tonight, right, Dave?

Stop it!

New girls arriving all the time. Never the same girl twice, ain't that right, Dave? I mean, unlike your wife. Same old, same old.

Hope is a great person.

Have a look at the new crop. You know you want to check them out.

He drowned out the voice by looking at the new wave of girls available for the night. There was one 15 minutes away. Far enough from home, yet close enough to visit her before hockey. He met her at a hotel. After they finished, he sat on his side of the bed dumbfounded. He really couldn't get rid of it. It was all so split up inside his mind. Part wanting to be free of all this. Part wanting to justify it and call it the new normal.

He hated that he couldn't control it—that it was bigger than him. He hated the guilt. Hated lying to his wife. Hated not being able to shut off his conscience.

Why do I have such remorse?

Who cares? Why would you let something as stupid as this bother you?

I … I don't know. I want to stop and yet I want to continue.

"Have a great rest of the evening," the young girl said. No names. No discussion. Who cares about her anyways? She wasn't really a person. Just some new body in town. Out with the old and in with the new.

"Why do you girls put your pictures up on the internet?" he asked.

Okay, trouble customer. Just get him out the door.

"Sorry?"

He swore at her. "You're not sorry." He finished getting dressed. "You're a low-life."

She kept her eyes down. She'd been through this before. All guys were thrilled when they came in. Not all of them were so thrilled when the reality of the money or their conscience or whatever set in afterwards. And they felt the weight of reality, which they had so desperately wanted to escape, begin to sink in again.

He stood up at the same time she did. They bumped into each other. In a fit of rage, he swore at her again and pushed her. She tripped and crashed to the ground. She turned over and looked at him with eyes full of fear. Smart girl that she was. If he was going to attack, she might as well be as prepared as she could be.

A wave of reality suddenly washed over him. It was as if his other self was suddenly transported into a room with a girl that he had just hurt. *What have I done?* He reached back for the door, opened it, and hurried down the hall towards the elevator. The place felt like a maze of dead ends. He made it through the lobby and got into his car.

Good going, Dave. Wow. You're a real hero. Yup, you got it all under control. You hit a teenage girl. Nothing to look at here, people. Move along. Move along.

Dave gripped the steering wheel. What just happened in there? It occurred to him that her bodyguard might not be too happy with the way he had dealt with her. He drove off. Then pulled into a parking lot at a mall in the vicinity of his house.

He looked at his hands, then tilted his head away from the rear-view mirror to make sure he wouldn't see his reflection.

That got a little out of hand. But, you know, hockey games have fights too, right?

Oh God. What have I become? He took in a deep breath. *This has gone on long enough. I'm out. I'm stopping.*

I'm sorry, what? Stop? Yeah, that's not exactly in the contract.

I don't care. I'm not doing this ever again.

I'm touched by your sentiments, Dave. Really. Got me right there. But you see, you don't actually possess the ability to stop. So, the wanting is one thing, but the stopping, well, you don't have it in you, Dave.

I'm filled with guilt.

Guilt? Well, Dave, why didn't you say so? We can get rid of the guilt.

I want this out of my life.

Let's continue down that guilt path. You want to be rid of the guilt, right?

Yes.

Fine. Here's how you do it. Go visit another girl.

What? That's what I'm trying to stop doing.

As luck would have it, that's also how you get rid of the guilt.

That doesn't make any sense. Why would I go back to what makes me feel guilty in the first place?

Why do you think alcoholics keep drinking? Because it makes sense?

I'd just be going around in circles.

Circles? Oh, I think you're missing the point, Dave. You aren't going in circles. You're spiralling down. We're making our way to the bottom. Figure it out, Dave. You're not getting out. Got it?

chapter thirty-one

Joy sat together with Samantha, Adrian, Desi and Elle in the small ready room. It connected to a large hall where media, members of Parliament, NGOs and police gathered to hear the testimonies. Joy glanced into the hall and saw it filled to capacity. Bright lights for the cameras. A buzz of anticipation.

She turned back to her girls. It took an incredible amount of courage to be able to face people and talk about what happened in their lives. She thought of Joel's words. *What if the reason they aren't on board is because they don't understand?* She hoped this would help. She hoped a living, breathing survivor telling them about human trafficking would help people understand.

"I'm so proud of each of you," Joy said. "All set?" They nodded. Joy led them in a brief prayer. She opened the door.

As they walked into the hall they heard the various conversations end and felt the focus shift onto them. Samantha had seen the room earlier when it was empty. It hadn't seemed so big then. Now that it was filled with so many people, she felt a rush of nervousness come over her.

Joy walked to the podium.

"Thank you for coming. Thank you for taking the time to hear the testimonies of survivors of human trafficking. Today you're going to hear first-hand about the dangers Canadian girls are facing. You'll hear about the unimaginable terrors they are put through by their traffickers. And you will hear how this entire trafficking network is fuelled by Canadian men willing to purchase sex that keeps Canadian girls enslaved."

She looked out into the audience. Saw Joel and Karen as well as other staffers at the front. Marian, her faithful assistant from Winnipeg, also came to show his support. Looking farther out she saw Thomas, the member of Parliament who had begged her not to bring this issue forward. Ian, the other MP whom she had threatened to go into his riding if he didn't vote for her, sat in the back, arms crossed. She admitted to herself that her tactics might have been a bit rough. They made eye contact.

"We are about to vote on Bill C-268. It's our goal that, after hearing the messages today, you will get the word out that we need to support this bill and stand up for the rights of Canadian girls."

Joy introduced Elle first. She came to the podium and read a prepared statement, as all of them would. How many hours had they pored over these speeches? So many tears. So many memories they had to relive.

"Sexual exploitation is a human rights crisis for women and girls," Elle said. "The harm of sexual exploitation extends throughout our whole nation. It begins with the individual, extends to the community, and then to the country. Trafficking restricts women's freedoms and citizenship rights. If women are treated as commodities, they are consigned to second-class citizenship. A country cannot be a true democracy if its citizens are treated as commodities. I stand before you as a survivor of the sex trade, echoing the experience of hundreds of women who cannot be here today.

"Prostitution in Canada today is organized by criminals—namely, the mafias and gangs that operate the global underground economy, dealing for profit in drug and human trafficking. In my 10 years of experience, I have never not worked for organized crime and gangs.

"Highly organized groups have infiltrated essential social systems, such as licensing and government agencies and police forces, where they have built influential relationships with officials within these systems. These hidden power structures keep prostituted women and girls acutely vulnerable to continued abuse and exploitation."

Elle sat down. Adrian came up next. She looked out to the crowd and found it hard to make out faces with all those lights shining on her. When her eyes adjusted, she saw a sea of people. And she hoped her words would build a correct framework in their minds of how to think about human trafficking.

"Thank you to each of you for being here. I also want to thank Joy Smith for her fight to bring this here, not only for women like me but also for up and coming generations."

The formal introductions were the easy part. Now came the real message. Each time she shared her story, each time she talked about her past, she found herself healing, growing stronger and becoming freer. Instead of weighing her down, she discovered that the shackles of her past life in human trafficking were being turned into evidence to support her story and to encourage others not to follow the same path.

"I was sexually abused as a child and abused by many men as a young woman, something that clouded my judgment and ability to make healthy choices. I had no sense of self-worth and was used to being taken against my will, so getting paid for it seemed like a good deal.

"I have known and worked with hundreds of girls in the industry and have not met one girl who did not suffer some form of abuse before entering into the sex trade."

She moved her discussion to the johns who fuel the industry.

"I believe john school should be mandatory," she said, referring to one-day seminars for men who are caught attempting to purchase sex. Johns are given the option of having their picture appear in the next day's paper or attending john school where survivors of human trafficking explain the reality victims face in being forced to service men.

"I have taught in john schools across Ontario for many years," she said. "I can tell you that this fight is about changing the mindset of men. Men truly believe that prostitution is a case of two consenting adults. They have no clue why or how a woman entered to begin with or if she even is of age. They don't know the domino effect it has on her life or even on his own life, or his wife's life or his kids' lives. The men become oblivious to it. After I speak in john schools, I have men coming up to me and apologizing, some of them even crying. John schools should be key in educating the men who buy sex. And we know they work. Eighty percent of men who go through john school stop paying for sex."

Desi approached the microphone. She began by describing how she was trafficked.

"I was lured and debased into prostitution at the age of 12 from a child welfare-run group home. I remained enslaved for 10 years in prostitution. I was sold to men who felt privileged to steal my innocence and invade my body. I was paraded like cattle in front of men who were able to purchase me, and the acts that I did were something no little girl should ever have to endure here in Canada, the land of the free.

"Because of the men, I cannot have a child normally. To this day I have nightmares. Sometimes I sleep with the lights on. My trauma is deep, and I sometimes feel as though I'm frozen—or even worse, I feel damaged and not worthy.

"I was traded in legal establishments, street corners, and strip clubs. I even had a few trips across the Great Lakes servicing shipmen at the age of 13. The scariest thing that happened to me was being held captive for a period of 43 hours and raped and tortured repeatedly at 14 years of age by a sexual predator who preyed on exploited girls."

Samantha came up last. Her fingers trembled as she held her paper. She blinked away the film of tears, focusing on her words.

"I was lured into human trafficking through the internet. I met someone online. He made me feel special. He listened to me. He was patient. Never pushy. I later learned that he had reached out to hundreds and hundreds of girls across Canada. This is a common practise among many traffickers. What started out as a fantasy turned into a nightmare. He slowly pushed me into having sex for money. I never saw a penny. I was abused and beaten, and many times I thought I would die. I wanted to believe the best of my trafficker. I had wanted to leave but felt compelled to stay for fear of what would happen if I didn't. I eventually escaped because my trafficker died in a knife fight. My best friend was not so lucky. She had tried to leave, and he strangled her to death with an extension cord.

"Girls like me are being exploited all across Canada. We are young and impressionable, and we are looking for love just like every other girl out there. I am asking for your help to stand against the exploitation of the young, poor and vulnerable by the richer, older and more powerful. I am asking for your support in this bill."

For the next half hour Joy fielded questions, which she and the survivors took turns answering. She took notice of the reactions of the members of Parliament, particularly those who were opposed to the bill. It disappointed her that many of those who opposed her bill had chosen not to show up.

Joy closed the official part of the event by thanking everyone for coming and for thanking the survivors for their courage to share their stories. Many reporters gathered around for individual comments from her and the survivors. Eventually the room began to thin out, and the mood returned to that of a quiet, empty place, giving no indication of what had just occurred, much the way a lake shows no signs that a boat has passed through it.

A writer approached Joy and asked questions. He then asked if he could speak with one of the survivors. Samantha was nearest. After introductions, he asked if she wanted something to drink. She said she was fine with her water bottle.

"Where would you like to sit?" he asked.

"Anywhere."

He motioned to two red chairs near the front. She nodded. He pulled the chair out for her. They sat down.

"Thank you for meeting with me, Samantha."

"It's no problem."

"I really appreciated what you said. I can't imagine the courage it must have taken to share your story the way you did." She nodded, feeling at ease in his presence. "I confess I'm quite new to human trafficking. I need your help to understand some things, if that's all right?"

"Of course."

"You wanted to leave your trafficker and yet you felt compelled to stay with him. Can you help me understand that?"

"It's a process," she said. "When you're a young girl you want to fall in love. You want acceptance. You want affirmation. Somebody comes along, and you form a connection. Sometimes that connection happens quickly. Other times it forms over weeks or even months. Either way, you get this love from him—what you think is love—and you'll do whatever it takes to keep that. You throw out your objectivity. But he's playing you. They're very skilled at being able to figure out who they can turn. The girl who might not be fitting in at school. The girl who's having trouble at home. The girl who might be looking for a little more adventure. The girl who has been abused in the past." Her voice trailed off as she spoke those last words. The writer didn't push.

"And yet even when you're doing something you don't want to, you feel a certain connection," the writer said.

"Yeah. Look, the girls who are trapped in this—it's not about being chained to a bed."

"Really?"

"That's out there. But it's such a small, small percentage. The vast majority of us don't need the chains."

The writer took notes in a black notebook, making sure she was finished before asking his next question. "Can you help me understand that?" he asked, trying to think through how traffickers managed to exert control over their victims.

"He was evil. I knew it. His threats of killing me prevented me from leaving. But I still had this connection to him. Like once he got into my heart and mind I formed this bond with him. I trusted him. But he abused that trust and edged me closer and closer to having sex with him. Then when he turned me, that bond was still there. I still believed he loved me. And I wanted to stick with him."

They both paused. His mind turned over the information he heard from her and from the other girls. Then a connection was made. Something he had read about years ago. And now, here, it seemed perhaps to connect exactly with what Samantha was saying.

"Is this Stockholm syndrome?" he asked.

Her eyes softened. She felt the validation that comes when somebody really understands the other person. "That's exactly what it is," she said.

Stockholm syndrome is a condition where victims develop strong bonds with their captors as a survival strategy. It was named after a bank robbery attempt in 1973 in Stockholm, Sweden, where a bank robber took four hostages. After the hostages were released, none of them would testify against the would-be robbers, and they even defended their actions. The syndrome is difficult to understand because victims act exactly opposite of the way one would expect them to.

But why?

Researchers into Stockholm syndrome believe that victims develop these bonds with their captors and negative feelings towards police not because they actually agree with their captors but because they force themselves to agree with them as a survival method. Their need to survive outweighs their hatred of their captors. They would rather live under false pretenses than die under the truth. But the victims don't just pretend to like their captors. They actually force themselves to genuinely like them out of a fear that if they fake it, their captor might notice and punish them for their deception.

"I was sure he would kill me if I didn't do exactly what I was told. I became like a little girl. I couldn't speak. I wouldn't eat unless told to. I would have to ask permission to go to the bathroom. I was a robot in his control. He would throw me a bag of takeout and I would suddenly think he was the best guy in the world because he didn't kill me, and not only that, he gave me food to eat. So in my mind he was a great guy."

She closed her eyes. Not out of agony. But out of relief. She wanted that feeling of knowing in her consciousness that she was in Ottawa. In a room with a decent guy. And not in any of those hundreds of other rooms with any of those thousands of other guys.

"Traffickers can either be solo operators or they can be part of organized crime. Either way, they know what they're doing. They prey upon us girls. They use our naïveté against us. We trust them. Looking for the love we so desperately want. But they use that against us. We keep serving them because we need the love, and they keep using us and getting rich off of our misery. We realize we have to play a game with them in order to survive. And we don't even know we're doing it. I didn't until I got out and went through a program. I looked back and realized how I had been manipulated. You get it?"

He nodded, so she continued.

"That's why the physical chains aren't necessary. He had me. Mentally and emotionally. And all I could do was to pray to be rescued and pray that I lived the next 24 hours. I lucked out. My trafficker died."

He put down his pen. The shock of the unimaginable evil Samantha had lived through ripped through his mind.

Samantha brushed her hair out of her face. "But you know, can I tell you something?"

He nodded. "Okay."

"The johns who use us are just as bad."

"As the traffickers?"

"The johns make it all possible. Their minds are all screwed up. They believe the stupidest lies. It's like inside their heads they have to justify what they're doing. I mean, get serious. What self-respecting 15-year-old is going to willingly have sex in an apartment? But they get around that by assuming every girl is 18. Then, they figure it's just money. It's helping her. It's paying her way through college. It's all a lie, but they'll convince themselves of anything because they want the sex so badly. Their minds just go crazy."

She took a drink from her water. "The traffickers are all wacked, too. Crazy, crazy people. They want money, and they figure the girl agreed to do this so she's getting what she deserved. Hello. You sold me on a dream that you would love me. You're older. You lied, knowing where this was leading. I was vulnerable, and you took advantage of me. But they don't care, because they need to convince themselves of a lie, that we wanted this. That way they can justify all the money they make."

She took in a breath. Paused a moment to clear her mind. "So you have the traffickers lying to us girls because they want money. And you have us girls forming a trauma bond with our traffickers because we want the love so badly and want to stay alive. And the johns convince themselves it's not hurting anyone, because they want to do it with a young girl. And that's the whole cycle. A cycle of lying. Everyone being deceived. Pretty sick, don't you think?"

He nodded, unable to respond while processing everything she was saying.

"And you have this bill that will put traffickers in jail for five years. It's great. But doesn't that tell you something?" He tried to piece together where she was going. "How sick have we gotten as a culture when a man forces a girl to be raped thousands of times, makes money off of her, and we're having a debate about whether he should be put in prison for five years. My God in heaven. How did we sink this low?"

Joy and the other survivors finished talking with the last reporters. They waited. Patiently. Not in a hurry to rush Samantha or him.

"Can I ask you one last question?"

"Sure."

"If there was one thing that would have made a difference—if there was one thing that would have prevented you from getting involved in being trafficked—what would it be?"

She responded so fast that it seemed to him she had long since concluded how all of this got started.

"If only my father would have paid more attention to me."

He felt his eyes begin to sting with tears forming. She took another drink of water and continued.

"Something happens when a daddy takes lots of time for his little girl. It's like there's this protective net that gets built around her. Enables her to feel real love. Enables her to spot creeps. But when Daddy's not around, or if there's sexual abuse, it's like that covering disappears and we're open prey. Every girl I've talked to—every single rescued victim, to a one—they all say the same thing. If only their dads would have taken more time with them. I'm not saying dads are always to blame. It's just what the girls I've talked to tell me."

She finished her water bottle.

"I want to thank you for your time, Samantha," he said. She could see he was visibly shaken.

"You heard more than you bargained for, I bet," she said with laugh.

How was it that a woman like this could have suffered so much and yet be the person before him today?

She raised her eyebrows and stood up. He stood as well. They hugged each other. It felt both strange and welcoming for Samantha. How many times had she been abused at the hands of so many men? And yet it felt somehow hopeful to be held, even just for a moment, by someone who only wanted to give, and not to take.

"Thank you again, Samantha."

"You have a chance to do something good," she said. "I'll hope you'll do that."

chapter thirty-two

Watching the fallen snow going by on the side of the Trans-Canada felt hypnotic for Abby. The simple and constant shade of white was a welcomed, if only temporary, change compared to the unending stress and worry of her life. She leaned back against her headrest. The new leather smell had long since disappeared. How many kilometres had they logged in this vehicle? She hated this car. It felt like a john that wouldn't leave her alone.

As they drove through Kenora, Ontario, and crossed the Manitoba border, Abby noticed the Trans-Canada signs change from Highway 17 to Highway 1. Looking farther out her window she saw the land stretch out as far as she could see. Snow covered the unending prairies like a massive blanket tucking in the soil until next year. She wanted Jake to stop the vehicle. Wanted to get out. Walk in the crunchy snow. Feel the wind. Experience the cold weather under the bright sunshine. Look around in every direction and not have anything impede her view.

To have sight without limit.

They passed the Perimeter Highway and entered Winnipeg. For most people, seeing the lights and buildings of the city brings relief that they're arriving at their destination. For Abby, it brought only fear and anxiety about whether she would be able to survive another city.

Decorative lights illuminated Portage Avenue in the festive spirit of Christmas. She had loved this time of year. She loved buying gifts, being in the hustle and bustle of the mall, hearing Christmas carols and feeling the excitement of setting up a Christmas tree. All of that was gone now. The anticipation she used to feel was now replaced with the hope of living to see another Christmas Day.

Jake fixed her up in a hotel downtown. She saw six guys that night. Saw more on Christmas Eve. She finished at two a.m., making it technically Christmas Day. Jake was nice enough to leave her a bottle of wine. She finished it. Lay down on the floor of the hotel. *Merry Christmas to you, God. The only thing I'm asking for this year is that you get me out of this. Please.*

She thought about all the Christmases she spent with her parents and grandparents. She remembered the feeling of coming downstairs and seeing the wrapped presents under the tree, and the smell of turkey dinner. That was back when life was simple. When it was predictable. She looked at the empty wine bottle. If only the alcohol could go on like the prairies and last forever. She rolled onto her back and looked up at the light. What a wonderful way to celebrate the birth of baby Jesus in a manger all those years ago.

New Year's went all night, as was expected. All of them drunk. All of them oblivious to her pain. She wondered if perhaps this trip across Canada would bring her different men. Good men. Men who would see through the fake facade and recognize her immediate peril. But the longer she did this, the more she gave up on someone rescuing her. So many people willing to take advantage of her. So many men willing to lie to themselves about what she was doing there. None willing to see her misery.

Jake moved her around from hotel to hotel and finally settled them into an apartment. They left on a warm February day, warm for Winterpeg anyway, and continued west. They passed through Brandon and crossed into Saskatchewan. Jake filled up at a gas station near Moosomin. Abby stared out the window, watching a man pumping gas into his black SUV, noticing an iron ring on his right hand. She wished she could get out, switch vehicles and switch back to her old life. If only it were that easy. Jake got back in. As they drove off she made brief eye contact with the stranger.

They set up shop in Regina. In March, he moved her up to Saskatoon. In April, he hauled her up to Edmonton, where they spent the next two months. He moved her around as much as he needed to. Too long in any location and people would get suspicious.

Hotels and apartments were the only real options. They both had their advantages and disadvantages. Apartments got tough because other renters could raise questions about why people were coming and going at all hours of the night. Busy hotels made it more possible for the johns to blend in. But paying in cash at the front desk was always a dead giveaway. So was trying to make Abby look older than she really was. Her age was an issue. But the real problem was her dead, vacant stare.

The vibrancy she once possessed had long since disappeared. Now, without makeup, she looked like she had walked out of a morgue. She was beaten down from exhaustion, depression, anxiety and fear. But what was a businessman like Jake to do? He had to keep the show going. And Abby's condition was nothing a good coat of cosmetics couldn't fix.

They moved down to Red Deer for a week. And at the end of June they made their way to Cowtown. Just in time for the Calgary Stampede.

Sporting events drew massive crowds of people from all over. Particularly men. Particularly men with money. Particularly men with money without their wives.

He rented two furnished apartments for the month. The owner showed them in. They made small talk. Just a couple of good ole rodeo fans in for the stampede. Some more friends would be coming in. The owner warned about making a mess. Jake assured them they wouldn't. The moment the owner left, Abby collapsed into bed. She didn't worry about locking her door.

She was pretty sure Jake had that covered.

Abby slept for six hours. It never seemed to help. She was in a perpetual state of stress and exhaustion—one that no amount of sleep could help. It was the feeling of Jake kicking the bed that woke her.

"Got something new for you," he said.

Abby sat up and stretched her neck to try to work out a kink that wouldn't seem to leave. Jake threw her a set of lingerie. Nothing new there. He told her to put it on. She did.

"Get out there and earn some money."

Get out there as in figuratively or literally? She stayed on the bed.

"Abby, get outside and walk the street. It's going to be crawling with guys."

A whole new wave of debasement pulsed through her body. How many levels of humiliation are there in this world? It was bad enough that all these guys were coming in one after another, city after city, province after province. Every one of them had decided to pay money for sex. She had a 100 percent success rate, if that's what it could be called, with guys paying to see her. But walking the street would be different. Most of those guys weren't going to pay for sex. She could already feel the stares. The judging. Especially from the wives. Looking at her like a whore trying to steal their husbands away for a night.

What to do? Argue with Jake? Reason with him?

This was going to be so unbelievably embarrassing. Unbearable shame at its very lowest. Jake saw the disgrace in her eyes. All the better. The lower you beat them down, the more likely they are not to run.

She changed. Took the elevator down. By herself. The doors opened. *I just want to die.* She walked through the lobby. Avoided eye contact with the crowds of people passing by. She walked through the glass doors. She'd had a dream once where she had forgotten to wear her clothes. But at least she could wake up from that. No such privilege here.

She stepped outside and wanted to disappear. She wanted to run in front of a car and fall into a coma. No one noticed her at first. But then it started. A group of college-age guys came by. They wore cowboy hats, big belt buckles and boots. The whole outfit.

"Hey, whore! Looking good. How much?"

They swore at her and called her names. That was bad, but it was their laughing that hurt her the most.

Husbands and wives walked past her. The wives pulled their husbands to cross on the other side of the street, shaking their heads. Yup. There were the stares. No words necessary. Eyes tell it all. *You sick slut, get off the street.*

People packed the sidewalk. She saw more guys laughing at her. Some called out humiliating offers. Fifty cents. A quarter.

There are so many of you, she thought. *So many of you on this street. Can one of you please help me? Please.*

More catcalls. More jeers. Guys passed by her.

Would any sane girl want to do this? I'm wearing lingerie, for crying out loud. Can even one of you—just one of you—please have the decency to help me?

Guys touched her. Grabbed her. Like she was a mannequin on display. But even mannequins in stores get treated better than she did alive on the streets. She gritted her teeth. How on earth do you try to look attractive when you feel so debased?

What about any of you women? You have to believe that no self-respecting girl wants to do this. Can you please just come over and ask me if I'm all right? You rich women have all these fancy houses in Calgary, don't you? All it takes is to ask me if I want out. I can be rid of this nightmare from hell in five minutes if you just ask me if I'm okay. Can you step out of your world for just a moment and be a good Samaritan?

But they didn't. The crowds kept passing her by. Some ignored her. Some looked at her. Some made jokes.

No one stopped.

At least not to help.

They aren't stopping, because you're pathetic. They know you want this. Admit it. You love Jake and you love doing this. This is what you are meant for.

It's so embarrassing.

You shouldn't have picked this then.

Please someone stop.

Stop wishing for them to stop. You and I both know what would happen if that fictitious good Samaritan stopped. You would change your mind. You would reject their help and keep doing this.

No, I wouldn't.

Oh, yes, you would. And do you know why?

Why?

Because deep down inside you know you're not worth anything else.

That's not true.

It's completely true. We've already had the boyfriend discussion. You know that you're not getting a guy after what you've done. You're not good enough to do anything else. That leaves you with walking the streets and sitting in hotels.

I want out.

You want in. You were meant for this. This is all you're good for.

She waited outside until the cover of darkness. Then the offers started getting serious, and she took guys upstairs.

The stampede couldn't end fast enough.

That evening, as she lay on the floor, she tried to wash away the anger she felt against all the people who turned a blind eye to her.

Not one. Not one of you in this city full of people bothered to stop? I get it for places when I am indoors and johns already have their brains so screwed up by the time they come to my door. But so many of you are decent people. Why didn't you stop to help me? Or do you live in your own glass cube as well, oblivious to what's going on around you, not wanting to interrupt your me-focused life? Or maybe ... maybe you just don't understand.

Is it as simple as that? Is it as simple as you needing a little education to see that a girl wearing lingerie and walking the streets is in need of help? Of your help? Is there no one out there to help me?

She found herself sinking into despair.

All right. Don't lose your mind. Don't lose hope. You can't count on people rescuing you. So what's next?

There is no next. Just fall in line and resolve yourself to doing this forever. See. Told you.

Abby struggled against the oppressive thoughts. She squinted and fought for all she was worth to focus on whatever speck of optimism she could find.

Okay. Okay, she thought, doing what she could to shake off the utter humiliation of today. *Calling my mom didn't work. Hoping for a good Samaritan didn't work. Think, Abby. Think.* She rubbed her forehead. Forced her mind to push through the depression, PTSD, anxiety, hurt, shame and anger.

Is there another way out?

chapter thirty-three

Even after all this time, Talia couldn't accept it.

She sat in the police office in Toronto. Her face revealed the exhaustion, worry and depression she had been fighting ever since she received that message from Abby. She found no safe place for her thoughts. It was as if her mind was running around on the second floor of a burning house with all the windows sealed shut and the staircase engulfed in flames. No matter where her thoughts went, she was greeted by one disaster worse than the last. Abby being raped. Abby crying for help with no one, especially not her mom, able to do anything for her. Abby dead in a garbage bin. And because there was no place for comfort, her mind continued to push the reality of Abby's trafficking away, in a vain attempt to escape the torture of reality.

Her heart was riddled with guilt. *If only. If only. If only.* There were times when she attempted to convince herself that no matter how hard you try, you can't control all your circumstances. But the discussion always proved pointless. In the end, somewhere out there, someone was making money off her daughter. Somewhere out there, men were lining up to use her. Men whom she had probably passed on the street.

An RCMP officer sat beside her, looking over Abby's file. She carried the tough yet compassionate combination cops need to have in dealing with both criminals and victims. They discussed the online searches they were doing for Abby. Talked, without the specifics, obviously, about the informants and undercover operations in finding trafficked girls. She knew the overwhelming odds against missing youth being found. What side of that statistics line was Abby going to be on? All Talia could do was replay the parking lot scene over and over in her mind. She had been so close. So very, very close.

The officer handed her a box of tissues. Talia thanked her for all the time they'd committed on and off work hours to finding Abby.

Talia stood and left the office, walking through the crowded lobby past other people whose lives had also been crushed by evil.

———

Joy stood at her desk in her private office, strategizing about her bill. Her open door to the rest of the office area brought in the commotion of staffers and volunteers. Bill C-268 had reported back from committee and had been added to the bottom of the private members' bill list. This meant that the third and final reading, consisting of two debates of one hour each, would get pushed to October and February.

Joel had pitched the prime minister's office about bringing Bill C-268 forward earlier for debate and a final vote. It was suspected that the Bloc would vote against the bill. So bringing the bill forward would show the Bloc being on record voting against minimum sentences for human traffickers just before the next election. The PMO warmed up to the idea of moving private members' bills forward, allowing members to switch spots.

Ed Fast, the MP for Abbotsford, BC, exchanged his spot on the order paper so that Joy's bill could be debated sooner. Ed understood the battle Joy faced. Three years earlier, Fast introduced his own private member's bill to increase the maximum sentence from five to ten years for luring a child over the internet for sexual purposes. Parliament passed the bill.

Jeff Watson, MP for Essex in Ontario, also exchanged his spot.

The help from these two members allowed the bill to be debated and voted on within two weeks instead of four months. It gave the green light for Joy and her team to make all the final preparations for the third reading.

Joy assumed that the Bloc with 52 seats would oppose the bill en masse, save for her friend Maria. That meant that the 50 percent plus one of the

307 seats (308 minus the Speaker)—or a minimum of 154 votes—would need to come from the Conservatives, Liberals and NDP.

Her phone rang.

"Joy Smith."

"You're going to take down that bill of yours," the voice said. It didn't sound like a member of Parliament. A disgruntled citizen? Or maybe …

"Who is this?"

"It doesn't matter who this is. There are a lot of people who don't like you, Smith."

"I have a lot of work to do, so if you're a reporter—"

"I'm not a reporter. I'm in the business you're trying to shut down." He swore at her.

Joy paused and gathered her thoughts. "If someone were trafficking your daughter, would you allow it?"

"You take your bill down, or I'm going to find you and kill you."

"You're pathetic and a coward!" Joy shouted. "We're coming after guys like you, and you're all going to get what you deserve!"

Joy slammed the phone down. She looked back at her computer screen. Only then did she realize what she had done. Had her response unnecessarily aggravated the caller? Joel came in.

"Everything okay?"

She told him. "You can't back down to threats," she said, turning back to her computer.

She continued working.

That evening Joy left the office late as usual. She exited the parliament building and walked towards her car. As much as she wanted to block the threats out of her mind, she heard the caller's words playing over in her mind. Like he was approaching right behind her, saying it over and over again to her. *You take your bill down, or I'm going to find you and kill you.* She quickened her pace and glanced back to confirm that her ears weren't wrong in hearing silence. Seeing no one coming after her, she continued to her car, clicked unlock long before she got there and locked the doors the moment she was in. She started her car and drove past security, glancing at the rear-view mirror.

Joy entered her apartment. Put on a kettle of hot water for her evening tea. Sat down on her couch. Folded her hands. Prayed for strength. Prayed for the bill.

And for the vote that would decide it all.

In a surprising turn of events, the Bloc Quebecois introduced a motion to remove the mandatory minimum sentences of the bill. They had tried to accomplish this at the committee stage but failed. As such, the entire first hour of debate was dedicated to their plan to gut the essence of C-268.

Joel and Joy reviewed her speech. On September 15, Joy defended her bill in the House.

"This evening we are debating a motion by the Bloc Quebecois to gut the heart of the bill—to remove the mandatory minimums that form the intent and scope of the bill. Bill C-268 was drafted with one clear intention: to create a separate offence of the traffickers of children in Canada and to ensure that the penalties reflect the gravity of the crime.

"Let us be clear about one thing: the opposition of the Bloc Quebecois to mandatory minimums for the trafficking of minors is not only reprehensible, it is unacceptable in our country. To openly oppose serious penalties for those who sell and abuse the bodies of minors does not just suggest approval for this horrific abuse of human rights, it virtually endorses this grave form of exploitation.

"Canadian girls and boys from across our country are being sold for sexual exploitation and forced labour. This harsh reality exists even in Quebec, regardless of whether the Bloc acknowledges it or not.

"Years ago, a member of the British Parliament, William Wilberforce, a great abolitionist and personal hero of mine, captured the essence of what motivates me to combat this modern-day slavery. He said: 'Never, never will we desist till we have … extinguished every trace of this bloody traffic, of which our posterity looking back to the history of these enlightened times, will scarce believe that it has been suffer to exist so long a disgrace and dishonour to this country.'

"History will remember those who fought against this evil trade and it will certainly not forget those who are complacent when faced with it."

The NDP justice critic Joe Comartin also called out the Bloc's intentions.

"It is important to know that the motion brought by the Bloc is really an attempt to gut this bill. I do not think there is any other way of addressing it. It does not fit the essence of what the debate is about."

The second hour of debate took place two weeks later. The final vote was scheduled the following day.

That morning, Joy got up early. In those early hours she prayed for success and prayed for those enslaved in Canada. At the office, Joy sent out an email to all the members of Parliament with a message from a survivor of human trafficking who would be sitting in the gallery that evening watching the vote.

As a person who has experienced this horrific crime first-hand, and as a person who is now helping other victims by giving them hope and courage to go to the police and give a statement, facing the possibility that their keepers will walk or get a light sentence is the hardest part of my job.

Looking in a victim's eye, and telling her that the police will do everything they can, but it is now up to the law and the court system to make sure that these guys will never hurt her again can be really scary to rely on.

Trafficking drugs and guns gets tougher sentences than trafficking a person.

I truly believe that if it was your daughter or sister, you would also feel that something is wrong with that picture. You have a chance today to change that. We, as victims, and the police officers are relying on your decision today.

Please give us hope and reasons to be brave and strong for giving a statement and testifying. Please reward the police officers who are doing a really hard work by giving them tougher laws to work with.

You have the power to do that!

The members gathered in the House of Commons. This was it. Yes, the Senate would be next if the bill passed the House. But it would be rare indeed if the appointed officials of the Senate overturned a decision by the elected officials in the House on an issue such as this. Joy made eye contact with the justice minister. She admired him and admired all those who were willing to learn about human trafficking and who were willing to believe they might not have had all the facts to make an informed decision. He nodded to her.

The House first voted on the Bloc's motion to gut the bill. The motion was defeated.

The Speaker of the House took the vote on Bill C-268.

The bill passed with 239 in favour and 46 opposed, with 24 who were absent from the vote. The Conservatives and Liberals all voted in favour of the bill. Nearly all of the NDP voted in favour, with 3 voting against. All of the Bloc voted against the bill. Some abstained from voting, including Maria Mourani, who had repeatedly supported Joy.

The House of Commons cheered for the bill's success. Members of Parliament gathered around Joy to congratulate her. As the crowd dispersed into the lobby, Joy looked out at all the seats. It had been a long journey that started all those years ago in her kitchen when her son Edward came over. He had been so distraught, so burdened with the evils of human trafficking. And now all these years later the journey was complete.

Or was it?

What a strange feeling. To come this far. To know you have won. To know Canada has won. And yet she had the distinct feeling that somehow this was really just the beginning.

The justice minister approached. Joy turned. He stretched out his hand. Joy shook it. "You were right, and I was wrong," he said.

Joy felt a sense of connectedness in that moment. Joel was correct in his assessment. It wasn't that people, most people, simply opposed it. They just didn't know. And once she explained the facts, they understood.

"Thank you for your support," Joy said.

"Thanks for your ... tenacity in all of this."

"If that's what you want to call it," Joy said.

They both smiled. They hadn't been smiling all those months ago in his office when things got heated. Tempers flared. People blasted each other with harsh words. Girls were dying, and Joy did not have time to be concerned about egos. Now here they were. In an otherwise empty House of Commons.

The two of them walked out together.

chapter thirty-four

A bby was always relieved to leave a city.
But the relief was soon replaced with the dread of arriving at a new one. The relative victory of surviving Calgary would soon be eclipsed by wondering if she would make it through Vancouver. Strictly speaking, Jake only promised to take her across Canada. What did he say? *Here's what's fun. I say we get out of Montreal. We go out to Halifax. Then we make a trip across Canada. What do you say?* He never promised to take her back.

The flashing lights grew brighter as they approached. The familiar combination of red and blue caused her to look closer in her side mirror, trying to make out the reflection through the pouring rain. Jake took his foot off the accelerator, hoping the police cruiser would pass by. It did not.

"These guys hate you, baby," Jake said, signalling to the right, then pulling over onto the shoulder. Always the law-abiding citizen.

This is it. This is your chance. Tell the cop everything.

Are you kidding me? That cop will just use you and make life even worse for you.

Worse? How could anything on earth be worse than this?

Seriously? Things could be a lot worse. Does Jake give you food? Yes. Does he give you a place to sleep? Yes. Does he let your ride with him? Yes. No cop will do that.

"You just tell them the truth, Abby. Tell them you're my girlfriend and we're going to Vancouver."

Jake rolled the window down. A young rain-drenched officer approached.

"You have a tail light out," the officer said. Jake noticed the cop's Glock out of the corner of his eye.

"Oh, I'm sorry about that, officer. Must have gotten kicked in last night. I don't remember hitting anything."

"Where you headed?"

"Vancouver."

This is your chance. Do it. Say it now.

That cop will pick out his Glock and gun you down right where you sit. You want that?

Excuse me? A cop shoot a girl in the car? Are you crazy?

The cop looked at her. But she didn't look back. Not directly. Outside of her working hours she never looked anyone in the eye. If she did look another man in the eye it meant she wanted to leave Jake for the other guy. A mistake like that would cost Abby a fierce beating.

Or worse.

"Ma'am, are you all right?"

No! No, I'm not. He's going to kill me if I ask for help. Wait, won't you kill me too?

For crying out loud. He's a cop! He suspects something is wrong. He's got a gun. It's there to shoot Jake if need be. Not you.

Abby smiled her shy, slightly crooked smile. She looked over but stared at the steering wheel instead of meeting his gaze, to fulfill her obligation of following Jake's no-eye-contact rule.

"I'm fine, thank you," she lied. "How are you?"

The cop went back to his vehicle.

The door is open, Abby. Click the handle and run for it.

You unbuckle your seatbelt, and Jake will strangle you to death before the cop gets back.

The cop returned. "Here's your ticket," he said.

"I'll get it fixed in Vancouver, if that's okay?"

Nice guy, eh, Abby? Asks the cop if it's okay to get his tail light fixed but doesn't get around to asking if it's okay to traffic you across the country.

This is your chance. You said you were looking for one.

"Safe travels."

"Thank you, Officer."

The officer left. Jake put the Mustang in gear. "Good job, Abby."

Yeah. Real good.

They took the Trans-Canada though Kananaskis into Banff. She leaned her head out the window. The soothing pale-blue water of the Bow River drew her in, making her wish she could get on a canoe and paddle as far away from Jake as she could. The noonday sky had cleared, allowing the sun to reflect off the snow-covered mountain peaks. Evergreen trees stretched out between the Bow and the jagged Rockies. She was sure this was supposed to look amazing, that it was supposed to make her feel in awe. But instead of feeling she was really there, it seemed to her like she was looking at a postcard. Or sitting inside that familiar glass cube. Where everyone and everything moved on, but she was trapped in her own world. Like everything was fake.

Dear God, get me out of here. If you can create these mountains, you can get me out of here.

They passed through Lake Louise, a quieter and less commercial town than Banff. They ate lunch at a picnic table. Hamburger and fries for her. The sun felt good against her aching body. She breathed in the clean, cool mountain air, wishing it could reach inside her and clean her thoughts and her past as well. She stretched her neck, but the never-ending kink was giving her a headache. They got back in the car and passed through Revelstoke, Salmon Arm and Kamloops.

Driving south from Kamloops they took Highway 5 all the way down to Hope—the iconic city where, as her dad had taught her, *Rambo: First Blood,* starring Sylvester Stallone, had been filmed. She could use Rambo right about now. Ask him to wrap that bullet belt around his arm and unload his M60 right into Jake's body.

Was it wrong to wish for that?

They transferred onto the Trans-Canada. Passed through Chilliwack, then Abbotsford, and then on to their great reward in Vancouver.

"We did it, Abby. Abracadabra."

Right. Abracadabra. Would be better if she could make herself disappear.

They parked on Cordova and walked onto the waterfront past Canada Place. Up ahead they found a restaurant. Jake told her where to sit. She did. He ordered food. No lobster. No checkered cloth. Not like in Halifax. But lots and lots of water in front of her. She watched a father and mother playing with their little boy in a red sweater near the water.

"I'm going to go down to the water," she said. That was different. She could feel Jake's thought. *Did I say you could go?* It didn't matter. She was working tonight. It was a public place. He couldn't afford to beat her. Not now.

She walked down to the water. Taking off her shoes she felt the sand between her toes. The little boy in red laughed and jumped up into his father's arms. Abby's heart was crushed within her. She turned away, hoping to relieve the weight she felt and the tightness of breath.

Reaching down, she dipped her finger in the water. She brought it to her tongue and tasted the salt. It reminded her of doing the same thing in Halifax. Coast to coast. She had survived it. "This is going to be a trip of a lifetime," Jake had said. He was right about that.

Only a shell of her had survived the trip from the Atlantic all the way to the Pacific. Her body, at least, was intact. That's what was most important for Jake. And for thousands of others she had the misfortune of meeting along the way. Much of the rest of her seemed to have slowly dissolved along the Trans-Canada.

Not one. Not a single person had reached out to help her, except perhaps that rookie cop in Calgary. Thinking back on that moment troubled her. Even when presented with an opportunity for escape, something strange went on inside her mind, and she didn't take it. Was that her last chance? A gift of a get-out-of-jail-free card that she turned down? If she got another shot, she would have to work on combatting that feeling of shirking away from a rescue opportunity. She would have to fight that debilitating chain Jake had tightened around her mind.

Looking out at the ocean, she wondered what it would be like to get on a boat, sail out and be free again. What would it be like to be rid of him? And would that be enough? She wanted more than that. Being rid of him would not be the only goal. She also wanted to become someone again outside of him. Away from him. Without him—

"Abby, time to go."

Of course it was.

He rented a furnished apartment on a monthly lease not far from the waterfront. It didn't have a view of the ocean. No point in spending his hard-earned money on unnecessary frills. They bought toiletries, makeup, granola bars, booze and drugs. He sat down on the couch and poured them both a glass of rosé wine. She guzzled hers, then thought about doing a line of cocaine. But it was too early. She knew it. If she did she'd need more of something else—that rainbow-inducing drug—later this evening. For now she had to get the image of the little child being held by his father out of her mind. The alcohol worked its way into that place where it does its job of numbing pain. She walked over to the balcony, opened the door and looked down at the street below.

You could end it all right here.

No.

No? How are you going to escape?

Not this way.

So you want to, what, go across Canada over and over again? Make the trip back and forth and back and forth? Keep dipping your finger in each ocean until you forget which one is which?

He's not going to win.

He already has. You had your chance when he sent the very first message. You had your chance again when you left school to go with him on a romantic getaway to Moe-ray-ahl. Again in Halifax. Again with the cop in Cowtown. You want to get out and you want to stay. And you've proven that in the end, you choose to stay. Makes sense. After all, he's going to follow through on that promise to give you a great life. Isn't he, Abby?

Glancing down again, she spit and watched it fly down and hit the pavement.

Abby walked back inside. Jake had pounded back a number of drinks. He looked so chill and relaxed. How was that possible? He looked at her, shook his head and cursed at her.

"You're so useless, you know that? Completely. You're pathetic, Abby. Everything about you. Be thankful you found me. You never would have found another guy. Nobody would ever have taken you. And especially not now. There are used car lots. And then there are cars you have no chance of bringing back to life. Know what I mean?"

THE TRUE STORY OF CANADIAN HUMAN TRAFFICKING

The words wouldn't have bothered her so much if they didn't already echo the ones she was hearing over and over again in her own mind.

He approached her. Kissed her. "Time to get ready, baby. Guys will be showing up in an hour."

He received a call. Left the apartment to take it. That was odd.

She fought through her exhaustion to find a rare moment to think and evaluate why she hadn't left when she had the opportunity. Could she still turn him around? Could this all still have a happy ending? Was she addicted to the drugs? Was she addicted to that other person she could become whenever she was high so she could dissociate herself from all of this? Or was she more addicted to the idea of what they could still have together?

She washed her face. Steadied her resolve. Looked up in the mirror.

No way. No way was she going to go all the way back to Halifax.

Somehow. Someway. This was going to end.

chapter thirty-five

Joy's steps on the hospital floor echoed down the hall, stopping when she reached Bart's room. She opened the door and saw him lying on the bed. He looked so exhausted. *Is this what a person looks like when they get near the end?*

She put on a brave face, though in her heart she wanted to cry. She kissed him on the forehead. After sitting down in the chair beside him, she pulled herself in closer so he would not have to strain to meet her gaze. He smiled in a way that looked painful and asked how she was doing. She deflected the question at first, wanting instead to inquire about his health. But he asked again. She waited, deciding whether to be strong or honest.

"I'm worried," Joy confessed.

"You shouldn't worry."

"I know. But I do."

"I'm not afraid of death," Bart said. "I know where I'm going. Whatever happens, we will meet again someday in heaven."

It was true. She knew it. So why didn't that make her feel better?

"There are people praying for you all across Canada," she whispered. She chose her words carefully. Not knowing which ones might be the last she would share with him.

"Tell them I appreciate them all."

"I will," Joy said, brushing away the first hint of tears forming. "I wish I could do something for you, Bart."

Bart tilted his head. Thought. "I could really use some juice."

Joy smiled. "All right," she said. "But you're not dying on me while I'm gone, all right?"

"I won't."

"Promise?"

"Promise."

Joy walked down to her car and drove to the nearby supermarket. She looked through the refrigerated section for the flavours he liked. A mother and her two children wearing soccer uniforms walked by. In the section beside her a young man stacked meat into the display case. Everyone carried on with their lives. How different everything seems when the life of a loved one is hanging in the balance.

The cashier had to ask twice how she would pay. She opened her wallet and used her credit card. She carried her bags to her car under dark skies. After placing her groceries in the back seat, she got behind the wheel and started the engine. She wanted to sleep and get some much-needed rest. Then she wondered if that would help her see this any differently.

How could she possibly?

Her phone rang. Not the ideal time for a call. She glanced down and saw Joel's number.

"Hello," Joy said.

"It passed! You did it, Joy! You did it!"

Did what?

"Joel?"

"It's official, Joy! Congratulations."

The juxtaposition between what she and Bart were facing in the hospital and whatever good news Joel was sharing proved to be too great at the moment.

"What's official?"

"What's official?" Joel asked. "Your bill! It passed the third reading in the Senate! It received royal assent. Your bill has become law!"

No more hurdles. Official victory.

Joy was so consumed with Bart's illness that she had completely forgotten that today was the day.

"Thanks for letting me know, Joel," she said. "Thank you for all your help. I couldn't have done it without you."

He picked up on her tone.

"How is Bart?"

She didn't respond. Not at first. "We can use your prayers," she said, doing the best she could to sound positive despite the circumstances.

Joel's soft, even tone matched his character. "We'll continue."

Joy pressed her lips together. Waited. "Thank you."

"Please say hi to Bart for me."

"I will. And thank you, Joel. For everything."

"You got it."

She returned to the hospital and gave Bart his juice.

"Did I pick the right one?" she asked. Bart nodded.

He'd been through an unsuccessful run of chemo. Radiation had been unsuccessful as well. And if the doctors' assessment was correct—and she hoped it was not—the stem-cell transplant had not worked either. They were out of medical options.

Joy and Bart received a call to see the doctors at Cancer Care. Bart had lost 40 pounds. He often felt weak. A once energetic, strongly built man was now reduced to a walking skeleton.

The drive there felt longer than it was. When you're younger and heading out on a date, you can't get there fast enough. But as the years pass and the destination becomes a face-to-face visit with doctors after they've tried everything they knew of, you lose the desire to get there quickly.

Walking up to the counter, Joy wondered who felt weaker, she or Bart. They sat down in the waiting room and were called in shortly after arriving.

Please let it be months. Not weeks. I need time to prepare. And not days. Definitely don't let it be days remaining.

They sat down across from the doctor's desk. How many times had Joy been to see members of Parliament on this same side of the desk trying to garner their support for the bill? She had used statistics, the need to protect children and, yes, even threats. She had an arsenal at her disposal then. But here, now, she couldn't influence the outcome.

The doctor looked down at his folder, reviewing something for what seemed like a long time before delivering the news. He wore glasses and a blue shirt, without the typical white doctor-type coat. Joy pegged him to be in his late forties. Maybe early fifties. These guys looked younger and younger every time she came here.

"Bart, you are in complete remission."

He didn't just say that. Couldn't have. Walls that had been closing in on her suddenly stopped. She could breathe again.

Words so different from what Joy was expecting to hear.

"All of our tests show that your cancer is gone. There's no sign of the tumour. No evidence of disease at all."

That's the problem when things are too good to be true. You just have that nagging sense that maybe you didn't hear right. That maybe you heard only what you wanted to hear, and not the real facts.

They thanked the doctor. She felt shell-shocked. Her number had been called again.

Driving back, they realized they could do something they hadn't done in a long while. They could plan for a future.

————

Abby was not as fortunate. She cycled through the Vancouver-Calgary-Edmonton route more times than she could remember. Jake kept her on the move. Different places. Different pictures of her. Some from the side. Some just text advertisements. Law enforcement laid an increasing number of traps through sting operations. But he was as cunning as he was evil, and he managed to avoid them.

He pushed her through Saskatoon and down to Regina and on to Winnipeg. She couldn't shut her mind down after each horrific night. It was always on, always racing, always paranoid. But her survival demanded this of her. She had to be suspicious. You were guarded or you were dead. Every guy walking in that door was a potential killer. And even those who weren't had figured out a way to drown out or appease their consciences to believe that a frail girl like her was in it for the money to pay for college. Any of those guys could turn violent, so she had to be vigilant. And that kind of a self-defence mechanism didn't just go away when her shift ended.

Plus, drugs pounded through her system to keep her up long enough while she was "working," resulting in an increasingly painful crash afterward. And she would force herself to regroup, only to do it all over again.

They left Winnipeg and headed into Ontario. She had vowed she would not go all the way back across Canada. That she would get out. But how? She couldn't go to the police. They were worse than Jake. She couldn't get to her mother. Jake made that clear. She was not allowed to talk to anyone. Jake made that clear, too. She wanted out. Yet she believed, regardless of what she actually thought of Jake, that he was her future. Her security. The only man who would love her. The only man who could give her a sense of belonging, warped as it might be.

If she rejected his love by running away, she would discover what it meant to be dismembered and shoved into a garbage bin.

This is my life. I both hate it and need it. It's both destroying me and keeping me alive. I want to run from it, yet I want to hide in it. I want to break away, but I want to cower in shame and disappear with the drugs. Jake is the worst person and the best person who's ever happened to me. He's the picture of deception, yet he's the beacon of hope.

I keep spinning around and around. Unable to decide what to do.

But a return trip to the GTA was going to make all of this clear to her.

chapter thirty-six

It didn't feel like home.

Abby recognized the highways, the buildings and especially the landmarks. Canada's Wonderland. The Air Canada Centre. The CN Tower. She grew up here. Went to school here. Her friends and family lived here.

But it felt like a foreign city.

Driving along the Gardiner Expressway she found herself looking at BMO Field. Home of Toronto FC. She wondered what it would be like to watch a soccer game there again. To hear the roar of the crowd. To study the players as they moved like chess pieces on the field. She thought of the last game she played at school when that defender smashed into her nose. She heard that awful cracking sound and saw her shirt full of blood.

How strange to see BMO Field so close and yet to be so far away.

The sun beat down on them as Jake drove with the top down on an unusually warm April afternoon. She felt a warming sensation over her skin. Perhaps some sunshine would do her good and help darken her pale and morose complexion.

Jake told Abby to sit in the lobby as he went to the desk to check in. She knew the drill. Don't look at people. Look alive. Not like the strung-out addict she was. She did as she was told. Watched businessmen checking in. Who knows. Maybe she would be seeing them again later this evening.

Families walked by. A little girl wiggled in her mother's arms, anxious to get down and try out those legs at walking again. The mother placed her on the ground and held her by one hand as the child wobbled. She took a step. Wow! The child cheered in excitement. A whole step. It wouldn't be long now and she would be off on her own. The father had walked on ahead to check them in, not hearing the joy in his daughter's cheer.

"Let's go," Jake said, without looking at Abby and not noticing the child.

Abby broke her gaze from the young girl.

She stood in front of the bathroom mirror longer than usual. The sun helped her skin a little, but it gave her a slight red tone instead of the brown she had hoped for. She was used to red. How many times had she been slapped?

A knock at the bathroom door. She didn't answer. Jake opened it.

"You hear me knocking, babe?"

She caught his eyes in the reflection by accident. It scared her to make eye contact, even if it was through the mirror.

"I'm sorry."

"I knock, you answer. Right?"

She lowered her head in submission, wondering if there would be a beating later. "Okay."

"You have to get some more sun."

I'd have to be outside more for that, wouldn't I?

"Get going. Fifteen minutes."

A pulse of anxiety ripped through her. It chewed away at her psyche. Without realizing it, she gripped the counter, as if doing so could somehow prevent her from being dragged away. Perhaps it gave her something to hang on to when everything else in life was completely adrift.

She sat down on the bed and looked down at the grey carpet. She rubbed her temples to try to get rid of the pounding in her head. She took in deep breaths and tried to calm herself down, but her thoughts started spiralling out of control.

Get a hold of yourself!

I don't want anyone to come in here anymore. Why can't all of you just stay away? Why can't you just stay away from me?!

THE TRUE STORY OF CANADIAN HUMAN TRAFFICKING

What's happening? Why so panicky now? Oh, wait. No. No. Don't tell me.

She forgot to take her drugs. That piece of paper under her tongue to make a rainbow out of everything. Or a line of cocaine that helped her make the jump to light speed in an instant. But then she would crash so badly. Like hitting a star on a poorly charted Millennium Falcon course, just like Han Solo warned it could.

But the crash was necessary. How else to get through these nights?

A knock at the door.

Oh, God. Make it end.

Put on the act. Sell them on their fantasy. Play into their stupid deception that this is all a fun time where they get to be *the man* for a few minutes. Be the toy that they abuse and let them leave thinking they deserved whatever they wanted because after all they paid for it. And if a customer pays money, they own what they buy, no?

She stood. Gave up on trying to look normal. Opened the door. Smiled that ever so slightly crooked smile of hers.

He smiled back. Blue sports coat. Off-white shirt. Money. Lots of it. He came in with an excited look on his face. Must have closed a big deal today. Nice that part of the world still knows what it's like to feel good.

Abby walked over to the bed. Waited for instructions. Maybe she would luck out and someone would invent a lifelike robot to take her place. Wouldn't help the johns any. They would stay on their road of destruction. But it would spare her.

The man looked at her. A different kind of look. She hadn't been scrutinized by a gaze like that before. It was like he was remembering something. Or trying to. And then it all started coming back to the man.

"Do you remember me?" Dave asked. Wow. Was it her? She had been so lively back then. It couldn't be the same girl. How? This one had sunken cheeks. Reduced to skin and bones. She was so thin he thought a strong gust of wind could pick her up and smash her against the glass balcony doors.

She smiled her typical fake smile. "Of course I remember you."

Really? Really? Thousands of you. I've been with thousands of you creeps. And I'm supposed to remember you? Are you that crazy? Are you that arrogant? You think you guys have a personality that I can distinguish one from the other? You're all the same person. All sick. All guys I wish would drop dead.

Then something triggered. He did look familiar. Her mind raced through images of all the men she had been with. Was it possible to do that? No. Couldn't be. She wouldn't remember them all.

But it'd be reasonable that she would remember her first. Wouldn't it?

A rush of sadness came over her. Seeing him not only reminded her of how long she had been in this but also of who she was before all of this went down. Before she became a face in the crowd.

Before she grew apart from herself.

Dave tilted his head and squinted at her. His mind was suddenly overcome with a thought that puzzled him.

"You've been doing this all along?"

"It's a great party, right?" she said, trying hard to sound convincing.

Dave felt a chill come over him. He wasn't sure why yet. It was like in the deep recesses of his mind he had put something together that he desperately wanted to avoid recognizing. But his mind forced him to continue down this path of determining what bothered him so much.

He knew how much he spent per visit. He knew how long ago it had been since he started. How many men did she see a night? Multiplying it in his head, her presence didn't add up.

But the numbers never lie. He would know that. She would have made hundreds of thousands by now. Way more than enough to get into school. So why was she still doing it?

For the money, idiot! Now do what you came for and get back to Hope.

"Can I ask you a question?"

"You can ask me lots of questions," she said, but the politeness in her voice didn't reach her eyes.

"You don't have enough money yet?"

"When is enough? We can always use a little more, right?"

"You don't have enough for school?"

Objection, Your Honour! This question is suggesting an answer to the witness.

"Can we just get on with it?" she asked.

"I don't understand this."

You don't understand? Really? Someone actually thinking about someone besides themselves for once? Someone actually considering that a girl selling herself might not want to do that? The obvious suddenly becoming obvious to you?

She closed her eyes. *Imagine if he walked out and talked to Jake. Could you imagine the repercussions?* Forget the wind. Jake alone would smash her into thousand pieces. Dave picked up on her expression.

"You don't want to be here?"

"Get on with it," she said in an angry tone, wanting to avoid a potential beating from Jake if this guy started putting the facts together. She wanted someone to look at her like a person. To figure the whole thing out. But now that someone was putting the real story together, she realized she wouldn't be able to deal with the fallout.

Dave's heart sank. He wanted to run. Wanted to clasp his hands on either side of his head to prevent his brain from exploding.

"Then why are you doing this? You're making good money. You're—"

Or maybe not, Dave. Maybe she isn't making good money.

Abby raced through the scenarios. He was not going to let this line of questioning go. And if she didn't tell him what he wanted to know, maybe he would ask Jake.

"Stop it," she begged.

"If you don't want to do this, why are you here?"

No options left. She had tried lying, but he had seen through that.

"You don't know?"

"Know what?"

"The guy you gave your money to?"

"Yeah."

"He's going to kill me if I don't keep doing this."

The blood rushed out of Dave's face. He couldn't breathe. A chill ran up and down his back. It all started making sense. "Seriously?"

She swore at him. "Are you for real? You think I want to take money from you for sex? You think I sit in rooms like this night after night because I want to?" It was the first time she had ever voiced her feelings about this. "Is that how sick you are? You actually believe that?"

Dave's mind was swirling. *All fun and games, eh, Dave? No harm in this.*

"I've been beaten countless times," she said. "I'm a drug addict. I'm a sex toy that gets abused every single day." She cursed a blue streak at him. "And if I don't, I get set on fire."

Dave felt like falling to the ground. "I'll call the cops for you."

More cursing. She was out of control. She rubbed her face in an erratic attempt to keep whatever glimmer of sanity she still had left. "You really are that sick? You don't get it. I'll be dead before they show up. And they will kill me."

"They're cops."

"They come through that door just like you do. They don't believe me."

"They will."

"Who's going to tell them? You? Or maybe your wife can come and vouch for you?"

"I'll leave an anonymous tip."

"And if they don't believe me for whatever reason, I'm dead. I can smell the smoke already."

Dave backed up, wishing he could go back to that happy guy who had walked in earlier. He turned, opened the door and hurried down the hallway. He hit the elevator button. Then again. And again. He took the stairs down. The feeling of movement helping to convince him he was leaving his problems behind.

He got behind the wheel of his car. Started the engine. Took off. That was a mistake. A car behind him that he cut off hit the brakes. Honked at him. He gunned the accelerator. Maybe the farther he got away from the scene of the crime the less the horror would fill his mind.

How does it feel, Dave? How does it feel to be part of making money for a guy who minute by minute keeps a young girl like that in perpetual fear of being killed?

How did I miss it all this time? How is this possible?

Because you were helping her make money for university. It's a little harmless fun. Smooth getaway, remember? No one to see your tracks. Eagle. Snake. Ship. Remember? Nothing leaves a trace. Except your conscience. I forgot to mention that.

This isn't how it was supposed to be.

And that whole part about the police? Very chivalrous of you and all. But I would advise against it. After all, you're paying for sex. And you're paying for sex with a minor.

What? She's not 18?

Hahaha! Oh Dave, you are priceless. I mean, if you could see the look on your face now.

A minor?

Dave, stop! Stop. I have to catch my breath. Yes, Dave. Minors. Did it never occur to you to ask any of these girls their ages? Getting caught might put a slight damper on your business, your marriage, your—

His throat closed up. He felt a pounding in his chest. He began to sweat.

You're a sick person, Dave. But don't worry, I have just the girl who can help you.

Stop it! Once and for all!

We'll get you set up tonight.

I'm done! I am done with this.

Sorry, Dave. You know the rules.

He walked in through the garage door. Hope said hello from the kitchen. He said hello back.

I beg you, Hope. Tell me you can see the guilt on my face.

He walked downstairs to turn on the game, grab a drink, something, anything.

"Hey, Dad," Nathan said, looking over from the TV. "How was hockey?"

I'm tired of lying. Just avoid the question. He sat down next to Nathan. "Who's playing?"

"Habs-Leafs just finished." Nathan offered the remote to his dad as he stood up. "I'm off to bed."

Hey, maybe you could introduce your son to a few girls. You never know. It could become a family tradition.

"Sleep well."

Dave sat down on the sofa. Turned off the TV. Saw his reflection. He looked at himself. Was that really him?

You look fine on the outside. Your reflection looks good, doesn't it? But you and I know what's really going on, don't we, Dave? We know what lies beneath that surface. There's two of you. And the man inside doesn't match the man on the outside. If I could paint a picture of the real you, what would it look like? You're a rapist. A liar. A deceiver. You hate your wife. You're an adulterer. You hate women. You detest young girls especially. Tell me, Dave. Tell me. What does a picture of you—the real you—what does that look like?

chapter thirty-seven

Abby sat down and took her familiar place huddled against the window of the red Mustang. Toronto faded away in the rear-view mirror. Every second she moved farther away from her mother. From her hometown. That was the bad news. The good news was that she had survived another city. Hopefully Montreal would be as kind to her.

Again.

She stopped caring about the scenery. Stopped noticing it altogether. It wasn't the inside of a hotel or apartment. That's what mattered most. The trips gave her time to have an anxious rest. A countdown to when the terror would start again.

They stopped for gas and fast food in Cornwall. The four-hour drive in the same position should have caused her to feel cramped and sore. But she was accustomed to hurting. And on the pain threshold, car cramps were the least of her worries.

They pressed on to Montreal. Jake led her into a furnished apartment. "Sleep," he said.

She crashed on the bed. An hour later he woke her up. She blinked. Had she slept at all? Deep sleep had long since abandoned her. The best she could ever manage now was a glorified nap. She was stressed beyond comprehension. Afraid. Exhausted. Drug dependent.

A trafficker's dream.

She sat up in bed. Saw Jake. Saw a girl her age, maybe younger, standing at the door. Short blonde hair with blue streaks. Short skirt.

Jake saw Abby looking past him. He turned. Saw the girl. "Go back, I said. I'll be right there."

"Okay," the girl replied.

The two girls made eye contact. It spooked them to recognize the fear they saw in each other. The girl left.

"Who is that?" Abby asked.

"That girl? She's your competition. You're doing good, Abby. But it's like hockey. Fresh faces are coming up all the time. If you want to stay number one, prove it. This one's a little younger. Bringing in a lot of money. She's got attitude though. That's her only drawback." He stood up. Walked to the door. Talked to her without looking back. "Half an hour. Get ready."

Abby gathered the courage to ask for drugs. Jake swore. "Sorry, babe. Slipped my mind." He put a small plastic bag on the counter. "Don't share with the guys."

The door closed. She got ready. Started by getting high.

She went back to the plastic bag over and over again that night. She wasn't sure if it was her memory or the drugs, but the guys were getting angrier. Yeah, there was the odd rookie. The odd quiet demon. But the rest were brutal. If she hadn't been high she wouldn't have been able to deal with them. Jake came in as he always did at the end of her shift. He congratulated her and sat down on the bed beside her. Abby looked at the door. No sign of Blue Streaks girl.

"Can I talk to the other girl?" she asked.

Jake worked through her question in his mind. That sick, illogical, immoral place where he processed information in such an evil way. "I'm going to say no."

Abby dropped her shoulders just slightly. Enough for Jake to notice.

"I mean, in theory you could," Jake said. "But not in reality."

That made Abby felt sick. The drugs had worn off. She needed something right now to deal with what Jake was going to say. He leaned forward. Put his face in front of her so she had nothing to see but him.

Dear God, please not a beating.

"Abby, you're a great girl. Not every girl is like you. You're obedient. You do what you're told. That's love. The other girl had a hard time listening. People who have a hard time listening have a hard time being in love. You know what I mean?"

She didn't. But she wasn't going to let Jake know that.

"If you really want to see that girl, I can take you there, Abby. But I'm telling you now you don't want that. You know why?"

His voice sounded different. Sinister. It sent a shock through her body. Like his words had a direct connection with the circuitry in her brain to make her hurt like that.

"The reason you can't see her, Abby, is because she's in a dumpster. Okay? Not pretty. Gruesome sight, if you ask me. I don't want to subject you to that, Abby." He leaned forward and kissed her on the forehead. "But you are a keeper, Abby." He got up. "Just keep doing what you're told."

Jake left.

Abby collapsed on the floor. In part because she wanted to be off that sickening bed and in part because she felt somewhat safer being closer to the ground. Like she was in a hurricane and debris was flying all around her in the high-speed wind.

That's going to be me. He's going to kill me. You have to get me out of here, God. Please. Please, I'm begging you. Get me out of here.

She didn't sleep that night. She stayed on the floor with a bedsheet wrapped around her chilled body. She stared out at nothing the whole night. She was optimistic she would live to see the coming sunrise.

But not too sure about the sunset.

"I'm out of makeup," Abby said as they walked out of the apartment and got into the Mustang. They'd stay in Montreal but at a different apartment. Keep moving. Different locations. They couldn't put down roots. Wouldn't want any of those pesky johns having an attack of morality and spilling the beans anonymously about their location. Secret sins were for God to listen to. Not the local police.

He drove to a drugstore. Handed her cash. Then waited in the Mustang while she went in. She found the makeup section. The salesclerk approached.

"Can I help you?" she asked. The woman had a perfect makeup job. Abby would have agreed if she had noticed.

I think I'm going to die. If not now, then soon. I get sold for sex across Canada. Yes, I need help.

"No," she said.

The clerk left. Abby looked through the colours. Bent down. Red lipstick caught her attention.

Abby, it's time to make a break.

Oh, really? Really? I should leave this? Thank you so much for stating the obvious. I would never have thought of that. I get it. I just don't know how. I just … When am I ever going to be rid of this guy? Nothing happens to him. I'm raped. Terrified. A junkie. And he's got money hand over fist.

She studied the red lipstick. Heard Johnny Cash on the store speaker.

I've been down on bended knee talkin' to the man from Galilee.

She gripped the red lipstick. Then looked at eyeshadow. Her eyes didn't need to look any darker, but she glanced at the heavier shades all the same.

Jake's been a liar from the beginning.

You didn't know him then. You were deceived. Cut him loose.

How? Nobody will believe me. If I go to someone here they'll think I'm crazy. Jake will come in and stuff me in the same dumpster with that other girl.

She straightened up. Having escape thoughts like this scared her. She was sure Jake could read her mind. Even from the car. Piecing this all together about her wanting to get out.

Grabbing a deep purple eye shadow, she looked for another colour.

Think, Abby. How are you going to get out?

I can't go to the police.

Why not?

Because they're in on it.

What evidence have you seen to support that?

Jake told me.

Jake the liar? Jake the murder? Jake the midnight rider? That Jake?

She thought hard. Had she been wrong about the police? Her mind shifted back and forth between believing what Jake had filled her mind with and what she knew of the police before she met Jake.

It doesn't matter. I can't get to the police.
Maybe you don't need to go to the police.
Then I'm screwed. No one else will believe me.
Maybe you can get the police to come to you.
They have no idea about me.
But they will. They'll come pay you a little visit.
How?
What is that in your hand?
Abby looked at the lipstick and eyeshadow.
Makeup.
It's your way out.
What?

Two simple pieces in her hand. How on earth—?

And then it made perfect sense. She put them in her pocket. She looked around to see if that girl saw her, but she was nowhere to be seen. Why was it so hard to find a salesperson when you really needed one?

Abby grabbed a number of more items off the shelf. Leaned back so the security cameras above had an even better look at her. She stuffed the items into her shirt. Put the lipstick in her pockets. Thought about Jake.

> *You can run on for a long time ...*
> *Sooner or later God'll cut you down*

She kept filling her pockets with makeup. It was getting embarrassing. She walked down the aisle towards the exit. *Come on, guys. How much do I have to stuff in here before you guys get off your—*

She felt a presence behind her. Jake. Had to be. He read her mind. Figured out her plan. He would make her return the stolen goods and convince her to go with him. Then she could talk to the blue-streaked hair girl as much as she wanted.

"Miss? You're going to have to come with us."

Not Jake's voice.

She turned. Two security guards. Young. Built. Hope never looked so good. *Make sure you arrest me, boys. Make sure. Because if you don't, I'm a dead woman.* She waited for them to take her by the arm. When they didn't, she reached out and grabbed each one of them by the wrist and clung onto them. That was strange, and they exchanged a brief glance. They led her down the hallway. She glanced behind her and saw Jake in the red Mustang. His face focused on his phone, lining up the evening appointments. He disappeared from her view as they led her to a room in the back.

"Can you empty your pockets please?"

She began to hyperventilate. Was she free? Was she out? Her hands began to tremble. A wild look came to her eyes. Jake was coming. Had to be. What if he came in here and told the guards she was crazy? Fed them some lie, convinced them to let her go so he could take her on to her garbage bin reward?

"You all right?" one of them asked.

She tried to sit down, but missed the chair. Crashing to the ground, she pushed herself backwards, as if expecting Jake to burst through the door. She started sucking air in quick bursts.

"He's in the red Mustang outside. Red Mustang outside. Please help me. Please help me. Please help me! Red Mustang. Red Mustang."

She was going full-on hysterical. The other guard reached for the phone. Called the police. Gave the location. "We picked her up for shoplifting. Just a young girl. She looks strung out if you ask me. But she keeps talking about a guy waiting in the parking lot." He angled his head slightly to avoid her hearing the next part. "She's freaking out, okay? Something's not right here."

The guards offered to help her up. But all she could do was watch the door with those crazed eyes of hers, begging them to keep the door closed.

A few minutes later, the door opened. A rip of fear raced through her. A tall police officer with a shaved head entered. Her pulse lowered. He crouched down. Introduced himself to Abby. Quiet voice. Like he knew all about what he was dealing with here.

"Everything okay?" he asked.

She looked at his gun. Looked at his eyes. *Am I out? Am I out?* This was it. Abby began to cry. She bit her lip.

You can't trust cops. You can't trust cops.

All she could do was shake her head. "I'm not okay," she whimpered. The officer reached out his hand.

"I want you to tell me all about it. Okay?"

Don't talk to police.

"Can I have your name?" he asked.

"Abby."

"Abby, everything's going to be all right. We're here to help you. My partner and I are here because we want you safe. Okay?" Abby glanced behind him. Noticed another officer behind him. She had the same blond hair colour as her.

Abby explained what happened. The deception. The forced sex. Coast to coast. The terror.

"Abby?" the officer said. Abby looked down. "Abby?" he said again. For such a big police officer he had a soft voice. She looked up. "I believe you, Abby."

She cried again. A steady stream flowed down her cheeks.

"We're going to get you help, okay?"

She nodded.

"Do you want to call your mother?"

She nodded, and one of the security officers gave her the phone.

The tall officer left the room. Called for another unit to come in. As it arrived, the officers approached the Mustang. The tall officer tapped on the window. Jake looked up from his phone. When he saw the uniform a jolt of adrenalin shot through him. He rolled it down.

"Are you Jake?"

"Yeah."

His confidence disappeared. His face looked pale. Where was Abby? That sick—

The officer put his hand on his gun. "Please step out of your vehicle."

Jake opened the door.

"You are under arrest for the trafficking of a minor." The officer turned Jake around. Gave him his rights as he handcuffed him. Put him in the back seat of the cruiser.

"You guys are pathetic, you know that? I'm going to be out in a month."

The strong officer finished typing the charges into his computer. "You listen to the news much?"

"What's that got to do with anything?"

In her home in Markham, Talia heard her cellphone ringing. She glanced at the number. Area code 514. Isn't that Montreal? Must be a telemarketer. Don't know anyone in Montreal.

Unless …

She touched the green receive button. Her heart pounded.

"Hello?"

chapter thirty-eight

Hearing her mother's voice on the other end of the call brought a wave of relief to Abby. Nearly two whole years since this started. Abby had spoken with her briefly, under massive duress, and then watched, from a distance, from that apartment window while her mom sat in the parking lot. But now she was free. Now they could both talk without hurrying. Without panicking.

Without fear.

"Mom, it's Abby."

A flood of tears erupted and streamed down either side of Abby's face.

"Abby! Are you all right? Where are you?"

"I'm with the police," she said. "I'm out, Mom. I'm out."

Saying it out loud felt like fiction for Abby. Like she was going to come off this high and find herself in some apartment somewhere. With Jake telling her to get ready for her first trick of the night.

"Abby, are you sure? Where are you?"

"I'm in Montreal." The tall police officer came in. "Mom, you want to talk to the police?"

Abby handed the phone to the officer. He introduced himself to Talia and said they would take excellent care of her daughter and would be taking her to the hospital right away. He also told her they had the man in custody.

His kind, firm voice gave Abby the feeling of security. She wondered what his job was like. What was it like for him to track down people like Jake? To rescue girls like her?

He gave the phone back to Abby.

"I'm coming to Montreal, Abby. I'll see you in a few hours, okay?"

"Thanks, Mom," she said. "I love you. And I'm sorry."

"There is nothing to be sorry about, Abby. I love you too. I'm coming to see you right now."

"Okay. Thanks."

Abby waited in the medical examination room at Montreal General Hospital. The tests had been completed. The nurses said the doctor would come in to discuss the results. Down to the waiting now. It was one thought that Jake could have killed her at some point for disobeying him. Another thought that one or more of the hundreds and hundreds of johns had given her death by disease somewhere along the way.

The doctor entered. Tall. Athletic. She introduced herself to Abby. Sat down beside her. Went through the results of her tests. Abby held her breath. The verdict? Yes, there was damage. Yes, there were medical issues. But if she stayed on the treatment plans it was expected she could make a full recovery. It was likely, though not guaranteed of course, that she would be able to have children.

Great news, all things considered.

Abby thanked her. Then the doctor paused a moment, absorbing the horrors Abby endured. She indicated that a nurse would follow up with her to transfer her information to her family doctor.

The doctor left. Abby lay down in the bed. Looked up at the ceiling. Jake was in custody. The doctors gave her a relatively good report. So why did she still feel so awful? Why would this news not be enough to reset everything back to normal?

Abby's mother came in, followed by her father. They hugged. Cried. They held each other for so long, Abby wondered if anyone would say any words at all. And if they were even necessary. Her mother pulled back first. Abby saw the pain in her eyes, revealing how much her mother thought Abby had changed.

"We love you, Abby," she said.

Abby stayed in their embrace. Felt her father's arms around her.

They stayed at a hotel for the evening. All in the same room at Abby's request. They had dinner together in the hotel restaurant. A quiet place. Dim lights. That helped. Abby sat with her back to the wall, scanning the restaurant, looking for Jake. As much as she forced herself to admit he was in custody, she still imagined him bursting in with a shotgun aimed at her and finishing her off once and for all.

She didn't need to know the time or see the setting sun outside to tell her that it was evening. She knew it. Could feel it. She almost felt like having to excuse herself from her parents and go upstairs to service the men Jake had lined up for her tonight.

She wasn't hungry. None of them were. A plate of nacho appetizers sat uneaten in the middle of the table. Her body craved a high. Or at least a bottle of wine. Something. She shared a few memories. Nothing major. Hard to do that without drugs in her system. She wasn't going to go into the unbearable shame of what she had been put through. Why hadn't someone invented a drug that could make you block out entire portions of your life? Like a scene the director decides to take out in the editing room. Just splice this moment in the restaurant here with the moment when she got the first message from Jake.

Why wasn't there anybody there to warn me? How could I have been so stupid to believe in Jake? How could I have been so unbelievably gullible?

Of the three people sitting at the table, it was her father who felt the most guilt. The most shame. He felt he had failed his daughter in not being there to protect her. She was back safe and sound now. And it caused him to wonder where he had gone wrong. He wondered about all those soccer games that his daughter had invited him to but he declined because he had too much work to do. Too many committee meetings to attend. Too much blah blah blah. Was he being too hard on himself? Not hard enough?

"Abby, there's a friend of mine who has done a lot of work to rescue girls who have been trafficked. She's the one who got a bill passed that will put—" Talia had a hard time saying his name. She felt if she spoke it out loud it would acknowledge his presence when all she wanted was to be rid of the thought of him. She settled on "him in jail for at least five years. And I want to offer it to you; if you would like to speak with her, she could help you. Help you in ways that I … that your father and I can't."

"We've been told it's a journey back," her father said. "It's up to you."

They visited the tall police officer the next day. He told them the prosecutor would be in contact with her. Her testimony would be crucial. She thanked the officer.

The three boarded a flight for Toronto.

They went home.

Joy drove to Markham, following her GPS to the Summers' residence. She knocked on the door, and when Talia answered, she opened it as wide as it would go.

"Hello, Talia," Joy said, smiling.

They hugged.

"Thank you so much for coming, Joy."

Abby sat in the living room, fighting her fears about having to tell her story. She had thought this visit through on the trip home, then late in the evening in her room, then again this morning at the kitchen table with her parents. As much as she wished she could forget the last two years and act like nothing happened, she knew closing her eyes to a fire like this would only reap further destruction down the road. She didn't want to process what happened. Processing involved reliving it. Wouldn't it be easier to block it out and believe there was nothing wrong with her and just get on with life? But she needed a reset, a time to heal.

Abby heard them approaching and stood. When she saw Joy's smile she let her guard down, sensing the genuineness of her character. No hidden agenda, unlike Jake. It was as if her mind had become hypersensitive, detecting the true intention of a person after having been deceived with such dire consequences.

"Hello, Abby," Joy said. "I'm so glad to meet you." Joy gave her a hug. "I am so glad you're safe, Abby."

Abby's father greeted Joy and thanked her for coming. Abby sat down between her parents.

"Abby, thank you for taking the time to see me. I also want to thank you for trusting me to come here and talk with you. You have been through an unimaginable ordeal. And I want to share with you about how I can help you, if that's what you and your family decide."

Abby nodded. Joy asked her to share her story. Abby thought, was she really going to do this? And if so, how many details to give out?

Abby started and eventually got the whole story out. She broke down many times, the memories proving to be too painful, causing her to take long pauses. Joy listened to Abby, her eyes compassionate. Three hours later, Abby finished her story.

"I have rescued many victims of human trafficking. Many girls from across Canada. And I work together with excellent people who help girls heal. We do this by first taking girls to a safe location run by a government-recognized organization to ensure they are protected. We help them transition out of the life they were in and help them reintegrate back into society with dignity."

Abby's gaze drifted over the kitchen. As if in a time warp she saw herself at the fridge. Getting out vanilla ice cream. Getting ready to watch the Toronto FC game. Receiving that first message from Jake.

The room became quiet. Joy was careful not to interrupt Abby's silence.

"I feel so stupid," Abby said, closing her eyes, trying to wipe away the image she just remembered. "I feel so gross."

No kidding. Look at everything you did. That's worse than gross.

Abby crossed her legs and covered her face. Her brain was not able to push away the memories. They crashed over her like a massive tidal wave, destroying everything in their path. "I am so ashamed of what I did."

You should be. You deserve all the guilt you feel. You chose that life. You picked Jake out of your own free will.

Abby swore. She suffered in silence. Overcome by the weight of shame that packed onto her with every man who went to see her.

When she knew the moment was right, Joy spoke to her.

"Abby?"

Abby kept her hands over her face, feeling unworthy of hearing anything that would convince her otherwise.

"Abby, you're a wonderful person. Your mother has told me all about you. We've spent a lot of time together. She tells me you love soccer. You do well in school. You have a friend, Kedisha. And one day an evil young man decided to deceive you. He took advantage of your trust and kindness. And he made you do things that you would never want to do."

Abby felt Joy's words resonate within her.

No. No, it's not true. This is your fault. You did those things of your own free will.

I didn't. I wanted to love someone. I wanted to believe he was a good guy. I would never, ever, ever have met with him if I had known what he was planning.

Are you sure about that?

"Abby, he's a criminal. He planned to do this. And it's not your fault."

Finally. Finally, someone understood. Someone who lived in the world of sex trafficking who knew what she was feeling. Abby raised her head. Focused on Joy.

"Abby, you are the victim here."

The tidal wave reversed its course. A sudden realization flooded her mind. Abby began to see everything in a new light.

That's not true. You willingly took part in this.

I was deceived.

You should have known better.

He should have known better. He lied to me.

"Do you believe that?" Abby asked.

"One hundred percent. That man took advantage of you. He lied to gain your trust. And once he had your trust he used you to do all these things to make money for himself. That took you off course, Abby. And I want to help you get back on track."

Abby glanced back at the fridge. If only there was a way to undo things. Jump back in time and not respond to his message. But there's no delete button in life. She resolved herself to that. And now it would take time to get right again. In just these few moments she felt the slightest shift in a positive direction, giving her hope that more could be in store. She looked back at Joy.

"How?"

chapter thirty-nine

The view out of the window from Joy's car as they drove north of Toronto felt different than anything Abby had seen in quite some time. She'd had her fair share of looking out at the Canadian countryside. But that was with Jake. In that Mustang. Being with him clouded everything she thought, did, said and saw. She now began to see the beauty of trees again. She saw their branches bend and their leaves flutter, making her wonder where the wind comes from and where it's going.

She decided she would make a trip across Canada again sometime. Down the road. See it coast to coast. Get out and experience the cities and the towns and the farms instead of the inside of a hotel or apartment.

She had spent her first two months after being rescued in a psychiatric ward. As much as she hated having to admit she needed mental help, it proved to be a critical and welcomed stage in her journey of recovery. The doctors and nurses both comforted and challenged her. She began to take control of her thoughts, exercising her brain and her mind towards better health.

She learned how to cope with the trauma bond she had unwillingly formed with Jake. As evil as he was, Jake was no idiot. He knew how to create diabolical cycles of reward and punishment so Abby would build a dependent connection with him. The doctors indicated that even if she still at times sensed a connection, she had a skill set she could use to combat those feelings. The safe house was a step in the right direction.

Joy pulled off the highway and took a few winding turns. They found a dirt road with towering trees on either side that eventually led them to a quiet, idyllic large house with light wood siding and a red door. Joy stopped the car. Abby got out.

She wasn't sure exactly what a safe house should look like. She had in her mind a place that provided physical security, something with high walls and a fence to protect from outside intruders. But someone had done their homework about this particular place. Because when Abby saw it, she felt an immediate ability to relax.

Abby didn't realize it then, but she had won the lottery with getting into a safe house. In spite of the massive human trafficking problem, there were precious few places available for girls who were exiting the game. Some girls couldn't go back home because their parents would disown them. Discard them for what they had done. *How dare you tarnish our good family name?* Other times, girls simply had nowhere to go. No NGO safe house available. Not enough people with the interest or the skill set or the vacant room in their home or combination thereof to take in a girl. And so sometimes girls wanted out but there was no mom or dad to be able to help them out and no space for them anyplace else. In some government-run shelters, girls were even allowed to continue working as prostituted women while staying there. Not the best environment for a girl who wants out.

Joy pulled Abby's belongings out of the trunk. "I can get those," Abby said.

"It's no problem," Joy said, leading her up to the door.

They entered. Alexandra and Samantha came to the entrance. They made introductions. Samantha took Abby to her room as Joy and Alexandra met in the living room.

Abby followed Samantha up the stairs and down the hallway. Samantha opened a door for her. A skylight allowed the bright sunshine into the room. It featured a bed with white blankets and pillows. The wall was clad in a soft pine siding. It felt like the inside of a cabin, homey and warm.

"How long have you been here?" Abby asked.

"Almost a year."

"Okay."

"You can stay as long as you like."

"I just meant that you look like you have it together. Trying to gauge how long it's going to take me."

"Alexandra and me and the other girls—we're all here for you. I'm not going to lie to you. It's going to be hard. Especially the beginning. You've taken a beating inside and out. All of us know what that's like. We've been there. And now we're out. And that's going to be you, too."

Abby sat down across from Joy in the living room. Samantha and Alexandra left for the nearest town to pick up groceries. The other girls were in their rooms.

"I'm proud of you, Abby."

"For what? I haven't done anything."

"Sure you have. You've come here."

"Big deal."

"It *is* a big deal. You know what this means?"

"It means I'm freeloading."

"It means you are willing to let people help you."

Abby stood and walked to the window. Looked out. Swore.

"What am I doing here, Mrs. Smith? I'm a whore."

"You're a wonderful girl."

"Spare me."

Just because you're here doesn't change anything. You want to go back to it. Don't you?

"It's the truth, Abby."

Abby leaned back and exhaled. "You're a member of Parliament, and I'm a slut from the streets."

"You're right about the first part," Joy said with a laugh. "But I would disagree with you on your assessment of yourself."

"It doesn't change what happened. Just tell me, why are you here? Why do you stick your neck out for girls like us? Why are you of all people doing this?"

It was a fair question. Joy could have saved herself countless hours of work. Countless fights on the Hill. Many death threats. But reflecting on it, she wouldn't have had it any other way. She thought about her brother being beaten so badly as a child. Thought about Edward. Thought about her daughters.

"I'm doing this because I love you."

Those words pierced Abby. "Why? How could you possibly?"

"Abby—"

"Why on earth would you love me? I don't have any money. I don't have anything to give you. I don't even live in your riding. I can't vote for you. I can't do anything for you."

"Abby."

"What?!"

Her face screamed worry. Confusion. Anger. But she made eye contact with Joy. Which was good. Because it was important for what Joy would say next.

"I love you because I love you."

Abby turned back to the window. "That doesn't make any sense. You politicians are always talking in circles."

Joy laughed. It filled the room and was probably heard by the girls upstairs. Abby smiled a moment, then returned to that familiar sorrowful expression.

It was something Joy couldn't explain either. She loved Abby. Loved all the girls she had rescued. Even the ones she would rescue in the future and didn't know their names yet. How do you explain unconditional love—when you commit to loving someone no matter what? Some of the girls were downright difficult to help. Violent tempers. Incredible mood swings. Their minds not able to think clearly, and so they would threaten one day to go back to the traffickers who apparently loved them and the next day take it all back and apologize to Joy, all the while wondering what drove them to think that way in the first place. Walking with a girl on the path of restoration was no easy challenge. Typically, it took three months to see small changes, and bigger changes would happen in a year. They would start by working on major trust, worth and anger issues. And when they were ready, they would reintegrate into society. And even then it was a hard step to convince them to go, like a mother bird that pushes its young out of the nest. Sometimes girls resisted that final step to get back into life.

Joy stuck with them through all of it. She had done it with Samantha. And now Abby.

Joy had developed a love for children with her own six kids. And she saw the victims as an extension of her family. As part of her life. As her children.

Joy stood and joined Abby at the window.

"I'm guessing Jake told you he loved you because you were beautiful. Then he told you he loved you because you made money for him. Then he told you he loved you because you wouldn't leave him. Then he threatened to stop loving you if you didn't bring in money and that you would never find love apart from him."

Abby nodded.

"He didn't love you," Joy said. "His love was conditional. It came with strings attached. Mine doesn't." Abby turned to face her. "I'm no angel, Abby. I have my fair share of shortcomings. I'm just saying that I love you. And nothing you do is going to change that. And I'm going to keep loving you."

Abby felt tears beginning to form. Joy hugged her.

"Thank you, Mrs. Smith."

"You are so welcome. And we're going to get through this, all right?"

"If you say so."

The door opened. Alexandra and Samantha entered.

"I think that means it's time for us to make supper. Want to help?"

"Okay."

Joy continued to visit Abby. They spoke often on the phone. Abby began to trust people more. As if on schedule, some three months into being at the safe house she began to look in the mirror with more confidence. She became less angry. More loving. Kinder. She studied hard and worked on her high school diploma by correspondence.

The crown prosecutor met with her to discuss the upcoming trial. As much as she wanted to be rid of the thought of Jake, she agreed to testify, knowing he would be in prison for at least five years, hopefully more, if she did. And that him being in prison would prevent him from recruiting another girl in that time frame.

Joy sat in the courtroom watching as Abby took the stand. She glanced at Jake, then forced herself to look back at Abby to dissolve the thoughts forming in her mind.

Abby wondered what seeing Jake would be like—if being in the same room as him would cast her under his influence again. But when their eyes met as she testified, she discovered she felt nothing for him. Even though she had to relive what Jake put her through, she took encouragement from being able to see Jake and not feel any attachment for him. She didn't feel under his grip anymore, didn't think he could read her mind and didn't believe he could force her to do things. He sat there with the weight of evidence piling up on top of him, but if he sensed any wrongdoing he gave no indication that he felt guilty or remorseful.

During the trial, it was revealed through other witnesses that Jake had contacted dozens of girls online. Abby was one of a number who responded. The girl with the streaked blue hair was never found.

Jake was convicted and sentenced to prison for seven years.

Joy met with Abby in spring of the following year. They went for a walk by a small lake a short distance from the safe house. The ice had melted. Abby approached the water.

"Sometimes I feel like I'm just repeating myself over and over to you, Mrs. Smith."

"It may seem that you're going in circles. But in reality, you're spiralling upwards. Every time you share about your life with someone you trust, you are choosing to deal with the painful memories."

"Do they go away?"

"No. But you see them in a different light. What was evil stays evil. But even bad events can be used for good."

"I don't see how."

"Look at Alexandra and Samantha. It's terrible what happened to them. But they used the difficult things that happened to help others. In a sense, the past and the present can work together."

Abby thought back to the first time Jake took her to Montreal. She had seen the old buildings and the new buildings near the Notre-Dame Basilica, and she noticed the past and the present working together there. Somehow it all fit together.

Abby walked to the water's edge. She crouched down and put her finger in the cool water. She brought it to her lips and tasted the fresh, clean water.

Abby finished high school by correspondence at the end of May. She, Joy, Alexandra and Samantha sat outside on lawn chairs under the warm sun to celebrate. She looked out at the view around her. She'd seen it for months now, but it looked more beautiful than ever. Like what was always there was suddenly being revealed to her. She watched the tops of the trees blow in the wind. Saw the rustling of the leaves.

"I want to help here," Abby said. "You guys have been so good to me."

"And you can," Alexandra said. "But I agree with Joy. You need to get out there. You're ready."

"I don't know if I can live a normal life again."

"Look at me. I'm living a normal life," Samantha said.

"Yeah, well, who says you're normal?"

They all laughed.

"I have a couple things I'd like to do," Abby said.

"Okay," Joy said. "What are they?"

chapter forty

How many times had she pulled out her cellphone to check the time? And how many times had she said this would be the last look? Abby put her phone back into her purse and sat back in the large chair in the office lobby, feeling out of her league. And as soon as she did she felt bad for feeling that way.

The online application said no experience was necessary. That was both good and bad. It meant she could apply, but it would also open the door to potentially hundreds of applicants. So maybe being here wasn't that great of a sign. But she had been called in for an interview. That was something. Wasn't it?

It would be her first interview ever, not counting the one with Jake, and she wanted to make the best impression possible. She went clothes shopping with her mom, and in the end they settled on this outfit: black pants (not a skirt—she wondered if she would ever wear one again) and a white button-up shirt. She looked the part, feeling both comfortable and classy. But whenever one of the guys in suits would walk past, she involuntarily looked down. Confidence would come with time, Samantha told her.

"Abby Summers?" the woman behind the counter asked.

Abby nodded and stood. The woman introduced herself as Mary and appeared to Abby as being kind and well put together. Abby wondered if the woman could see right through her frail shell, and it made her all the more scared heading in.

They're going to see what a phony you are. They will see right through you. This woman in front of you? That's a real woman. You? You're cheap trash. You're going to get bounced out of here so fast.

The woman knocked on a door at the end of the hall, opened it and smiled at Abby.

I wish I could be half as good as you.

Abby entered. A middle-aged man stood from his desk. His smile and the life behind his blue eyes put her at ease. He introduced himself as John. What were the odds? Mary indicated to Abby to sit down across from John in a red chair.

Oh no. You're staying too. It would have been better with just one of you. Two is a little more intimidating. But I get it. All kinds of legal issues these days, right?

"Thank you for coming in, Abby," John said.

Thank you for giving me the opportunity to be considered for something other than my body.

"Thank you," Abby said, counting it a step forward that she could maintain eye contact with him.

"We've had a chance to go through your resumé," he said.

Yeah. All of three seconds it took you. There's nothing on it. I should have applied at a fast-food joint. I should have stayed at home in my living room eating a tub of ice cream.

"You're a soccer player?"

"Used to be," she said, following her policy of being totally honest no matter what. She'd been lied to and nearly died as a consequence. She wasn't going to carry on that tradition, no matter how small and inconsequential the lie might seem.

"And you've finished high school by correspondence," Mary said. *Yeah, because I'm an idiot.* "That takes a lot of guts," she said, looking to John, who agreed. "I don't know if I would have had the determination to do high school that way. Congratulations."

Are you serious?

They were. And it caught her off guard.

"Quite impressive to have a member of Parliament be a reference for you," John said. "I don't think I could get that on my resumé," he said with a laugh.

Abby smiled. It felt good to do so. But she was knew what was coming. It was inevitable.

"It seems like there are a couple of years here where there's a gap. You did correspondence in what I would say is record time. I'm staggered that you plowed through it so quickly. It just seems that there's a couple of years here unaccounted for."

Don't say it. Don't hint at it. Nobody wants to be around cheap trash.

Be honest. What would you prefer? To get this job because of a lie?

You want a job, or you want to go back to putting your face on creepy websites?

Abby folded her hands, then rubbed her fingers. She touched the place where Jake's ring had once been. Somewhere in all of this it had been left behind in some hotel room. Just as well. She felt sweat begin to form on her forehead and was sure Mary and John could notice.

If you want to heal, you need to be honest. If they decide you're not a fit for whatever reason, no harm done. You were honest. They were honest. But you will not continue to get better unless you allow people to reject you.

"I was a victim of human trafficking," Abby said. It sounded surreal at first. Like it was someone else saying it. But as soon as the words came out, the fear about revealing the truth was broken.

Abby didn't look up at John or Mary. She had a good enough view of them out of the corner of her eye to notice their contained gasps. The tension left the room, as it often does when it gets replaced with something far more important.

"I was 15 when I was lured in. I got out last year. I went into rehab." That was the wrong word. But everyone in the room knew what she meant. "I'm now volunteering at helping other girls who have gotten out. It would have taken me forever to finish high school had I gone back to school. I'm smart. So I did it by correspondence. Faster that way."

She felt good to say that with confidence. She was smart, and she knew it. There was nothing wrong with being humble and honest about her abilities. "I got off course. And I want to get back into the swing of things."

She noticed that Mary's face went pale with empathy. Like she could feel part of what Abby had gone through. Like she wanted to be careful with whatever she said next so as not to accidentally cause any more pain.

"And so I'm not going to lie to you. I haven't had a job before. Not like this. I just need a shot."

The room stayed quiet. It was John's turn to go next. They all knew it. And he waited with the wisdom some men have when they're in the presence of a woman who has suffered at men's hands.

"I want to thank you for your honesty. I ..." He looked visibly shaken by what he had heard.

You think that's bad? Let me tell you about just one night in the life of Abby Summers. You'll run for the sink. Take the rest of the day off. Maybe a month.

"I confess I'm new to this," he said. "And I don't how to help you, except to say two things."

You can hear it already, can't you, Abby? Number one: Get out. And number two: Don't ever come back.

"First, you have the job. We welcome you here with open arms. And number two." He glanced at Mary for confirmation. Her eyes were filled with compassion. "We need you to tell us what you need. What can we do for you to help you succeed?"

Kind strangers. So very different from what she had lived.

"I picked this office assistant job because—" Her mind shifted gears. "I suffer from PTSD." She shrugged her shoulders. "I know people think that's for veterans, and it is. But it's also for people like me who live our own war. There are times when I need some patience. Sometimes it takes me a little longer to do things. I'm still processing what happened. But I'm dependable. And I'm a real stickler for details. If you want to rethink your decision to hire me, I'll understand."

"I'm not wrong about you, Abby," he said. "You have the position. The work requires mostly on-the-job training. You'll spend a couple of hours with Mary learning how the filing in the office works. And take whatever time you need. As things change, let us know. We really want this to be the kind of place where this business helps you grow. Okay?"

Yeah. Yeah, that's going to be more than okay.

"Thank you," Abby said.

"Sure thing." They all stood. "What position did you play in soccer?"

"Midfield."

"The most running. Takes a lot of endurance to make it to the end."

Abby walked down the street in Toronto. Saw the outdoor patio at the café up ahead. Saw Joy and Joel at the far end. Saw their eyes light up when they saw her. It did Abby's heart good. She felt the connection that came between people who love not only in spite of what's happened but because of it.

Joy hugged her. A mother's hug. She shook Joel's hand. They had met numerous times over the past months. Joel had helped her with her resumé. Joy raised her eyebrows in anticipation.

"I got it," Abby said.

"Congratulations!"

They sat down, and Abby began talking about how nervous she had been and how good her new bosses had been.

"I want to continue volunteering with Alexandra and do this job as well. Get my feet back on the ground. Then look into maybe nursing or education. And keep hanging out with you guys."

A pause. Abby didn't understand it.

"Abby, I love you. And I will always be here for you. I want you to know that."

"I do, Mrs. Smith."

"You've come a long way. And I've helped you as much as anyone can. But you don't need me anymore."

It felt like a cord of security had been cut. Like she had been pushed out of a moving vehicle.

"Don't say that."

"It's true. A mother bird pushes her younglings out of the nest. But she doesn't do it until she knows they're ready."

"So you think I'm ready?"

"Absolutely."

"I don't feel ready."

"You will when you fly out of the nest," Joy said with a laugh.

"You're sure?" Abby asked.

"I am."

"But I want to help you."

"I don't think you want to be on the Hill. Joel, convince her," Joy said with an even deeper laugh.

"It's a challenge, for sure," Joel said. But they both knew what she meant.

"I don't mean the Hill," Abby said. It got quiet at their table. It was as if all of Toronto suddenly disappeared, and all that was left was the three of them, a table and the outdoor air. "Like maybe there's something in the future you'll do that I can help with."

Joy's phone rang. She looked at the number. Glanced at Abby. "It's a girl who needs my help. One moment."

Joy left the table.

"You did really well, Abby," Joel said. "It takes a lot of courage to apply for a job and to tell them what happened. It's very impressive."

"Thank you, Joel. Thank you for your help."

"Of course." Remembering something, he pulled out his phone. He looked through his documents. "You had asked me for information on NGOs, churches and other organizations involved in combatting human trafficking. I assembled a list for you. I can send that over to you."

She saw him cycling through his files to find the one he had prepared for her. How many hours did he spend at his work? And how many additional hours did he spend fighting for victims of human trafficking?

"You're a good man, Joel."

It caught him off guard. He glanced up.

"Thank you for all you've done," Abby said.

"You're welcome," Joel replied. Then, to break the awkward silence, "I've emailed it to you."

Joy returned to the table.

"Thank you for everything, Mrs. Smith."

"You are most welcome, Abby. You have a great future."

Abby glanced out to the street, taking a deep breath in preparation for what she was about to say. Finding no objection in her mind, she continued.

"There's something else I've been thinking of doing," Abby said.

Joy watched her eyes. Saw conviction in them. Whatever it was Abby was referring to, it would be both difficult and right. Strange how often those two go together.

Joy leaned forward. Wondered what Abby was thinking.

"Okay," Joy said. "What is it?"

chapter forty-one

She felt more nervous here than she did for her job interview, and with good reason. In many ways, much more was at stake.

Abby stood to the side of the stage, behind the curtains. This all seemed like such a good idea—right up until now. She knew this moment would come. Knew she would want to back out at the last minute. And so she told herself why she was doing this. Yeah, some would blame her. Some would judge her. Fine. But there were bigger things she was concerned about. Like her reason for doing this.

She wondered how many people were out there. Hundreds. Some would have no idea who she was. No clue. But that wouldn't matter. They would hear the truth. And those who did know her? They might be the worst she would face. Literal finger-pointing would be easier to take than the condemning look some people would have in their eyes. Like those women when she walked that Calgary street in lingerie.

Here she was. After all this time.

Back at her high school.

The principal came up on stage to give announcements. The way he walked indicated he had played a lot of sports in his life. He spoke in the way principals do when they connect with their students, seamlessly transitioning his welcome into the introduction for today's guest speaker. Through her nervousness, Abby heard him refer to the Canadian land-scape as transforming with such speed that students had to be more and more vigilant in light of an ever-pervasive darkness. He introduced the topic of human trafficking.

"Most people think of human trafficking as foreign girls brought here under false pretenses who end up as sex slaves. That is tragic, and it's happening. But girls are also being trafficked right from within Canada. From coast to coast. From reserves. From upper-class neighbourhoods. Lower-class neighbourhoods. And everything in between. In fact, it happens right here in Markham. In our very school, one of your classmates was trafficked. If you think it can't happen to you, think again. The dangers are real. And I am going to ask you to listen very carefully. If you're a girl, I want you to listen because of the dangers that directly affect you. If you're a guy, I want you to listen so that you don't become an unwitting participant in this awful crime. Please join me in welcoming Abby Summers."

Her past flashed in front of her. She recalled being a student here. Meeting Jake. Getting dragged across Canada. All those men. In Vancouver, the temptation to jump and end it. She resisted that. And now, here, she was tempted to quit. To give in to the shame. But she resisted. One of her favourite Tom Petty songs played in the back of her mind.

No I won't back down
You can stand me up at the gates of hell
But I won't back down

Abby stepped onstage, feeling the looks of her former classmates. Were they judging her, or were they genuinely interested? The lights blinded her until her eyes adjusted. She had debated about whether to bring notes, and in the end, she trashed them. But now, all alone at the microphone, she wished she had the comments in front of her so she would not have to look at the students.

Abby saw Joy sitting at the front beside her mother and father. Their presence gave her reassurance.

Just be honest. Speak from your heart. Remember why you're here. Remember your reason. Don't worry about anything else.

The clapping stopped. Silence fell.

"My name is Abby Summers, and I used to attend here."

The first sentence was out. She suddenly felt at peace. Like she was just having coffee with a friend.

"I played soccer. Did well in school. Came from a good home."

She was about to look down at her mother but decided against it, for fear of breaking down. From all the conversations she had with her mother since being rescued, Abby knew what her mom was thinking. *It was my job to look after you, Abby. I feel so awful for what you had to endure. How on earth are we supposed to make sense of any of this?*

"I walked these hallways. Went to the classrooms. Hung out in the lunchroom. And one day a guy contacted me on social media. He seemed cool. And he made me feel really great. I had fun with him. And he liked me. That's what I thought at the time. I gave him my heart. And then he started to suggest I do things with other men. Just for fun. Just to try it out. One thing led to another. And I was used by men every night for two years."

Just stop it already. You're making a fool of yourself.

We do what's right because it's right.

"I know what you're thinking—Why didn't you just leave him? Believe me, if I could have, I would have. I'll get to that in a moment. The bigger question, in my mind, is how do they do it? How do traffickers—or pimps as some people call them—how do they lure girls? How do they turn a girl like me?"

She glanced out of the corner of her eye. Saw Kedisha. She looked devastated. Abby had talked to her, assured her it wasn't her fault, but she knew her friend still felt guilty—like she could have done something to prevent Abby from going down that dark path. Abby smiled at Kedisha—a sad smile, but it was returned.

"Trafficking has a million faces. My friend Joy Smith is here today with my parents," she pushed herself to look over at them. That was hard. Harder than facing the students. Joy and her parents had been there for her, and, most of all, they took her in when she was at the very bottom. She felt her hands beginning to quiver. She looked back to the sea of students, took in a couple breaths to calm herself. "She said that all the stories are different, and yet they're the same. And this is why they are the same.

"Traffickers seek to gain the trust of their victims. Mine was very cunning. I couldn't see through it. You might be thinking I'm a dumb loser and anybody should be able to spot a creep. If that's what you think, I'm praying for you in particular, because girls of all types have been lured in."

She cleared her throat.

"He showered me with gifts. Clothes, jewelry. Gave me tons of compliments. Took me on great dates. Every girl wants to be loved. And so somehow I gave in to him and trusted him. And he knew this. Knew what he was doing. Knew how to string me along. This process of getting me to trust him is what we call *grooming*. He's getting me ready for what's next. He then started planting thoughts into my mind. And I began to fight within myself. It was so gradual. And that's the key. He never did anything abruptly."

Abby glanced beside Kedisha and saw the rich girl. The one with the designer jeans, perfect makeup and flawless skin. The one with the fancy car who drove all the girls to the mall that day, all of them except Abby. She remembered the lottery of there not being enough seats in the rich girl's car for her. The rich girl only vaguely paid attention, typing on her phone every few minutes and shifting in her seat, bored.

"He turned me against my parents. He was really sly about that. He knew what he was doing."

She took a quick look at her parents. A surge of emotion ran through her, so she turned back to the crowd.

"He sold me on a dream. That's what this whole thing is based on. Getting a girl to believe the dream. To believe that a guy wants her and considers her worthy of being the girl he wants to build a life together with. And I bought it."

She saw the soccer defender on the other side of Kedisha. The one who had smashed into Abby, cracking her nose. The girl looked in anguish, grieved by what Abby had to go through.

"And once I bought it, a bond was formed. It clouded my judgment. I started doing things. With lots of men. And for all the guys out there who think it's fun to go and pay for a girl—you need to know that she does not love you. She will pretend to love you. But she is terrified of you. She just wants to go home. She doesn't want to be there with you. She wants to be anywhere other than with you. It's all a lie. All of it. Even the money. For any girl out there looking for quick money, you need to know that I never got to keep any of it."

She paused a moment, letting the quiet comfort her.

"Traffickers keep you in line in two basic ways. One, they keep feeding you the line about the dream. 'You're beautiful. We're going to have a great life together. I love you and I know you love me,' they say. But that eventually wears thin. And when I said that I wanted to leave, he turned violent. I honestly thought he would kill me. He even threatened to burn me alive if I tried to exit. You'll believe me when I tell you that a threat like that is a strong motivator to stay. I wanted out, but I was trapped. And it left me powerless.

"A girl was murdered, and I thought I would be next. He had brainwashed me into thinking the police were my enemies. You see? Everything is one big lie. And it worked because I wanted to be in love."

She felt the contentment that comes with speaking from the heart. Effortless. And, hopefully, impactful.

"I want each of you girls to know two things. First, you are being targeted. I know we want to live in a fun, free world. But that's not what this world is. There are many, many traffickers, and they are hunting for you at malls. At community clubs. At places of worship. And especially online. They're reading your profiles. Studying what you say. Figuring out a way into your life. Second, I want you to know that no matter what you're going through, you don't need to sacrifice yourself for love. You were created wonderful and unique. And if a guy really does love you, bring him to meet your family. Creeps hate families. But real guys will want to know your parents and friends. A real guy will respect you, honour you and build you up."

She looked over at the principal. A patient man, he gave the indication he was content to let her continue. Some things don't need to start and stop on a schedule.

"We all have a part to play. Girls, we need to protect our hearts. Parents need to love their kids. Guys need to treat women like women. And say no to paid sex."

Abby paused. She wondered who she was reaching. Wondered how they were receiving it.

"It's great that we have politicians like Joy making laws. It's great that we have cops busting traffickers. And we need to admit that the battle starts in our minds and in our hearts. I hope you'll have the faith to believe you are who you were designed to be. Thanks for listening."

Many of the faces registered shock. Did they just hear what they thought they heard? And what did they think of her? Loser or hero? One clap started. It escalated to everyone pounding their hands together. They stood in ovation for her and gave loud cheers.

Abby felt awkward and had a sudden desire to go home, curl up on the couch alone and watch a soccer game. The principal came up and thanked her. He challenged the group to consider her words and announced that Joy would be speaking later in various classes. He dismissed the group, but most didn't leave. They stayed and talked with each other, trying to absorb what they heard. Abby came down and answered questions. She spoke with a reporter from a local paper. Afterward, she talked with Kedisha, the defender, and the rich girl.

"I'm sorry, Abby," the rich girl said. Her eyes were soft, like she had gained an insight into a world of suffering. "I'm sorry about everything that happened to you." She *had* been paying attention. So much so that she reached out and hugged Abby, who acknowledged to herself she had misread the rich girl. She wasn't the same girl Abby knew over two years before.

The foursome made plans to get together again soon.

Joy waited until the end.

"I'm proud of you, Abby."

"You think so?"

"I do."

"You think it made a difference?"

"Would it have made a difference for you had you heard a talk like this?"

"Yeah."

Abby looked into Joy's eyes. Full of reassurance. Full of approval.

"You did the right thing, Abby. You warned people about how they can be enslaved. That takes guts. I admire you."

Abby believed her.

Her parents congratulated her. They were all about to go out for lunch when Abby turned to see a young girl, about the same age she was when she was being trafficked. Abby broke away to talk to her.

"Hey, I'm Abby."

"I'm Cassie. Thanks for your talk." The girl wore green hairclips in her fire-red hair. "You know, as you were talking ..."

The girl glanced behind her, even though she knew no one was there. But something made her look. The feeling that someone was always watching her, perhaps.

"As you were talking, I realized that … I realized I'm being groomed. He gives me tons of stuff. Never comes to the house. He's been asking me to go off with him for a weekend. He's starting to suggest I see a couple of guys. Just for fun. I'm in grade 10. And I love him so much. I just … I'm confused. I haven't told a soul about this."

"It's real simple."

"It is?"

"Yup. Pull out your phone. Tell him goodbye. And then block him."

"I can't do that."

"Do you want to be standing up on that stage in a few years?" Abby said. "Or even worse?"

"This was a mistake. He's not that bad. I gotta run."

Cassie turned to leave.

"Are you that afraid you can't make it without him?" Abby asked.

Cassie stopped. Turned back. That's the trouble with people who have been where you are. They know exactly what's going on in your thoughts. She pulled out her phone. Swallowed. Texted him that they were through. Blocked him.

"That's weird," Cassie said.

"Like a cloud's been lifted? Like you were in a glass cube that has suddenly vanished?"

Cassie exhaled as if she were getting rid of whatever remnant of him had been left inside her.

"More than that." She stood there quiet, recuperating. Had she really just gotten rid of him? "I believed him."

"They're good, aren't they?" The school bell rang. "You got plans for lunch?" Abby asked.

"No."

"You do now. I'll make sure there's room in the car."

Abby and Cassie joined up with Joy and Abby's parents. As they left the gym, Abby thought about the disaster Cassie had avoided. About how the conversation with her only took place because Abby took the courage to get up on that stage. She had massive doubts before getting

308

up there. But Cassie averting tragedy confirmed her reason for giving the talk. Yeah. It was tough.

And worth it.

The newspaper ran a story on Abby's testimony. They put it up on social media, and people shared it. Around and around it went, eventually making its way from Markham to Dave's eyes in Mississauga. The headline caused him to stop and read the story. A rush of adrenalin pushed through him, followed by a feeling of deep sadness. He looked at the picture. It couldn't be. He looked closer. Sure enough.

He recognized the girl.

chapter forty-two

It was the texting that got him in the end.

Hope made an honest mistake. Her phone looked similar to Dave's, and she had picked up his by accident. When she realized what she had done she was about to put it down when she saw his latest message. He had been good at deleting his conversations but not perfect. Be sure your sins will find you out.

He came down the stairs and saw her sitting at the kitchen table. Or, at least, what must have been her. She didn't look herself. Not at all. A ghost. A shell of a person, really. She was ashen grey, sitting there in shock and unbearable grief. It was as if someone had made a wax statue of her, leaving her as only the outward appearance of a woman, hollowed out, like she was some empty jack-o-lantern after Halloween.

She didn't look at him. She was too busy trying to figure out answers to so many questions. *How long? Why? What's wrong with me? I never was good enough, was I? How did I not recognize this?*

The evasive presence of evil.

So many lies.

He sat down at the table just as she stood up. She put her hand on the chair to stabilize herself, the pressure of everything making standing difficult.

Who was this man she was living with?

She placed her hand on her throat and tried to regulate her breathing. The house suddenly felt cramped, like a mining tunnel in the dark ages. It was as if the lights had gone out and she was fumbling around in the dark. She covered her face with both hands and began sobbing uncontrollably.

"Hope, I'm sorry. It's over. I'm not doing it anymore."

She grabbed her car key and went out to the garage. Check stood up from her blanket and barked. Dave followed after Hope. She got in the car and backed out. She drove off without looking back.

He wondered if he would see her again.

Late that evening, he looked for Abby on social media. He found her and recognized her unmistakable face. He wondered if he would be able to recognize each and every girl he had been with. Could he pick each and every one of them out of a lineup? Probably not.

How had it all come to this?

How did he get to the place of believing all those lies?

How had he become so stupid?

He sent her a message. *Would you be willing to meet for coffee?*

It had gotten so late that Dave figured she had decided against it. He'd been waiting in the back of the coffee shop for half an hour and assumed by now she wouldn't show. He couldn't blame her. Why would a girl like Abby want to meet him anywhere? He decided all the same to stick it out the whole evening if need be. He could make the drive from Markham home to Mississauga in the dead of night. Nathan was gone for the next week, so Hope had no obligation to come home and pretend everything was all right for their son's sake. Dave wondered where she was. He'd sent her messages and received no replies. She was probably in a hotel somewhere. Or with her parents a few hours away. It felt strange to have no one to go home to.

Abby came in and sat down in the armchair across from him. She'd been sitting outside for an hour. Debating. Wondering. What was the point of this anyways? But she did have a few questions of her own. Answers that, perhaps, might help in the healing process.

"Thank you for coming."

Abby raised her eyebrows and did what little she could to get all those images of him out of her mind.

"Can I get you something to drink?" he asked.

"Dave?"

"Yeah."

"What do you want?"

I want to undo what I did.

Yeah, sorry. Doesn't quite work that way.

"I want to ask your forgiveness."

She paused. Thought.

"How did you get started in this?"

He'd racked his brain on this very question. Was it the isolation at work? The financial pressures? Was it looking for a thrill? What caused him to cross the line? To throw away his manhood in the search for it?

"I don't know."

"Sure you do."

Or maybe it was a trap that had been set for him years and years ago. And slowly it creeped in towards him. Perhaps he had said yes quietly in his heart over time without even knowing it, and then when the opportunity finally sprung on him he was already predisposed to saying yes.

"Pressure at work. Getting older and—"

"You're not trying very hard, Dave."

He felt his face pulse with humiliation. This was a bad idea. Or was it? Maybe the idea of them meeting was good, but this experience was difficult, making him second-guess it.

"If I could undo this, Abby, I would. The damage I caused you is unspeakable."

"You got that right."

His coffee was cold. She still had nothing, and it bothered him.

"You're sure I can't get you a coffee? Tea?"

Abby looked at him, feeling the freedom that came with not having to do what he said or asked.

"I had a good life," he continued. "Wife. Kid. House. Cars. Vacations. Great job. Lots of stuff. Anything I wanted, I got. And it spooked me."

"Because?"

"Because it wasn't enough," Dave said. "I talked to some other guys who visited girls."

"Visited."

So much code. So many words to downplay what they were doing. Like they needed to have softer phrases to keep their consciences from figuring out what was really going on.

"I believed the lie," he said. "I believed I wasn't hurting anyone. I even believed that by giving you money I was helping you. And because I had the money, I thought I had the right to do what I wanted with you. With all the others. I used to think that a guy who beat up girls was a women-hater. But then I realized I was, too."

You don't hate women. It was all in fun.

Yes, you do hate women. And you've finally admitted it.

He stopped. How in the world did he manage to keep these two people alive in his head and soul for so long?

"I'd meet other johns in the elevators. Hallways. I'd talk to them. Sure, some of us were richer. Better dressed. And that gave us the illusion we weren't like those bad johns. But I realized we all share a common rotten core. Some do it because they're lonely. Some do it because they're angry. Some—"

"And you?"

"I did it because after all I had achieved, after I had everything, it occurred to me that it wasn't enough. What was left? Alcohol? More business? Drugs? They just didn't interest me. But I was looking. Without even knowing. And some guys on my hockey team showed me a website."

"And it never occurred to you I didn't want to be there?"

"I needed to believe you wanted to be there."

Abby turned to the side. She heard what he said. She believed him. But in spite of it, she had a difficult time wrapping her mind around how someone could be so deceived. As she thought about it, she wondered if he might have been thinking the same thing about her. Maybe he had put it together that she had been deceived by the guy he gave his money to.

"I'm sorry for what I did to you," Dave said. "And I'm sorry that Jake lied to you."

"My need for love was greater than my ability to think clearly," she said. "You ever think that what you were doing was wrong? Even after spending time with a girl?"

"At times I felt guilty. Somehow I sensed it was wrong, but seeing girls became a drug. An addiction. And the need for being with a girl clouded my judgment. It wouldn't take much for me to lie to myself and drown out my conscience. She needs the money for university. I'm not harming anyone. It's not cheating if I don't know her name. And suddenly, there I am. At your door. Deceived. Ready to destroy you. And able to switch back into that other person five minutes after leaving you."

Dave put his hand on his cold coffee but didn't take a drink. It felt wrong to be sipping anything during a conversation like this.

"I kept hoping that one of you guys would help me," Abby said. "That one of you would come in with a clear head and get me out of there. I told myself I never wanted to see a man again for the rest of my life. So I guess sitting here is success to some degree."

"How can I help you, Abby?"

Abby squinted. Searched her mind. "I can't think of anything," she said. "But maybe you should think about taking a stand the next time guys in a hockey dressing room show you a website." She stood.

"Thank you for meeting me," Dave said.

"Take care of yourself."

"You too."

She began to leave, but then stopped. She turned and looked him in the eye.

"I forgive you, Dave," she whispered.

Abby walked through the café and out the door and disappeared into the black of night.

Abby got into her car and drove home. She talked with her parents. Her father was home more now, and they discussed the day over ice cream. She poured a heap of strawberry sauce over hers. Afterward, she went up to her room and sat on her bed.

How long had she been out of it? Yet part of her still expected to hear a knock at her bedroom door and to see a john waiting there for his turn. She instinctively glanced at the window, trying to think through her escape routes.

She knew her mind was full of instincts and impulses built from her past and that she had devised many clever schemes to help her survive. She wondered how long it would take to rid herself of those destructive old thoughts and build new ones.

She got ready for bed, turned on her table lamp first, then shut off the main light switch. Climbing into bed, she debated about praying. She had so many questions. How to piece this all together? How to make sense of it? Could she even? She thought perhaps she would never understand it or see the big picture or the greater purpose for why this happened.

It was hard to trust God, who hadn't seemed present through her struggles. Hard to build faith again. She decided to thank God that she was still alive, and she wondered why the girl with the blue-streaked hair had not been spared. She prayed for all the girls in Canada being held against their will. Then she prayed for her racing mind to settle down. That all those desperate, chronic thoughts of survival she had trained her mind to think would be replaced with thoughts of protection and love.

She rubbed her neck. Her body was tense throughout the day, as if bracing for impact, and she had to continually remind herself to let her muscles relax. *I'm safe now. I'm safe now. I'm safe now.*

As she lay in her bed she was suddenly struck—not by the presence of something, but by the *absence* of it. She recalled her life in captivity. How she was still physically in the world but felt like she was living in a glass cube, watching but unable to interact with people around her. Like the real her was invisible, leaving her with an incredible sense of loneliness. It made her feel that people could only react to a shell of her, that they wanted only her physical body and didn't want to know about or care for the real her.

But lying in her bed, for the briefest of moments, she found herself *without* the feeling of loneliness. For just a second, Abby felt like Abby again. And it gave her an incredible rush of freedom. It was like taking a step forward, or backwards, in time. She wasn't sure which. And it gave her an insight into not just who she was but who she could become.

Grabbing her faded red teddy bear, she imagined angels around her bed. Enveloping her. Protecting her.

She wondered if she would ever be able to trust like she used to but reminded herself that getting better was a process. There were days where she took a step backwards, but there were days like today of taking a step forward.

She was too close to herself to see weekly progress. But she kept a journal, and month after month, she admitted, she was becoming stronger.

She was able to trust more and to experience the freedom that comes with being be able to look back at an experience with the advantage of time. It was like she had built a bridge spanning a river and had taken the courage to cross over it. And while she could still look back and see the other side, the water in between here and there provided increasing comfort.

She felt herself growing tired, a welcome change to the rank exhaustion she used to feel. Abby glanced at her clock. Looked at the date. Something triggered.

She smiled.

Yes, tomorrow would be the day.

chapter forty-three

The deal between Dave and Hope was simple. He agreed to go to counselling, where he admitted he was trapped and felt powerless to change himself. He also agreed to get himself tested for STDs to make sure he wouldn't send Hope to an early grave. She got tested too, hoping he hadn't put her on that path already. Both of them came out clear. And last, if he ever did it again, he would be out. For good. Part of her still felt that was too harsh. The other part of her felt she should have cleaned him out when she first discovered it.

Hope stood there in that precarious place between grace and judgment. Her heart still crushed. Her soul still wounded. So many angry thoughts to fight off.

Dave joined her on the deck in the warm Mississauga sun. Would they get back what they had before all the lies began? Would the wounds he gave her ever totally heal? He thought it creepy to be Jekyll and Hyde at the same time. How his outer shell could look like a pristine picture but the inside of him a hideous creature indeed. And what concerned him the most was that even if he managed to clean up the outside, would he ever have the power to cleanse the inside?

———

Joy stood at her desk in Ottawa, looking out at her office. Countless conversations had been held here. Many late nights. She could hardly believe what it took to get the bill passed. It had driven her to her knees. Pushed her right to the end. And there she discovered that her faith could do what she could not do for herself.

Glancing to her left, she noticed the quote from Wilberforce that had inspired her so many times. "*You may choose to look the other way but you can never say again that you did not know.*"

He had done well. So had she.

Joy picked up the framed copy of Bill C-268. Read the wording.

An Act to amend the Criminal Code (minimum sentence for offences involving trafficking of person under the age of eighteen years) ... Her Majesty, by and with the advice and consent of the Senate and House of Commons of Canada, enacts as follows ... every person ... who exercises control ... over ... a person for the purpose of exploitation ... is guilty ... and liable to a minimum punishment of imprisonment for a term of five years ...

She had gone from being that poor little girl in a country schoolyard who was too afraid to intervene in her brother's beating to standing here today. She had vowed that day never to back down. And looking back on it, she thought that sometimes life's most bitter failures can be turned around to shape a person to enable them to win against incredible odds. Especially if that included intervention in a private members' lottery.

The suite felt so different when it was empty. Like it needed recharging after everything it had been through. The staff had left for the summer. Save for Joel, who stuck around to make sure Joy had everything she needed before she left for Kildonan-St. Paul.

"Well, Joel. You weren't bored," she said with a laugh.

He stood up from his chair. His bag was packed. Ready to go. He smiled. He had been there for her no matter what. That's the key in a fight. You needed teammates who would walk through fire with you.

It was his turn. He needed to respond. And Joy could tell there was something heavy on his heart he wanted to share. Hours serving in the trenches. Threats by traffickers. No spotlight. No applause. But Joel's satisfaction came from a deeper place.

"Thank you for the opportunity to serve with you, Joy."

He could have bolted at any point. And would have had good reason to. But he didn't. Yes, he believed in the cause. Yes, there was personal fulfillment in working in the shadows and seeing their team win. But it was deeper than all of that for Joel. Much deeper. He cared for the girls. Cared for them in their slavery. Cared for them being trafficked across Canada. Gave everything he had to help them. You couldn't counterfeit that kind of love. And Joy had seen that in him since the very beginning.

"You had so much pressure," Joy said. "Late nights. Death threats. I think you got more than you bargained for, Joel."

"Thank you for the opportunity to be part of something that made such a difference."

He reached out his hand. Joy shook it. It felt so formal. She gave him a hug.

"Thank you, Joel," she whispered.

They pulled back.

"You've done an incredible work here, Joy."

"You did too."

"Say a big hello to Bart for me."

"I will. And you say a big hello to your family. Have a great summer. We'll stay in touch and see you in the fall?"

"Of course," he said. "It was a great victory."

Joy nodded. Joel turned toward the desk and collected the last of his things.

"It really was," Joy said. In that moment, something came over her. An impression. A thought. A conviction. It felt as strong, if not stronger, than when she started fighting for the bill.

Joel looked back at Joy. Saw the resolve in her face.

"Although I have the distinct impression my battle is just beginning," she said.

Joel met her resolve. "I'm looking forward to it already."

They left the office and walked out of Parliament.

Soon to return.

chapter forty-four

Abby thought she was seeing an earlier version of herself. Not in terms of looks but everything else. The inside. The frantic yet vacant look in the eyes. The feelings of worthlessness, shame and guilt.

Abby had volunteered to help rescue victims of human trafficking. Girls like Jen, who sat with Abby in Alexandra's living room, her face buried in her hands against her knees. She wore a black hoodie, her strands of black hair draped down all around her. She was scrunched up like a ball, as if she had trained herself to constantly brace for impact. Jen had been lured into human trafficking while living on her reserve and was trafficked across eastern Canada.

"I'm telling you, this is a mistake," she shouted, loud enough to hurt Abby's ears. She got up and walked towards the front door. "I'm out of here."

Jen touched the door handle.

"You might want to reconsider," Abby said.

Jen turned around, her face flushed with anger. Abby recognized it as a typical cover to mask unbearable hurt.

"Yeah?" Jen asked. "You give me one reason why I should stay. You got five seconds, or I'm out of here."

Five steamboats. Not much time.

"I'll give you three reasons. Number one. I have been exactly where you are. I know what you're feeling. I know what you're thinking. I know what scares you. I know about the trauma bonds you have with your trafficker.

"Number two. I'm sitting here now. I changed, which means I know you can change too. I know that you can go from where you are to where I am. I want you to take a good hard look at me. I finished high school. I have a job. And later today, I'm doing something that I've wanted to do for years and finally have the courage to do.

"And number three. We're miles from anywhere. You have no car. And it's too far to walk, so you're stuck here."

Abby cracked a smile. Jen laughed, taking her hand from the door handle. In that moment Jen caught a glimpse, just a split second when she felt she consisted of someone besides her memories and addictions.

"Seriously, though. If you want to leave, I'll drive you. But I want you to ask yourself one question. Do you want to stay the way you are, or do you want to have a life again?"

Jen returned to her seat and rubbed her forehead, like she was trying to get rid of all the events occupying her memory.

"You were like me?" Jen asked.

"Yup. I'm still a work in progress. But I'm going to promise you something." Jen kept her eyes closed. "Jen?" She opened them. Focused on Abby. Looked for any sign of hope. "I'm going to be here for you. We all are. Joy, Alexandra, me, the other girls. They helped me, and we're going to help you, okay?"

Jen nodded. Abby gave her the box of tissues. "Thanks," she said, wiping her eyes. "So what are you doing this afternoon?"

An idea came to Abby. "You want to come?"

Jen shook her head. "Thanks, but I'm going to bed. I'm exhausted," she said. "What do you have planned?"

The combination of the warmth from the sun and the slight breeze down Hanna Avenue gave Abby the perfect temperature as she walked into a café.

"What can I get for you?" the barista behind the counter asked.

"Could I please have a large mochaccino?"

"Of course. Inside or to go?"

"Inside. Well, I'll take it outside to the patio," she said. "If that's okay?"

"I'll bring it out to you."

"You sure?"

"Of course. It's a beautiful day. No point waiting in here."

Abby walked on the white-and-black checkered floor and passed under a gorgeous chandelier before walking out the door. She took the concrete steps down and found an empty table. She sat down with her back against the wall and watched people walk by. She took in a deep breath. *Everything's fine. Everything is fine.*

Is it really? You can make a lot of money if you go back.

I'm through. And I'm not believing your lies.

You could work for yourself. Forget having a pimp.

No thanks. Not interested in dehumanizing myself.

You're welcome back anytime, Abby. Anytime.

That time is never. Get lost.

The barista placed a large white mug on a white saucer with a red napkin in front of Abby.

"Thank you."

"You got it."

Abby wrapped her hands around the warm mug. Breathed in the aroma of the coffee. Felt it fill her lungs. Heard the conversations around her. This area would start to get busy soon. Lots of people would be walking by. She could have come way later. But she loved being early. It had taken a lot of guts to get to this stage. And so far, so good.

She drank her coffee slowly. Zero hurry. Just turn the clock off. Sit. And exist for a while. Watch people. Get excited for what was about to happen.

When she was finished and ready, she got up and walked down Liberty Street to Atlantic Avenue, under the Gardiner Expressway, and crossed over Manitoba Avenue. There it was. Her favourite place.

For tourists in Paris, it's the Eiffel Tower. For visitors to Rome, it's the coliseum. But for Abby Summer in Toronto, her go-to place was none other than BMO Field. She looked up at the stadium. Felt a connection with it. Like she could watch a triple-header of soccer here every day for a month.

The attendant at the gate scanned her ticket. Abby walked into the seating area, the first one there. She stood by the railing, looking at the beautiful grass. She felt something calming about being in a sports facility in the stillness before everyone started arriving.

Abby walked back and negotiated around fans in the concourse. She found her familiar vendor and bought a foot-long hotdog and bottled water. She took the stairs and found her seat. She put on her red cap to match her jersey. Placing her feet on the seat in front of her for the time being, she watched Toronto FC take to the field for the pre-game warm up.

The sea of red eventually packed out the stadium. The capacity crowd stood to their feet for the national anthem. She removed her cap and sang as loud as she could.

"O Canada. Our home and native land. True patriot love ..."

She glanced around as she sang, engulfed in a sea of red jerseys, with the gorgeous afternoon sun shining down on her. Fans held up their FC scarves.

"The True North strong and free ..."

The sound of the stadium belting out the anthem had such a great ring to it.

"God keep our land glorious and free ..."

She closed her eyes. Heard the male voices in particular and a father, wife, daughter combo beside her. The anthem ended. They all cheered and sat down.

Toronto FC took their positions on the field to her left. Montreal Impact to her right. Finally. A live Toronto FC game.

Her phone chimed, alerting her to a social media message.

Abby put her hand into her pocket. Felt her phone. She placed her thumb on the power button.

Turned it off.

The chants started. Fans stood, stretching out their hands, then clapping in rhythm. Abby joined in. Screamed as loud as she could. *"TFC!"* Clap, clap, clap. *"TFC!"* Clap, clap, clap.

The TFC striker stood over the ball. Abby watch the inside right midfielder. Her position. The ball would likely be passed to him soon.

She felt her excitement rise. The fans were going crazy. She cheered.

The ref blew the whistle.

The game began.

THE END

afterword

Joy was right about her battle just beginning. The following year she drafted a proposal called Connecting the Dots, which provided recommendations for a national action plan. That plan launched two years later, and it emphasized awareness for vulnerable populations, the requirement for supporting victims, and the need for dedicated law enforcement efforts and for all Canadians to prevent human trafficking.

If it was fortunate to have her name drawn in third place for her first private member's bill, C-268, then it was astonishing to have her name called fourth in the lottery for her next bill, C-310. The bill sought to target Canadian sex traffickers abroad. If Canadians engaged in the trafficking of children or adults outside of Canada, they could be tried just as if the crime had taken place in Canada. MP Harold Albrecht exchanged his spot on the order paper so Bill C-310 could be debated sooner. The bill passed unanimously.

Joy later championed Bill C-36, led by the then minister of justice Peter MacKay, which made the purchase of sexual services illegal in Canada for the first time. It was patterned after the Nordic model that criminalizes the johns and traffickers instead of the prostituted women. The Nordic model was a revolutionary idea started in Sweden to deal with sex trafficking. It decriminalized those who were being prostituted, helped them exit and made the purchase of sex a crime. Instead of pointing the finger at the prostituted women, it shifted the blame to the johns who paid for sex. Swedish research proved that women were suffering terrible abuse, and it showed that prostitution had links to human trafficking.

Bill C-36 passed the House with a vote of 156 to 124.

In 2015, Joy left politics. She focuses all her efforts on the Joy Smith Foundation and works to ensure that all Canadians are free from human trafficking by educating the public and providing resources to frontline organizations that rescue and rehabilitate victims.

For more information:
www.JoySmithFoundation.com
info@JoySmithFoundation.com
(204) 691–2455

CASTLE QUAY BOOKS

AWARD WINNING TITLES BY

PAUL H. BOGE

Paul H. Boge is winner of the Word Guild's Best New Canadian Author award and author of seven other books: *Hannah's Hope*; *Father to the Fatherless: The Charles Mulli Story*; *Hope for the Hopeless: The Charles Mulli Mission*; *The Biggest Family in the World: The Charles Mulli Miracle*; *The Urban Saint*; *The Cities of Fortune* and *The Chicago Healer*. Paul works as a professional engineer and lives in Winnipeg, Manitoba.

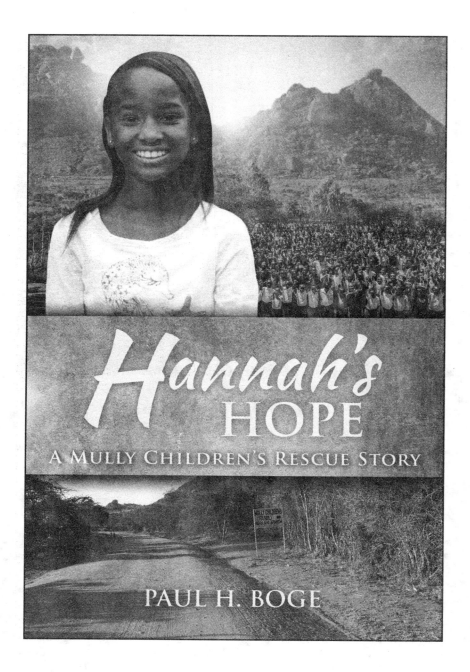

Hannah's
HOPE

A MULLY CHILDREN'S RESCUE STORY

PAUL H. BOGE

The Man. The Miracles. The Mission.

FATHER TO THE FATHERLESS

The Charles Mulli Story

PAUL H. BOGE
Foreword by Bruce Wilkinson, *Dream for Africa*

The Children. The Calling. The Compassion.

HOPE FOR THE HOPELESS
The Charles Mulli Mission

PAUL H. BOGE

Foreword by David Rowlands
Introduction by H.E. Hon. Daniel Arap Moi, Second President of the Republic of Kenya